LETTERS
FROM THE DRAGON'S HEAD

MARTHA WILEY'S
CHINA
1900-1947

The title for this book was inspired by a Chinese folktale in which the king of Foochow (Fuzhou) was visited by a Taoist priest who exclaimed that the city was indeed well positioned, for the hills of the region resembled a dragon, and the city had been placed on the dragon's head, while nearby hills formed the dragon's undulating back and tail. This placement, according to the priest, would ensure lasting good fortune and prosperity for the king.

ISBN 978-0-9824553-7-1

Library of Congress Control Number: 2014944027

Cover design by Kathy Langhorn and Nancy Wilkins

Book interior design by Nina Noble

Empty Bowl Press, Port Townsend

Printed in the United States of America

For
Mary Constance Wiley
1905-1987
who provided 32 of Martha's letters
and the inspiration to begin this project.

"I hope the integrity of China may be
preserved and that old China
may never be dismembered
by greedy nations."

Martha Wiley

LETTERS
FROM THE DRAGON'S HEAD

MARTHA WILEY'S
CHINA
1900-1947

EDITED BY PAT LANGHORN
& KATHY LANGHORN

EMPTY BOWL PRESS

Pat Langhorn

Enjoy Martha's journey

Kathy Langhorn

ACKNOWLEDGMENTS

We thank the Yakima Valley Museum and archivist Martin Humphrey for his invaluable assistance and patience.

We also thank the Wiley, McGinnis, Woodhouse and Rogers families for their generosity in sharing documents, photographs, and other useful information.

Also:

Ray & Jean Hoffman
Professor Harriet Mills
Jan Prichard Cohen
Mrs. Theodore Chen
Oberlin College Archives
Yale Divinity School Library—
    Martha Lund Smalley
Whitman College Archives
Claremont College Archives
University of Washington Alumni
    Association
United Church Board for World
    Ministries (formerly American
    Board of Commissioners for
    Foreign Missions)
Ellen T. Weiss
Bailian Zheng
Mabelle Hsueh
Frances Bingham
Eunice Bishop
Victor Chou
John & Agnes Alden

Elizabeth Alden
Virginia Stowe
Indianapolis Historical Society
Alden Matthews
Helen Perkins
Shirley Schuller
Irene Shockley
Nancy Rekow & Everett Thompson
Kim Anicker
Ruth Hansten
Howard and Henrietta Alsdorf
Mary Lacy
Agnes McClure
Lois Schutt
Richard & Janet Miller
Yakima Valley Daughters of the Pioneers
John Baule, Yakima Valley Museum
    director
Mike Siebol, Yakima Valley Museum
    curator of collections
Raymond Greeott
Jennifer Hager

Hugh and Mary Ann Wiley and children—clockwise from left—Charles, John, Wallace, William, James, Isabelle, Anna, Martha (kneeling) and George

Sharp Peak landing

CONTENTS

MAPS

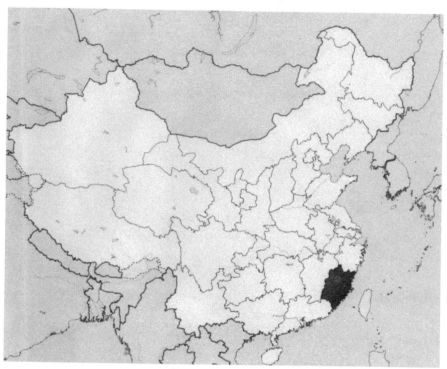

Map of China—Fukien province highlighted

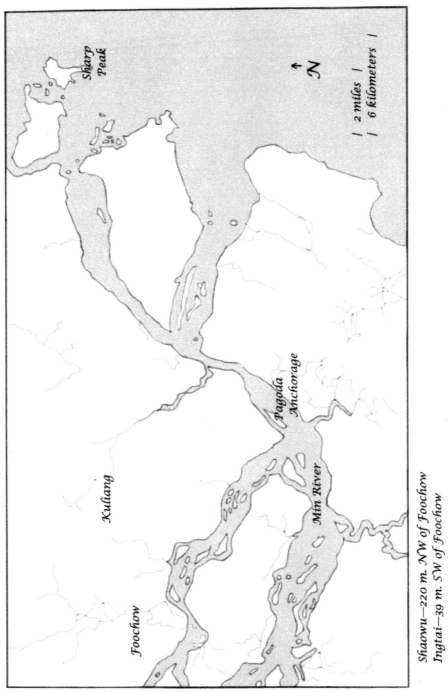

Foochow Region

Shaowu—220 m. NW of Foochow
Ingtai—39 m. SW of Foochow

Martha and sisters Anna and Isabelle

Most of Martha's collected letters were written to family members—mainly, her mother, Mary Ann, until her death in 1919, and her two sisters, Anna and Belle. She also wrote to several siblings, their spouses and children. Spouses are listed in parenthesis and children, in brackets.

William – (Annie) – [Vera, Ernest, Howard]
Wallace – (Nettie) – [Lenore, Hugh, James, Marian, Robert]
James – (Rose) – [Malcom, Marguerite, Madeline, Gordon, Clifford]
John – (Lovina/Vina) – [Constance, Jean, Irene, Arthur, Helen]
Isabelle/Belle – (Norman Woodhouse) – [Earl, Myron, Clark]
Charles – (Nellie) – [Cecil, Charles S.]
Martha – (never married)
Anna – (William Achelpohl) – [Doris, Jean, Margaret]
George – (never married)

EDITORS' NOTE

Our intent for this project has been to follow Martha Wiley's original plans for writing a book about her years in China. She had wisely prepared in advance by asking relatives and friends to save her letters so that they could be used in the remembering and retelling of her story. Unfortunately she was not able to finish that project.

When we, her grandniece and great-grandniece, discovered that more than 700 of her letters were housed in the Yakima Valley Museum, we drove the 200 miles to Yakima, Washington—ten miles from Wiley City, where Martha was born. And with the kindly help of Martin Humphrey and the museum staff, we spent several days Xeroxing letters, as this was 1992, before digital technology was prevalent. We then looked through Martha's collection and spoke with relatives in the area to gather information where we could.

After that original trip, we collected material through extensive correspondence to universities, friends and family, and surprisingly a few people in China who remembered Martha or knew of her work.

This book has been assembled in the format of Martha's letters, editing out only repeat information and what we considered to be extraneous or personal content that would be of no interest to the general reader.

Original word usage has been preserved. Punctuation has been added only where needed for clarity, and underlining has been replaced with italics. Ellipses (. . .) have been used to indicate obvious omissions in text only. Any added information has been placed in brackets.

TIMELINE

1868 — Martha's parents move to Yakima — the eighth family to settle in the valley

1874 — Martha is born in Wiley City (founded by her father)

1884 — Martha's father dies of blood poisoning (from splinter in finger)

1895 — Martha graduates from University of Washington with a Bachelor of Pedagogy

1898 — Martha graduates from Whitman College with B.A. degree, teaches in local county schools

— Boxer Rebellion begins (ends 1901)

1900 — Martha is appointed by the American Board of Commissioners for Foreign Missions to teach Mathematics at Foochow College (later, English and Bible courses)

— Departs for China

— Learning Foochow dialect

1904 — Severe case of mumps (only a few letters written in '04-'05)

1905 — China begins its change from ancient system of education to Western

1907 — First furlough, extensive vacation (Philippines, Ceylon, Aden, Egypt, Palestine, Italy, Switzerland, Germany, Belgium, France, England, Ireland, Scotland, Canada — Montreal and Quebec)

— In Quebec spends one month in sanitarium to recover from malaria

— Speaking engagements across U.S. (eventually speaks in all states but Maine)

1908 — Martha receives honorary M.A. degree from Whitman College

1909 or '10 — Departs for China

1911 — Overthrow of Manchu Dynasty

— Martha establishes East Gate School for Manchu orphans after the burning of the Manchu quarter

1912 — Republic of China (ROC) established

— Martha establishes industrial school in Maunchu quarter and also a Bible school with Emily Hartwell

— Trip to Great Wall, Mongolia, Korea, Manchuria, Japan, and tomb of Confucius

1913 — Sun Yat-sen establishes National People's Party (Kuomintang — KMT)

— Foochow College now teaches to high school level only

1914 — WWI begins

— Martha learning Mandarin dialect

1916 — Departs for U.S. to care for ailing mother

1917 — Donald Hsueh graduates Foochow College, attends Yenching University

1919 — Martha's mother dies

— Martha returns to China and devotes herself to the work for women

1921 — Chinese Communist Party (CCP) established — Mao Zedong a founding member

— Donald graduates Yenching University with B.A. degree, begins teaching at Foochow College

1922 — Donald and Catherine are married

— Provincial revolution

— Donald and Catherine have son that dies — he lives eight weeks

1923 — Martha almost dies from pneumonia, three months in U.S. hospital to recover

1924 — Returns to China

— Donald in U.S., receives M.A. degree in education from University of Washington

— Donald and Catherine have second child — Ella or "Little Boat"

1925 — Sun Yat-sen dies

— Foochow under martial law

1926 — Donald and Catherine at Teachers College, Columbia University, New York City

— "Little Boat" dies

— Martha recovering from typhoid

1927 — Living under Russian Cheka (Bolshevism)

— Martha is a refugee in Formosa (seven months)

— Donald and Catherine's third child is born in U.S. — Mabelle

— Donald becomes the first Chinese principal of Foochow College at the age of 32

1928 — Martha returns to Foochow

1929 — Donald and Catherine lose another child

1930 — Donald and Catherine lose another child

1931 — Donald and Catherine have another child (born in Hong Kong) — Marian

— Martha home on furlough

1933 — Martha returns to China

— Foochow College has all appropriations cut by American Board of Missions

— Donald and Catherine have another child (born in Foochow) — Elizabeth

— Another Foochow government "turn-over" — Foochow area bombed

1934 — Admiral Chen considers resigning from navy, later promoted to fleet admiral

1936 — Donald in military training camp, and again in '37

1937 — Chinese War of Resistance against Japan until '45

— Martha in U. S. for one year, Hsueh (pronounced shweh) family also in U.S.

1938 — Dugout bomb shelter built on Fairy Bridge property

1939 — WWII begins

1939 —Foochow bombed
　　　—Martha starts rice kitchen for refugees and destitute
　　　—800 Foochow College students move to Ingtai (40 miles SW of Foochow) with
　　　　the Hsueh family
　　　—600 Primary School students remain in Foochow

1941 —Foochow College moves to Shaowu (220 miles NW of Foochow)
　　　—Japan invades Foochow
1942 —Martha teaches at Foochow College again because of teacher shortage
1943 —Foochow College is divided between Ingtai and Shaowu for one year
1944 —Martha retires from mission service but remains in China
　　　—Foochow is occupied by Japan (four months)
　　　—Refugees in Ingtai—students sleeping in abandoned Buddhist temple
1945 —Return to Foochow
1946 —Fire destroys campus building of Foochow College, library and all books burned
1946 —'49—KMT—CCP Civil War

1947 —Martha leaves China for U.S.
1949 —Establishment of People's Republic of China (PRC), KMT retreats to Taiwan
　　　—Students of Foochow College refuse to pay tuition, salaries cut in half
　　　—Admiral Chen joins communist government
1950 —Admiral Chen now vice-governor of Foochow
　　　—Martha is teaching in Piney Woods, Mississippi
1951 —Martha receives news Admiral Chen is killed, finds this to be incorrect, years
　　　　later
1952 —Foochow College becomes a public school
　　　—Donald is re-appointed as an English teacher and head of library
1953 —Martha moves to Pilgrim Place cottages for retired mission workers in
　　　　Claremont, California
1957 —Donald retires

1961 —Martha hospitalized from auto accident (numerous injuries, shattered kneecap)
1966 —Cultural Revolution begins
1969 —Martha dies in nursing home after a fall
　　　—Admiral Chen dies of stomach cancer three weeks earlier
1979 —Donald dies in China from infection after an injury
　　　—Mabelle brings Catherine to U.S. Catherine dies one month later

INTRODUCTION

To understand the spirit of Martha Wiley, it is essential to begin with this pioneer woman's legacy. Martha was the seventh of nine children born to Hugh and Mary Ann Wiley, both second generation immigrants from Ireland, who married and lived in Minnesota before coming west to eventually settle in the town of Yakima, Washington Territory.

With the threat of Indian massacres after the Civil War, and the danger of traveling directly across the states, they decided to take the longer, safer route. And in the winter of 1865, they traveled from Minnesota to New York with their four sons and Hugh's brother Josiah, who was fresh from cavalry service in the Civil War, then boarded a ship for Panama, crossed the isthmus by rail, took passage on a steamer to San Francisco, and headed for Salem, Oregon, having been enticed by letters from a cousin who lived there. The family lived in Salem for two years until a fire burned their home and all its contents, which prompted the move in 1868 to the much talked about Yakima Valley.

Hugh established Wiley City just ten miles from the present-day city of Yakima, where Martha was born in 1874. At that time settlers had mixed feelings about the Indians in the area—some were friendly to the settlers and even helped the Wileys raise their first log home, but there were also threats of raids, which is expressed vividly in a Claremont Graduate School interview with Martha taken during her retirement years at Pilgrim Place in Claremont, California:

> In Washington there were uprisings all the time by the Indians. My first memory—absolutely the first thing I can remember in my long life—is being taken out to a field of timothy, where the timothy grew quite tall there in that valley, and being cached there at night. Everyone in the family was put down in a different place through that meadow. I can remember even to this day after so many years my father looking right on me as he put me down and pulled the timothy over me, "Now, whatever you see make no noise. Don't even whisper. Don't dare scream." So, I was put down there, in the night, my brothers and sisters scattered around the same way."

> The next morning we were gathered up and taken to a fort [a sod fort that the men in the family had built] and there we stayed for some days until the Indians were quieted. But, in the meantime, two neighbors were killed. So we were in real danger. That kept on and on for years. In spite of our lovely valley, there was always this undercurrent: being chased by the Indians when we went out riding.

Years later, Martha would develop respect and friendships with Native Americans in the area, enough so that she was given the name "Siwash." Although this term technically means "a Native American," the Indians' usage of it meant that Martha was "between being Indian and being White," in other words, not one or the other.

Martha's mother, Mary Ann, had stressed education for all her children, and Martha was an all too willing recipient. At not quite four years old, she protested so loudly and often, of wanting to go to school (which was held for the three winter months, being the only time the older boys were free from farm work). Finally her brother Wallace said he would take her for one day (along with her six older siblings), to show her that "it was not fun to go to school." That afternoon the teacher sent word that she was "no bother at all" and that "she might come every day" with the hope that Martha would be a motivation and example for the "playboys" of the classroom.

Martha's education continued at an accelerated pace. At age fifteen she attended Whitman College, and at seventeen, took the teachers' exam, and went on to receive a Bachelor of Pedagogy (the method and practice of teaching) from the University of Washington in 1895. She taught in local county schools until her return to Whitman College to receive a B.A. degree in 1897.

Hearing stories of China from Dr. Walker, a traveling missionary, who stated, "go out and do something for the world," and Miss Chittenden, a teacher at Foochow College, had expanded her interest in China. And when the American Board of Commissioners for Foreign Missions needed someone in Foochow College to teach mathematics, she was "very glad to get the appointment." She departed for China in 1900, at the age of twenty-six.

In 1908, during her first furlough, she was also presented with an honorary M.A. degree from Whitman College.

During her forty-seven years in China, Martha witnessed the fall of the last dynasty, the rise of a nationalist government, the Japanese occupation, and finally, the move toward Communism. Throughout these monumental changes, and up against every aspect of a culture in turmoil, she has been a correspondent with keen insight, evolving compassion, and wry humor. In reading her letters, we are allowed to experience her growing respect for the people and customs of China. Martha returned to the United States in 1947, thinking it temporary. To her dismay, she was not allowed to return, as it was considered unsafe for Americans to be in China at that time. She stated, "I would never have left China had I dreamed I could not get back" and further revealed that she hoped she could die in China and be buried there with her people.

While in China, Martha sponsored and/or found sponsorship for many of her students, enabling most if not all, to receive further education in the United States. Martha's intention was for her students to gain knowledge and skills in America that, upon their return to China, would allow them to assist their country in moving forward through its era of upheaval. Martha also focused on relief work for the displaced Manchus after the overthrow of their dynasty in 1911. She established educational schools for orphans and industrial schools for women. Seeing the disparity between the sexes, she stated, "There were men in the college getting a good education and going out into public life, every one of them, and here were the women almost waist-deep in mud in the paddy fields. Well, that was too much for my Western spirit of equality and so I got that [women's school] started."

In 1919, after three years at home in the States to care for her dying mother, Martha returned to China, and it was then that a focus on women's education became her priority.

In the women's schools, she taught girls and adult women to read and write, and to develop skills that would enable their self-sufficiency. In the men's school, Foochow College (one of the highest ranking and most respected schools in the area at that time), she taught many who went on to achieve prominent positions in business and government. One of those students, Chen Shao-kuan, became supreme commander of the Chinese Navy, and was also a lifelong friend. Another student, Donald Hsueh [pronounced shweh], eventually became the principal of Foochow College and was its inspirational and stoic guide through the many hardships it endured.

Throughout its history, Foochow College experienced many turbulent changes — repeated bombings, fires, and occupation by soldiers. Yet the students rallied with great spirit and increased dedication, even when the school took to the countryside for safety, where at one point they slept in an abandoned temple with no beds and little food.

When Martha first arrived in China in 1900, the school was teaching college level courses. In 1913 the status changed to high school level but Foochow College retained its name. Eventually it became a public middle school, and remains so as of this writing.

Over the years Martha gained the respect of people from many cultures. There were Native Americans she befriended in the Yakima valley, the Buddhist nun with whom she shared lively banter and exchange of philosophical and religious tenets, the Egyptian guide who allowed her to ride his fine Arabian horse "like a gentleman" around the pyramids, so impressed was he with her riding skills. And lastly, there were onlookers in the streets of China, wanting to get a glimpse of "the woman so wise she could teach men."

By receiving other cultures and customs throughout her life with openness and curiosity Martha Wiley invited respectful relationships and lifelong bonds that endured until her death at the age of ninety-five. Our hope is that she may live on through her letters and be an inspiration for the reader as she has certainly been for us.

Pat Langhorn
Kathy Langhorn
Silverdale, Washington
2014

*Edna Deahl and Martha on board Kaijo Maru — Osaka, circa 1910
with Japanese fleet in the distance.*

SAILING SCHEDULE

1900 – (Jan) – *S.S. Doric* – San Francisco, Shanghai

1907 – (Mar) – *S.S. Fungshun* – Shanghai, Singapore

      (May) – *S.S Teresa* – Port Said

      (Jul) – *S.S. Mongolia* – London, Montreal

      (?) – *S.S. Prince Eitel Fredrich* – New York

1909 or '10 – (Aug) – *S.S. (?)* – San Francisco, Shanghai, Manila, HK

1916 – (Sep) – *S.S. Empress of Asia* – Shanghai, Seattle

1919 – (Sep) – *S.S. Katori Maru* – Seattle, Yokohama

1923 – (Jul) – *S.S. Grant* – Shanghai, Seattle

1924 – (Sep) – *S.S. Grant* – Seattle, Shanghai

1931 – (Jul) – *S.S. Empress of Japan* – Shanghai, Seattle

1933 – (Jan) – *S.S. President Madison* – Seattle, Shanghai

1937 – (Sep) – *S.S. Empress of Russia* – HK, Shanghai, Japan, Seattle

1938 – (Sep) – *S.S. Empress of Asia* – Seattle, Shanghai

1947 – (Jul) – *S.S. General Meigs* – Shanghai, San Francisco

TIMELINE 1900-1910

1900 — Martha is appointed by the American Board of Commissioners for Foreign Missions to teach Mathematics at Foochow College (later she also teaches English and Bible courses)
  — Departs for China
  — Learning Foochow dialect
1904 — Severe case of mumps (only a few letters written in '04 – '05)
1905 — China begins its change from ancient system of education to Western
1907 — First furlough, extensive vacation (Philippines, Ceylon, Aden, Egypt, Palestine, Italy, Switzerland, Germany, Belgium, France, England, Ireland, Scotland, Canada — Montreal and Quebec)
  — In Quebec spends one month in sanitarium to recover from malaria
  — Speaking engagements across U.S. (eventually spoke in all states but Maine)
1908 — Martha receives honorary M.A. degree from Whitman College
1909 or '10 — Departs for China

1

A Time of Change

"I assure you of my appreciation."

Ahtanum, Wn.   November 9, 1899

Judson Smith D.D.
Boston, Mass.

Dear Sir,

Yours of November 2nd at hand. The notification of appointment had reached me two days previously, and I assure you of my appreciation of the opportunity to be of use in that field. As to the time for my departure, I cannot say anything definite until I hear from Miss Chittenden, to whom I have already written, but I do not think a preparation will necessitate a very long time. When I receive her reply and know just what is to be done, I can tell how much time will be required getting ready, and will write you in regard to it.

    With many thanks for your cordiality and kind interest, I remain,

Very truly,   Martha Wiley

[Note: Ahtanum is seven miles from the present day town of Union Gap (what was once the original site of Yakima City.)]

"I can begin at once."

AHTANUM, WN.   NOVEMBER 28, 1899

Rev. Judson Smith
Boston, Mass.

Dear Sir,

Your letter of November 22, also Miss Chittenden's of the same date, came to-day. I can have all needed preparations completed by January 15, and if satisfactory will plan to sail as soon after that date as possible. Miss Chittenden wrote me quite fully as to what was needed, so that I can begin at once to prepare to go.

I do not think the voyage will be trying to me, as before this I have been a "good sailor." Anything further that you may think I ought to know about the journey will be very welcome. I am anxious to be on the way but could hardly be ready before the above date.

Martha Wiley

"Are the travelling expenses from here to San Francisco met by the board?"

AHTANUM, WN.   DECEMBER 22, 1899

Rev. Judson Smith
Boston, Mass.

Dear Sir,

Yours of present date at hand, I enclose the receipt of $100 for outfit. Will the remainder for the outfit reach me before leaving the U.S.? Are the travelling expenses from here to San Francisco met by the Board, as well as those of the voyage?

Thanking you for the draft sent, I remain,

very truly,   Martha Wiley

"The police are as thick as flies."

FOOCHOW, CHINA   MARCH 4, 1900

Dear Sister and Relatives,

As you see I am now in Foochow, but as it is a long story, I must go back to Shanghai and begin there. The Doric anchored at the mouth of the Yangtse River, and a launch met us there. We then, went up the river about 14 miles and a branch of it six miles more, before reaching Shanghai. There are no cities on the coast of China; they are all inland.

Shanghai is preeminently the city of the East for foreigners—there is a large concession granted to foreigners, which is ruled by their municipality. The police are as thick as flies and they are of three kinds, Chinese, Indian and European. The Chinese cannot be trusted in case of riot against the foreigners. So the Indians watch them, and the foreign police watch the Indians. The latter are picturesque in the extreme—great tall, black fellows, with red shawls twisted into a turban.

The foreign concession is beautiful, with fine big houses for the various officials and for other residences. There is what is called "Old Shanghai" which is enclosed by a great stone wall. As it happened, Dr. Gracey, the U.S. Consul to Foochow, was aboard with his wife and the Consul-General Goodnow came to meet them.

The boat was small and smelled of oil. I had to sit on deck and eat oranges to keep from being sea-sick. The sea was smooth and quiet but every night we would cast anchor because we were so near shore among the islands. The coast is precipitous and dotted with rocky islands that jut out of the sea. It is not flat as generally supposed. We anchored at the mouth of the Min River for a day and night, and next morning, came up to Pagoda Anchorage, 20 miles.

From Pagoda Anchorage, we took a sampan up the river for ten miles; then, up a creek a mile or two and finally, finished in sedan chairs. We wound through the City on old South Street for two miles before reaching the Missionary settlement. The coolies met us at the landing with chairs, and I had a great time getting in. I backed in at last, but dropped my hat off in so doing. It took 14 coolies to move my baggage and me to the house and with the others, all single file, it made quite a procession.

To-day, Sunday, the program has been as follows: breakfast at 8:00; assembly for prayers at 9:00; Sunday School at 9:30; church at 10:30. I had a fifth grade class to teach by means of an interpreter. After church a number of Chinese called, most of them officials, to whom I had to pay my respects and drink tea with them. After dinner, the young postmaster called, dressed up in blue silk. He spoke English, and we had a pleasant chat. Mr. Peet tells me that this is one of the Foochow College graduates and he is already being rapidly promoted. Sunday School again at 3:00 where I had the Senior class to teach. They spoke English so we got along all right. I have not been here 24 hours yet, but I am knee-deep in work.

I wish I could tell you of all the things I have seen and heard. This trip has been a wonderful one in every way to me and I have wished so many times you could have the same trip. I would give all the money I have not, to see mother get into one of these sedan chairs, and some coolies carrying her, and have her "horses" stop. She would say "shocking" and never ride again. People consider these poor coolies just as we do horses.

I am staying at Mr. Peet's. He is president of the school. He has a wife and three children. Mr. Hartwell is just across the street and as the street is only four feet wide, the two houses almost adjoin. Foochow is very hilly. The missionaries live on the side of a hill with the City below them, a very healthful location.

Martha with mission child

The Chinese have given me a name already. Everyone here has an English name and a Chinese one. My surname is "Moi" which means "Dispenser of Food," I'm told. Ging Hok, one of the Chinese, writes the translation of his name "Yellow P. Bliss." "Ging" means golden and "Hok," happiness. So, he put them together and had Yellow Bliss. I have two hours of teaching a day, beginning tomorrow, and I recite two hours a day to a teacher. He is one of the graduates, a Cantonese by birth. We do not learn the Mandarin at all. The Fukien is what we have here, and the classical.

I believe I am going to like it here very much. My room is a great big affair and I feel lost in it. All the houses are one-storey houses and the ceilings about 14 feet. The outside walls are mainly double doors.

Mail for Shanghai closes tomorrow morning, so I am trying to get this letter sandwiched in before it goes. You do not get things for a song here. Everything is high. We must use Mexican silver, and you have to have a wheelbarrow to carry enough to buy some thread!

Love from,   Martha

"And I did some free gymnastics for a second."

FOOCHOW, CHINA   MARCH 11, 1900

My Dear Mother,

Friday evening, Miss Hartwell took me over the Min River with her, which I must tell you about. We have to cross the City through the narrow streets that I wrote you of before. The sights are very interesting. The first thing that came into view as we left our gate was a row of prisoners in stocks, i.e. places cut in a board for a man's head and feet. They are put in this position and chained beside the principal streets for punishment. Small pox patients were scattered along the way but nobody seemed to mind them. They are too common. My coolies ran into another chair and spilled me out and I did some free gymnastics for a second, in order to light on my feet.

Every place that belongs to foreigners has a high stone fence around it. So, the Consul's place has a fence about 12 or 14 feet high, and a servant has a little house at the grand entrance where he admitted us. We were then escorted to the hall by another servant and into a waiting room by the third, and a fourth took our cards on a silver tray to the Consul and his wife. A fifth came and showed us to the drawing-room, which was very handsomely furnished and where Dr. and Mrs. Gracey were receiving. We went through the usual ceremonies and were served with tea by another retinue of servants. Everybody in China serves you with tea when you call. If not, you have been slighted.

We visited the Martyrs' graves in a little cemetery on the river bank. They were killed here in 1895. Their remains lie buried there with a monument of an angel placed above them. The missionaries of Foochow at that time were away, or I suppose, these people I am with would have been killed too. A block or two down the hill from here is where the 26 Chinese were beheaded, who led the riot. If I meet a similar fate, I will have a pretty cemetery to rest in. The idea Americans have that Chinese have a great reverence for the graves of the ancestors would be shaken in many cases here. Every available space contains a grave but two stones alone show the place. All along the paths and walls coffins are piled up. They are so well sealed that they are one thing that does not smell rank. Some of these coffins have been there for hundreds of years. The baby towers [a stone structure roughly 8 feet in circumference and 6 feet high] are here and there, where they throw dead bodies. It takes too much room to bury them.

This is a land of graves. The people are said to think more of dying than of living. We are almost on the top of a hill so the well is above the graves. A high wall surrounds the premises and I have not yet learned all the ins and outs. Banana trees grow on each side of my windows. We people in the City are much more crowded than the other missionaries. Yet, I prefer this place and like this school better than any I have visited.

Mr. Peet is a nice old man and Father Hartwell is a nice old man too, and talks Chinese to me to encourage me. He has been here since 1849 and talks Fukien and Mandarin like a native. All the people speak Chinese and I stand with my mouth open and do not know a thing. I recite from 9:00 to 10:30 and from 11:00 to 12:30, and next week will also begin reciting from 7:00 to 8:00 P.M. My little dandy has gone home so I have another teacher for this week. He is such an improvement that I want to keep him. You would die to see some of the productions my Rhetoric class produces. A Chinese does and says everything just different from what we do. In the Bible classes they have a mania for remembering and telling about every man who had more than one wife.

You would be disgusted if I told you how many things I have had disappear already. I carry a handful of keys with me and hope to keep what I have left. I can yell "Lee," which means come here, and my special man servant appears on the scene, then the fun begins in making him understand. He brings me coffee and toast at 6:00 A.M. Everybody eats a little when he gets up, "to keep away malaria"!! He takes care of my room, does my washing, and boards himself, all for $4 per month, silver. The Chinese assistant-teachers here in the college get $15 silver which means just half that much in American money. We pay a coolie about 60 cash or about six cents for carrying our sedan chairs.

March 15 —— Mrs. Peet and I went to Ponasang to-day and I walked most of the way. On our way to Ponasang, we have to go through a busy street and there will be 50 Chinese following each of us and feeling of our dresses, and a band of kids usually brings up the rear, yelling at the foreigners.

A thief came to Dr. Woodhull's house and stole three armfuls of her things. She caught him carrying off the third and, with her sister, cornered him until Mr. Peet and his coolies got there. He had her medicine case, petticoat, soap and bath towels. He was tried this P.M. and will be posted up before the month of June, to be seen every time you put your head out. The punishments here are horrible. For the worst crimes, for the murder of parents, the criminal is put in a cage and slowly starved to death right in the streets.

To-day, Mr. Peet and I walked to Ponasang across the fields. There are high dikes that we walked on, and the fields are cultivated on each side. The present crop they are curing is rape seed, then they put in rice. The little patches of wheat that are planted are almost ripe. A great wall surrounds the City, and on this is a place to walk, several feet wide. Old cannons are placed in little towers every block or so of distance. Between the towers are openings, where great stones are piled up to hurl at an enemy in case of attack. This wall has four gates and after dark one candle is burned which means about half an hour, and gates are closed and guards keep out the thieves. This means that they shut them in. From this wall, the country looks grand. The mountains and fields, the river with little villages along it and the great banyan trees with the red-roofed temples under them—all are perfectly lovely! A great pagoda looks down on Mr. Peet's house just a few feet from our wall that was built at least a thousand years ago.

White Pagoda — originally built in 905

March 18 —— It has been a long time since the steamer has come to get our mail so I will add some more to my letter. I have just finished my classes for the day, as I have but two classes on Saturday. Chinese characters are clearly the invention of the devil. I am wading through John's Gospel in the characters and learning to write. My writing would make you laugh. I study the Romanized colloquial, which means the Foochow dialect reduced to a system of letters. Chinese is not so bad to translate, for one character means one word and one only but the sticking point is to remember which word and character go together. There is no inflection in the language, or any grammar whatever. I am getting so I can recognize a good many words but when they are talking, can't "catch on yet."

We live ordinarily well. We have fresh buffalo meat right along, whole wheat gems, oranges and bananas. Rice is our principal food; we have some Irish potatoes about twice each week; sweet potatoes the same. Bamboo shoots are also articles of some importance. Sweet articles are mainly conspicuous by their absence. Some wild game is killed in the mountains nearby but is too high for missionaries to indulge in. Butter is made of buffalo milk and is as pale and ghastly as Hamlet's ghost. Nuts, come from the Shantung province—which are like walnuts—and peanuts are raised here. Once in a while as a special treat we have some canned fruit from the U.S. It will be almost time for raspberries when this reaches you. They don't raise them here—I've been inquiring. Just think of me when you sit down to Sunday dinner with some good potatoes. I never knew before that potatoes could be a luxury.

Love from Martha

Members of the American Board Mission assembled outside of mission compound.
Martha—second row from back, second in from right.

"My name is Oi-Su-Gu."

FOOCHOW, CHINA   APRIL 14, 1900

Dear Sister and Family,

I have not been sorry that I came and like it very well. The Chinese are nice to teach; they are very good to their teachers; the language is going to be hard to get at, at least it always has been for people, and I suppose I am not so bright but that I shall find it so. I can jabber enough to make my wants known. Oh, but it is hard to remember the characters! I like to study the language, it is so strange, and is the opposite of ours in every way. I can read the Romanized pretty well, so a Chinese can understand me, but don't know much of it myself. My name is Oi-Su-Gu, (Wiley Miss) [Su-gu means teacher aunt]. I will have forgotten my "Boston" name by the time I am here seven years. I hear it so seldom.

The other day I was going along the street in my chair, a leper was on a box by the side of the street; his toes and fingers had come off and he was a terrible sight; as the streets are about six feet wide, I was pretty close to him, but I have not taken the leprosy yet. The beggars sit at the gates and almost grab onto you to get a penny. They are simply bundles of vermin. The country is beautiful but the City is a fright. There are a great many ruins on one side of the City, great walls overgrown with vines, where the Japanese destroyed them a great many years ago, and even as crowded as the City is, no one will live there.

The plain around the City is a regular lake, for the fields are flooded so that the second rice crop can be planted. Little stone paths are built up above the water to get over the plain. Everything here is built of stones. The bridge across the Min is built of stone—every bit of it. The Min is as wide as the Columbia. Think of building a stone bridge across it! The mountainsides are covered with tea fields. You should see the Chinese tramping tea leaves into boxes with their feet, and the sweat running off their legs into it. The native fruit is just getting ripe. The pears taste like turnips and the Babas are a half-ripe apricot. Many kinds are not good at all. The spiders here are as big as a saucer. I saw one coming toward me at prayer meeting and I made tracks. But they are not poisonous. Centipedes and snakes flourish here. Must stop and prepare my lesson.

A lady who came to Foochow lately, was walking on the wall one day and a soldier kept following along and finally he caught hold of her bustle and wanted to know what it was. Being alone, she made tracks for home. Yesterday, Miss Brown and I went to a temple to see the worship, and when we left, at least 200 followed us. You can't leave the house but a mob follows, and all try to talk to you.

Love from,   Martha

"I have been out on my wheel,
and oh, what a circus!"

U.S. CONSULATE   APRIL 21, 1900

Dear Mother and Relatives,

As you see, I am at the U.S. Consulate staying over Sunday "to get a rest" literally and fig-
uratively. Mrs. Gracey is a charming lady. A very cultured Boston Lady while the Consul
is a D.D. Mrs. Gracey thinks I may get homesick so she has me come over here as often as
I can get away, and I am only too glad to do so. It is perfectly lovely here and makes quite
a contrast to the Mission home, and I like the "Flesh pots of Egypt" enough yet to like to
get here pretty often. The room I have has eight great doors opening out on the veranda,
which is filled with beautiful plants and vines. The room is as large as your whole cottage,
with bathrooms, wardrobes, etc. opening off it. If I only had this room all the time I do not
believe I would grumble about no rooms as we girls used to do. Breakfast over and we had
a nice stroll over the consulate gardens. I wish you could see all the trees and flowers—orange, mango, lichees, bananas, pomelo and I don't know what all else. In the City we are
so cooped up that when I get here I want to give a big whoop.

Yesterday, next door to us at the Yamen [office or residence of a Chinese public official],
two pirates were punished with 200 blows. One was given 200 blows on the face for lying, while the other received them on his body. I can stand on the windowsill in my room
and look down into the Yamen. But I do not have any desire to see criminal proceedings!

April 25 —— To-day is the first day I have been out on my wheel, and oh, what a circus!
Miss Brown and I had Father Hartwell as guide. We went to a clear place in the temple
court near here. When the wheel was hauled out of hiding, it began to draw a crowd, and
the farther we went, the more the crowd grew and by the time we were through riding,
we had several hundred spectators. One of the college boys happened along and he ran
like a horse to spread the news, and here came a hundred boys with a half-dozen teachers at their head. The priests in the temple quit worshipping and came out and wanted to
see how we rode on wheels. The soldiers quartered near, came flocking about and wom-
en and children swarmed like fleas. Miss Brown and I fairly doubled up with laughing to
see the excitement we were causing, but they would ask the "slim See-Gu," which means
myself, to ride some more.

May 12 —— Next year I have to spend Saturdays with a woman's station class, and super-
intend two Bible women, but if I did not I should have to teach on Saturdays so I prefer
that, because I can get out more. I like it very well here. The Chinese are good students,
but perhaps my judgment is superficial as I have had only one Senior class which has had
eight years of drill. They are the silliest people in some respects. If I want to tell one of my

students anything about his lessons, for instance, and should happen to see him in the hall he would not walk the length of the hall with me, no more than in the company of an evil spirit because I am a *woman*. When the children are baptized, the man and his wife will not stand side by side in the church. It would be a breech of etiquette.

May 13 —— The rain is coming down in torrents yet and it is very cool. It rains every day nearly, and a few hours of intense heat always causes a shower. The city is a hot place. The only place we have to walk is on the wall. The top is several feet wide. That place to walk is of course, too rough for a wheel and too hard on shoe leather to be very enjoyable. I feel as though I have not thoroughly straightened out since I came here.

A lady in the U.S. gave $15,000 to Foochow College with which to build suitable buildings and the Mission is trying to buy more land, but it is slow work. You don't dare offer them a sum of money for land however small it may be, for then, they would think you wanted it and it would be impossible to get it without paying an extortionate price. So, a middle-man has to be found who suggests that perhaps the foreigners would buy if he would offer and then negotiations begin which last indefinitely.

May 18 —— "Gee Whiz" [Martha's Chinese language teacher] has come so I will "coo" tones for a while. It just saws holes in my windpipe to talk Chinese for an hour. I have to screech so and then the vocal chords used are apparently very different.

Love from,   Martha

"She thought she would have to sell the children."

FOOCHOW, CHINA   MAY 23, 1900

Dear Mother and Relatives,

Only two weeks more then we go to the seaside, Sharp Peak Sanitarium. I am getting my bathing suit ready and intend to be a "kicker" if I stay in China. Sharp Peak is at the mouth of the Min River and is a fine place for bathing, I'm told, but I do not believe it, for the water is too muddy, so much sediment is washed out by the rivers that the sea is perfectly muddy.

I wish I had a drink out of our home well or some other. I have not had a drink of cold water since I left the *Doric*. It is all boiled and never gets cool again. I saw the natives haul a man out of a well here. He committed suicide by jumping in, I suppose. The water got so bad that they investigated and a man was in it. They hauled him out and left him on the spot for a day and a night. I'm glad it was not our well. Suicide is so common, and you cannot blame the poor wretches very much. Their poverty is something terrible. One poor man near our house had four children and they were actually starving and not a way to make a cent. I went down to see if it was as bad as reported and found the children wailing for food and the mother wailing because she thought she would have to sell the children, and a slave dealer there trying to buy the children at $25. Think of that when $3 will keep the whole family a month. When we go on the street there is a regular train of Chinese that follows us and when we wait anywhere hundreds surround us. Foochow is just like an ant hill. The Chinese say there are "four brothers" in China that make much trouble: the piper (mosquito), the jigger (flea), "the dealer in wood" and "the dealer in cotton cloth." The first two are making it lively for me so I will quit and go into my mosquito house.

May 24 —— To-day I went to a woman's school and *examined* the pupils. Don't laugh, *I did*. The women began studying the same time I did, so they didn't know much. Miss Hartwell said she would settle the business while I did the "tek" so the native teacher trotted them into a room and I heard them recite hymns and Bible verses and go over tones. It was a fine lesson for *me*. I learn more that way than by sticking to my books. Miss Woodhull came a little later to examine candidates for her school and they wanted the "good-looking" (guniong) old maid, meaning me, to go on with the examination. (Think what the other woman must look like)—but I gave way to a more experienced questioner. It was quite funny to think of my presumption but I got along well and will try it again tomorrow.

"Gee Whiz," my teacher, and I have a row about once a week. He gets so lazy he will not correct me, so I lay a trap for him and he gets mad when he gets into it. At first I could not distinguish a word but now the words stand out as plainly as ours, though of course, I do not know so very many yet. I can make my wants known well enough.

I sold my wheel for $50. Wasn't that fine, so I'm going to 'blow it in" on a typewriter, perhaps. I need one badly. I have to pay 20 cents per letter postage as it is and it would economize stamps to use a typewriter.

May 29 —— You have read of that tired feeling, well out here we have it "bad." We almost wilt when the sun is out. One feels weak enough to fall over and lie anywhere. If it did not rain every day I do not see how we could exist. Nobody can complain of cold feet for six months of the year at least. A tailor has been at work making me some cool clothes. All my clothes are too hot. I pay him 12 ½ cents per day for very good sewing. The only objection is that his breath is like fury, and I hate to have him work on my clothes.

Love from,   Martha

"And ever so many birds are perched on the shutters."

FOOCHOW, CHINA   JUNE 6, 1900

Dear Mother and Relatives,

This week is examination and it is a great task—200 boys of all grades, and four of us have all the examining to do. Thank goodness it has been delightfully cool for a few days. As soon as school closes we will flit to escape the heat and smells.

June 8 —— It is lovely this morning. There has been a little shower and the drops are dripping off the banana tree that leans against the window, and ever so many birds are perched on the shutters. One old magpie hops up in the window and chirps every morning—the birds here are so tame. They do not seem to have the least fear. A great banyan that overhangs the yamen just across the wall is a perfect rookery. Most every kind of bird is represented. All the familiar kinds we have at home besides the birds of the tropics are here.

Love from,   Martha

"This is a literary center and very peaceable."

PAGODA ANCHORAGE   JUNE 21, 1900

Dear Mother,

I suppose you are reading all the Chinese news and wondering when I will become a martyr to the Boxers. We are so far south I very much doubt if there will be any excitement at all here. The Viceroy reported to the Consul that everything was perfectly quiet in the City and soldiers have been ordered to Ku-Cheng, near Foochow in case the Vegetarians become active. [Vegetarians in the south correspond to Boxers in the North.] I have been at the U.S. Consulate enjoying myself for a week and went back to the City and packed up. Just think of my packing again—and we packed everything so that if we should by any chance burn out this summer, we should not lose quite all our possessions. It seems like I did not escape packing by coming to China.

Everybody is very sad to-day over the death of one of the college boys, Gienu-Gu. He came to say goodbye day before yesterday and said he was not feeling very well but took the launch for Ku-Cheng and died on the way after being out but a few hours. He had what is called beriberi, a slight swelling of the legs, and heart failure following. It is almost painless and very sudden. Very few ever recover from it and it is really a kind of plague. He was the son of a native pastor and ranked first in his studies of all the boys, this past term, and he was such a good obliging young man that everybody liked him. He was the most promising boy in college both from a Christian and educational standpoint. He recited to me last term and so I came to know him very well. It is hard to understand the Providence that took him.

There have been other deaths among the boys but none seemed to take hold of the teachers and students like this one. Many of the students attempt suicide if reprimanded by the teachers or parents. One young man, the son of a very prominent man killed himself because his father scolded him. He dressed up in his elegant clothes, took opium and went to sleep never to awake. Dr. Woodhull was called but could not save him. He was buried just as he died and was put in a coffin just as he was dressed. While I was at the Consulate, Dr. Gracey went to the club one evening and as he was returning in the dusk, he heard a gasp and looked up and saw a man swinging from a tree. He cut him down and left him to recover, for if a man saves another he is supposed to furnish him rice for the rest of his life.

Sharp Peak—looking on Mat-su Island

June 22 —— We started from Pagoda Anchorage at 7:00 A.M. yesterday and the wind and the tide brought us here in five hours. It was a lovely trip and so enjoyable because the boat was clean and there were no bad odors to distress us. I am getting to be quite a sailor, as the roughest water never makes me sick. We landed at Chiong-Sich, a fishing village, and how the half-dressed coolies swarmed about us jabbering like so many magpies. We had a mile and a half to go across the mountains to Sharp Peak Sanitarium.

Sharp Peak Sanitarium

We were hungry enough to eat anything when we got here but the crazy servants had started without any breakfast so we let them get their dinner first, then we unpacked and are pretty well straightened up now. We have the east end rooms, which consist of a suite of three rooms and a veranda. We have the two middle rooms for sleeping rooms and the veranda and outside room for a place to study. We board with Mr. and Mrs. Hartwell. My bed looks like the one I had in Shanghai, a Chinese bed with springs on top of that and a wooden frame covered with netting around that. You would laugh to see it. The way I get in is to put on my bathing suit and get back and run and jump for it! But before this, everything has to be looked over to see if a stray centipede has taken up his quarters there. Sharp Peak is an island and the sea comes swishing up, up, on all sides, and the breezes blow all the time from the land or sea. It is almost like being on a boat except we do not move. The island is a sharp peak and the sanitarium is on top.

Sharp Peak landing

June 23 —— Consternation reigns in camp to-day. We can get no news at all except a little that leaks out of the Chinese telegraph operators. The Viceroy has ordered a guard of Chinese soldiers to protect the missionaries and other foreigners in Foochow City, and the foreign consuls have ordered all the Missionaries to the City from country districts. The whole city is organized for mutual protection in the case the Vegetarians rise in arms. The Vegetarians in this province correspond to the Boxers in the North. It is rumored that they are arming and the people are as much afraid of them as we are. They pillage and murder without discrimination. We get rumors of every kind and the very fact that we do not know how much is true puts everyone in a state of anxiety. Mr. Hartwell says he has no fears for this province for he has lived here 52 years, and during the British and French wars, you would not have supposed there was such a thing as war.

This is a literary center and very peaceable, though the highest military and naval officers are Foochow men. In case there is an uprising against foreigners, our lives would not be worth insuring. The Chinese have an idea these Vegetarians and Boxers have magic powers and they are ready to run at sight of them. The soldiers are worth so many tin soldiers, there is not a foreign gun-boat on the river and the pilots are afraid to pilot out the tea ship for fear of mines. The new forts with their great guns could blow up a fleet in short order. In the midst of the excitement to-day I drummed away on Chinese for six hours, and everybody wondered where my nerves were. I can't realize there is danger, though no doubt there is some. I do not know where we could run, for we can almost jump into the sea from the top of the island.

June 25 —— No doubt you have the news in America long before we have heard it here. There is a telegraph station here and one of the operators killed himself last night so we can't get any further items quizzed out of him. Yesterday was Sunday and as lonely as any day I ever awoke to see. Everybody had the blues so I climbed into my mosquito house and slept all day so that I would not get blue also. We are having the latter end of a typhoon at present. The wind is rising and the sea is lashed to a foam. The building we are in is a stone one-storey flat so I think we are safe from danger in that respect. It makes me so furious to not know what is going on. All the foreigners in North China might be killed and we would know nothing of it for six weeks.

Love from,   Martha

"Don't you worry about my head parting company yet."

SHARP PEAK   JULY 7, 1900

Dear Sister and Brother,

There are terrible floods in Foochow, which have swept out whole streets and drowned hundreds. This happened the day we left Foochow. Add to this a terrible typhoon with heavy rains attending and you have the physical situation. Hundreds of poor people would have starved if it had not been for the foreign tea merchants who contributed several thousand dollars, and the native Christians under the care of the Missionaries brought rice and cooked it for those impoverished by the flood. The City is in a terrible condition, dead bodies are taken out of most every place since the flood subsided. The Mission compound is on a little hill so it was not damaged. The crops are a total failure and starvation stares the people in the face for next year, as they will have nothing.

You know I told you I sold my bicycle for $50. Well, soon after, a poor woman right under our walls was starving with three children. So I thought that hateful bicycle was gone for a lot more than it was worth so I give the woman $2.50 a month until she gets some work. Just think of that keeping four persons a month. Miss Brown gave enough to buy some clothes and the woman nearly breaks in two making bows to us when she sees us. Miss Brown and I have a little fun about being the head of the family. The father is dead.

The Viceroy had said the river would not be closed to foreign trade. Then he ordered torpedoes set in it and some of us nearly got blown up. Just after our party got here at the Sanitarium a half hour from the place, a terrible noise was heard and a great column of smoke came up and we did not know or find out for some days that they were getting out torpedoes at the neighboring fort to mine the river, and one had a rusty screw, and a fool soldier tried to hammer it loose with the result that the magazine was exploded which demolished the massive fort and destroyed the crops on the hillside for a long distance around, and the boats of the river near were blow into splinters too small to pick up. Besides, and worst of all, there were 36 lives lost, that many soldiers were blown into atoms. They tried to keep it from the foreigners, they were so ashamed of their ignorance and deceit but of course, they could not.

The English Missionary Society has ordered all the missionaries to Hong Kong and they are going on every steamer. Our missionaries are going to Japan as soon as they can get off, i.e. those with children. That will leave Miss Hartwell and her father and myself on this island with our troop of Chinese who are ready to run any minute. If we have to leave, we will go to Hong Kong or Manila for the summer, but I do not anticipate any such trip. Don't you worry about my head parting company yet. We are on the coast where the ocean steamers can pick us up at any time and we have all our traps packed and ready to fly if the signal comes. I fear this is going to be disastrous to our school-work for some time. The summer term had to be given up. Of Miss Hartwell's 30 day-schools, all but three were washed away by the flood. One of the school boys wrote me a letter telling of the plague, as if this is not enough. China is a beautiful land, but Oh! dear, the suffering! Suffering stares one in the face on every hand.

July 8 —— I like the Mission people much better than I did at first. The Chinese and I get along famously, except my teacher and I, and I suppose I get mad at him because I can't get along faster. I have two teachers now, one in the A.M. and the other in the P.M. So, I am doing pretty well, I think. Chinese is not hard to translate — it is just fun — but the talking is a pinch. I like to study it. I never get tired of it.

Love from,   Martha

One of Martha's language teachers

"One must make up his mind to be deceived at least two-thirds of the time."

SHARP PEAK   JULY 28, 1900

Dear Mother,

The Chinese Christians are in perfect terror when the missionaries speak of going (to Japan). The persecution is held in check only by the persistency of the missionaries in having cases of persecution severely dealt with. Our consul has the right to interfere in such cases, so the native Christians fear with good reason that as soon as foreign protection is gone, their hard times begin. Rice is selling at three times the usual price and the looting of shops is a common occurrence. They can't trust each other and that makes half their trouble. There is no unity or agreement among them. They stand in open-eyed astonishment at the extent that foreigners trust each other, but most of all to see themselves trusted. One must make up his mind to be deceived at least two-thirds of the time or else believe everything is a lie. If the latter course is pursued, you defeat the object for which you came here; if the former, you feel so mad sometimes you could bump heads.

Love from,   Martha

"I have no inclination to die yet a while."

SHARP PEAK   AUGUST 1, 1900

Dear Anna,

I am sorry mother is so worried about me. I have no inclination to die yet awhile, and I shall endeavor to get away before anything serious happens. I was on my way to Japan once but fortunately it was too crowded to go and now the danger seems to have passed. The officers are very vigilant to arrest anyone who makes incendiary speeches on the street. One of our Mission walked on the street a few days ago to see if there would be any demonstration and the only thing he heard was a shopkeeper say, "kill him, kill him." He stopped and began to take the number of his shop and the fellow said he was telling his next-door neighbor to kill a chicken.

Love from,   Martha

"A shrine containing the tears of Buddha."

SHARP PEAK   SEPTEMBER 21, 1900

Dear Mother (and all the home people),

I went with Mr. and Mrs. Hinman to Kushan Monastery—the richest in all southern China and next best in the Empire. It is simply grand—the situation ideal, and so clean and cool. Water-works just as we have at home, are used and fountains come gushing in places among rocks so naturally that you can scarcely believe your eyes that they are made there. Great long walks bordered with gigantic banyan and camphor trees extend all through the place. Ponds and flower beds and beautiful plants are everywhere. There are some 20 great temples filled with idols and these are mostly covered with gold leaf. The great idols in the main auditorium are at least 30 feet high and the pedestal ten. There is a library of 10,000 volumes beautifully arranged and in the center of the room is a shrine containing the tears of Buddha, also his tooth! There are 150 priests there to minister to the idols, and all told, there must be some thousands of idols, as I counted some hundreds in one temple alone.

The Buddhist priests shave their heads, then, brand nine spots on top with a hot iron [this practice is typically done with cones of incense, which Martha later witnesses]. They wear long yellow robes when they worship. A delegation of nice looking young priests escorted us about and explained everything. We ate our lunch in a temple with idols grinning at us, and the priests brought us tea and fruit. While at dinner, the priests put on our hats and when we began to look for them, a row of priests were standing before their little mirrors admiring themselves, and one fellow had our colored spectacles on, and a foreign umbrella over him. We at once requested that they take them off but they skipped off carrying the hats along and came back by and by with them decorated with roses. We had a jolly good day and trudged back over the hills in the evening and found a big python in the path. As it began to get dark, the coolies had another tiger scare and stampeded and lit out as hard as they could run. No wonder though, for eight people have been eaten at Kuliang this summer. A boy was picked up in the yard with his mother looking on only a few feet away.

Next day a typhoon came on and we did not stir out of the house until Tuesday last when we started for Sharp Peak, Mr. and Mrs. Hinman and Miss Brown and I. We had three coolies to carry each of us and two for baggage. We got along all right going over the mountains but when we got to the paddy fields they struck for more pay. A paddy field is something beyond a foreigner's skill in getting through. We raised the wages a little and they went on for half a mile. Presently, they dropped me in that muddy field and wanted more money. Till this time, the rain was pouring down, but I sat as contented as crunched cookies and even *sang* a little. Presently I told my own coolie he had better go to the next village for some more men. How those scamps did pick me up and travel then! We went on until we came to a ferry across a canal and I stepped out of my chair and went down to my knees in the paddy. The head coolie came and dug me out or I should have been there yet. It is simply impossible to extricate yourself if you break through. The coolies said to themselves, she can ma (scold). I didn't know what a vocabulary I had before.

Yesterday, we hired a fishing boat in the A.M. and explored some small islands. We took our dinner and ate it in a great cave where it was so chilly that we had to have wraps. In the evening, we had our daily swim in the sea. I have got so I can swim now. All summer I have just paddled around and floated but of late, I can swim. Mr. Hinman explained the science of swimming and then he took me out beyond my depth and turned me loose. I forgot the principles but it was "sink or swim" and I preferred to swim and began to paddle with all my might, when a big wave took me up high and dry on the land, but I landed head first with a lot of salt water down me—it is great fun!

Foochow City, September 25 ——

A lady in Massachusetts gave $15,000 gold or about $32,000 silver to erect buildings, so you see we will have something good eventually. We are having a hard pull to get a ladies' house out of the fund, but we single ladies are set on having it, and probably will get it in a year or more. While most of the "kickers" are gone, we are going to get a tennis-court! We have to be politicians here as elsewhere.

September 29 —— The Chinese are a people with wonderful capacity for good when once they are brought out of the apathy, which the degradation about them has caused. In America we come in touch with the low class (which do not compare so very badly with our submerged tenth) and our judgments are hastily formed. An authority on China says that, to compare any other 400,000,000 people on the globe with these, for average intelligence, China would rank ahead. Then we are apt to get the Manchu Dynasty and the people confused. This dynasty commenced somewhere in the 17th century and is of the conquering Manchus. They are the Royalty and the Military, and consequently, the unscrupulous power that convulses China. How the people hate this dynasty—even worse than foreigners. Their shaved heads and their queues [braid of hair worn at the back of the head] are badges of their servitude. When the Manchus established this dynasty, they ruled that every man who did not wear his hair so, should be considered an enemy to the country, and so the fashion prevailed. There is no superstitious dread of losing their queues as we used to suppose.

. . .

I have five classes in the college and study with Gee Whiz three hours, so you see I have no play-time. When I have leisure, I go to the women's classes in the City to "examine" them. Don't laugh. It is a fact. The Peets are still in Japan and the Hinmans have that house and I am in the Hartwell house. Miss Hartwell and I have this big house to ourselves.

We went to a temple yesterday where there is a nice clean place to sit and as usual, in came a crowd. Mr. and Mrs. Hinman agonized over Mandarin and Miss Brown and I over Foochow, and when we made a remark in English, several of them laughed and we learned that they could speak English very well, and were enjoying our struggle over the Chinese. On our way home we stopped at the Garrison and some soldiers went through the drill with their Big Knives, of which, you have perhaps read. They have a handle as long as a pitchfork handle and similar, and on the end is the knife shaped like a pruning hook and knife. Every second man has an implement like a pike for impaling the enemy. The soldiers were most admirable fencers, but it looked so simple to see such weapons used in modern times. The commanding officer walked almost home with us and he really has a military bearing and is a good-looking man. These are Honan soldiers, said to be the bravest in the empire. Their uniforms are black with a red border around their coat-tails, and a round yellow piece of cloth with characters on it sewed on the back and breast of the coats.

When we returned a letter was awaiting us saying that Mr. Peet's little son aged six years had suddenly died in Japan, where they had gone on account of the troubles. They have one child buried in China, one in U.S. and two in Japan.

If you had my coolie Sing Joy, you would have a fine servant. I wish you might at the same price I pay him, 50 cents a week in silver, or 25 cents our money, and of course he boards himself besides supporting his wife on that. I gave him 50 cents to get him a couple of suits of nice clothes and he was overjoyed at my generosity. He does all my work now except cooking—my other men are gone. Our personal coolie waits on us at the table and looks after us generally. You may think this lazy but we could not possibly do our work if we had anything else to do. Besides if we did, we lose standing, if we did any of the work, for they would think we were coolies and what would be the use of respecting us? I have not done a bit of housework since I left for China except make some taffy one day. Thank Will for his information about typewriters. I will send to Boston for one and then I will not have to pay freight.

You and Dickie have taken up my favorite author this summer I see—Mark Twain, while I have been digging out Chinese. At first I thought it would be harder to talk than to read but now I have changed my mind.

Love from,   Martha

"And the devils were all hauled out of their musty corners and given an airing."

FOOCHOW CITY   OCTOBER 7, 1900

Dear Mother and Brothers,

A life in China not well crowded would be anything but desirable for there is nothing to do to amuse one's self. Between 6 and 7 P.M. I take what exercise I can get. Most evenings we climb U-sang hill and practice with a bow and arrow or fly kites. When we try to shoot we usually have such a crowd that we are afraid of hitting somebody. The Chinese have a perfect mania for kite flying. Literary men, soldiers and school boys, and everybody else but the Viceroy, flies kites. We foreigners get the craze too. Thousands of kites are to be seen over the City in the evenings. Most every kind of animal is circulating over our heads.

Next week, there is a holiday for everybody to fly kites. Tomorrow is also, a holiday to celebrate the intercalary eighth month. [A month inserted in the calendar to harmonize it with the solar year.] There are holidays galore here but then no wonder since they have no Sunday, and they want some time for play. On Saturday we have no school in the afternoon so Mr. Walker, Mr. and Mrs. Hartwell, Miss Brown and I walked around the City wall. In the Tartar city the soldiers were drilling and had fine guns, but they themselves were a sorry lot. They are big brutal-looking fellows, much worse than the Chinese proper. There were a thousand recruits being put through a genuine up-to-date drill, by very soldierly and good-looking officers—the officers are mainly fine-appearing men, educated abroad. The Tartar women dress just like Chinese men, and being so much larger than the Chinese women, if it were not for their hair it would be difficult to tell them apart. One old dame followed along with a big rock in her hand, glowering at us, and when we turned a corner, threw it at Mr. Walker, but like all women, missed him.

Yesterday, there was a big idol procession to "make peace" and the devils were all hauled out of their musty corners and given an airing. It is to be hoped the head devil has made enough trouble and quiet will be secured though everybody here seems to think this is but the beginning of worse matters. If that old dowager and Prince Tuang were gone it would be an end of murder for a while. It will be a disgrace to civilization if these abominable murders are allowed to go unpunished. If the German Minister had not been killed, I fear that the dozens of missionaries put to death in the most barbarous of ways would never be avenged. The Germans have sold arms and drilled Chinese troops, now they may get a chance to see how efficient their pupils are.

Your affectionate daughter,   Martha

*"Yet they cheat, in spite of the fact that their
head is cut off if caught cheating."*

FOOCHOW, CHINA   DECEMBER 8, 1900

Dear Wallace,

Yesterday a party visited the Examination Hall, what an immense affair it is! Ten thousand separate cells arranged in rows of 50 each. Candidates for literary honors present themselves and are looked over to see that they are not smuggling in anything, then they are shut in one of those cells two days and nights to write upon some given theme. A guard is placed at each row to see there is no communication, yet they cheat, and in spite of the fact that their head is cut off if caught cheating. There are two high walls around the cells and cobras imported and put between to prevent anyone coming over. Last exam five men were bitten by them and three died in the cells. Those who win a degree are eligible for office, and have a title.

December 12 —— The last I wrote I said there had been no excitement but now I have a little. To-day we all went to Nantai, the foreign settlement, to the monthly concert and as we returned a Chinese man spit in Miss Brown's and my face. Usually I keep an umbrella with me to drive off dogs, but to-day I rode in a chair and left it at home or I would have knocked him hard. Miss Brown was ahead and I behind, and this man spit in her eyes. I did not see him do it as there was an awful crowd, but he came next to me and stared in my face (as many of them do) and then he spit in my eyes too. I had two old vagabonds carrying me and they would not let me down or I would have chased him to a soldiers stand and had him arrested. Mr. Hinman said it was a good thing they did not or it would have precipitated an awful row. The Chinese are afraid of foreigners, if you just show a little fight, and I would not have been afraid to have given that fellow a good whack or two. When I get mad or excited I can talk Chinese first rate—I remember all the words I ever heard.

Last week a chunk of bamboo whizzed by my ear on a trip to the South Side in a chair. Yesterday a man on the street struck at Mrs. Hubbard and just missed her head as she dodged, and a crazy man followed Mrs. Hinman from Ponasang and she had a pretty hard time to give him the dodge.

Love from,   Martha

"Now I study the classical and translate into colloquial."

Dear Brother,

I am cramming Chinese again for next term. It is a good way to learn it—by teaching. Sometimes I get discouraged at my progress but when I think how perfectly helpless I was a year ago, and now I can "paddle my own canoe" all right, I think I have learned fast enough. Now I study the classical and translate into colloquial. I am paying a boy a dollar this month to teach me during vacation while my teacher is away, but it really amounts to his following me around and telling me new words. He gets it in his head that he is to do all the talking sometimes, when I want to talk, so I have to "sit upon him."

. . .

I am going to the consulate for a week this vacation. That is my usual retreat when I get a day off.

I wonder if you get tired of the length of my letters. I have known such things to occur—I will close with love to all.

Martha

"In spite of this terrible death rate the foreign consuls agreed there is no plague in the city. It would injure a lucrative tea trade."

Dear Sister,

The boys (students) are very much sobered by the ravages of the plague. Some have lost their young wives, their parents, others nearly every member of their families. They were very sad when it came time to disband this morning after prayers. Some go into plague infested homes and I fear that many of them may never return. Yesterday the grandson of the District Magistrate came home in the evening well and took sick this morning and died at 11 P.M. He was hardly dead until he was sealed in a coffin and hurried off. This occurred just over the wall from us. Coffins are almost as numerous as people on the street and it is a marvel to think that the people do not get in a panic.

They say repeatedly, ("Mo-huok") *"fate"* and they think there is no human aid. Consequently the idol "shindigs" are going on at a great rate now. In spite of this terrible death rate the foreign consuls got together and agreed there is *no plague* in the City. It would injure a lucrative tea trade, and of course a few thousand Chinese do not count.

June 21 —— There is a big flood in the river to-day so the people can't go to Sharp Peak. Miss Chittenden and I are planning to go a week from now, stopping over at the Consulate a few days. I think it will be a rest to be by ourselves a little while. I am going to do a lot in Chinese this summer, as I can progress much faster now.

I have not closed my women's school yet—there has been so much plague I haven't ventured out very much. There will not be many at the Peak this year, Mr. and Mrs. Hartwell, Miss Hartwell, and a cousin from Amoy, besides Miss Chittenden and myself.

I just heard a few minutes ago that one of our best preachers was taken with the plague and is now at the point of death, if not already gone.

The natives have also been telling me that this is a great shark season at the Peak and people can't bathe in the sea for fear of them. If that is true I will send you my new bathing suit for evening wear! Last summer I just got so I could swim a few strokes, this summer if the sharks do not interfere, I intend to do some great kicking.

Next year I will have you send me some men's socks—short ones—so that they will meet my dress skirts and no more. It's entirely too hot for hose.

June 23 —— People are dying at a rate that would be astounding in time of war. Yesterday I went to a shop and there was a plague coffin, which passed and Chinamen ran in all directions. Last night a woman screamed most all night mourning for someone. This was so near it kept me awake. I think we will clear out of here and ease everybody's mind, in a day or two. It is the custom that no one shall die in a strange house, so as soon as a man gets sick he is hustled off home and as the disease usually is fatal within three hours, there are many deaths inside the chairs on the streets. If a man dies out of his house he must be put in a coffin outside. If an unmarried person dies they must be taken to the street to be put in the coffin, so you see how it spreads. A Chinese cannot burn the infected clothes, but gives them away to beggars, and that also helps it on. I presume you are tired of this plague subject, but it is forced upon us almost every hour in some way.

June 30 —— Am now at Sharp Peak settled for the summer. It is more home like here than I ever have felt in China. No one here but the Hartwell's and Miss Chittenden and I. Don't scream, but we brought ten Chinese along. Do you think we will manage to get along? To-morrow I think I shall begin study—like a young Trojan.

Love from,   Martha

View from Sharp Peak house — Min River in distance

"The man who carried water for us."

**"They say the average is a hundred coffins through
each of the seven gates per day."**

FOOCHOW, CHINA   JULY 21, 1901

Dear Brother Wallace,

This summer I have been comparing Lao-tze's (the founder of Taoism) philosophy and
that of Pythagoras, one of the earliest Greek philosophers and find them so near alike

that it seems they must have drawn from the same original source, especially as they lived about the same time.

Originally Taoism was a philosophy of the cosmos. Just as Taoism speculates on the origin of matter, so Confucianism deals with practical ethics, and Buddhism with the future after death.

I keep my teachers sufficiently stirred up on these questions so that they do not get to sleep.

Yesterday I asked my Chinese man how much the hired mourners got for wailing at funerals, and he denied any such custom, but I am going to prove it to him tomorrow.

Speaking of funerals makes me think of the plague—in fact it is constantly brought up in some way. In Foochow I believe it is said the highest death rate in one day was 1300. Consternation is personified there. The people cannot get away from the City and if they did they would get into a place as badly infested, so they just stay and die. They say the average is a hundred coffins through each of the seven gates per day.

The day before we came here our most promising teacher died, having caught the disease by going to the door of a house where there had been a case. He was taken with the disease and died a day or two later. It is in three forms, one more malignant than the others. It seems to affect the blood and in three hours the patient is dead.

I surmise these Chinese cities are in just such condition as those in Cuba were before General Woods got after them. I was telling my teacher that Cuban cities had been cleaned, and hence the Chinese cities could also be.

It is rather strange that foreigners do not take the plague. Business goes on just the same, and the great shipments often get out every day, just the same.

Poor old China is having a hard punishment, but it seems that those who deserve the punishment escape and those who are not responsible must bear it.

With love to all from your affectionate sister,   Martha

"We can look down and see the city almost submerged."

KULIANG, CHINA   AUGUST 5, 1901

Dear Sister,

Now that I am shut in with no prospect of leaving for some days I am going to do up my tardy letter writing. Mrs. Peet invited me to stay with her during the annual convention at this place and I accepted very gladly as I wanted to hear the star speakers in China. It took us (Miss Hartwell and I) two days to get here, as the water between Sharp Peak and the mountain was fearfully rough and the wind contrary. The English ladies of the party were terribly sick.

We reached a little village at sunset and had ten miles up the mountains in addition before reaching Kuliang. [Kuliang is a mountain resort used in the summer to escape the heat of Foochow.]

The moon rose calm and serene and a lovely trip it was by chair, though really we walked most of the way. The coolies kept close together as we passed through the ravines, as they feared tigers. We reached here a little after 10 P.M.

The week of meetings passed off very well and Miss Hartwell and I intended to start home on Friday morning, but the evening before a typhoon came up and we could not stir. All the doors had to be braced and window shutters barred so the house was as dark as a tomb except for the lamps.

Kuliang cottage

This house has kept us dry so far, but it is beginning to leak. This is Monday night and no signs of it stopping. The flood in the plain below is something terrific. Between the rifts of the clouds we can look down and see the City almost submerged. Thousands of people must be ruined by this typhoon.

The ravages of the plague have been most appalling this season—it being said that 35,000 have already died of it.

At this weeks convention the variety of styles was as varied as the individuals. Ladies just from the continent and others from the interior of China presented a contrast that was striking to say the least.

Miss Way, one of the three missionaries who escaped from the terrible massacres of Shansi is here and will spend two weeks with us at the Peak. Mrs. Gracey is coming down to Sharp Peak in September and will stay a few days with me. You would die laughing to see the importance it adds to me to have the "Great American Consul's wife" visit me. The Chinese think it is wonderful to be on good terms with an official; the servants pretty nearly have a panic on such occasions. The clatter and bang and yelling of my retinue and the party she brings is deafening.

With love from,   Martha

BEGINNINGS AT KULIANG

GLEANED FROM MANY SOURCES

Naturally the early missionaries looked about for a cooler place than Foochow in the summer for the children and began taking turns going to Kushan monastery for periods of two weeks each. Now we wander over the hills for a day's outing at the monastery and return along beautiful paths to our comfortable cottages at Kuliang, tired and happy. Sixty years ago and after, each family took in turn a stuffy little room over the "fish pond rest house" at the monastery and then another plunge into the intense heat of their homes in the City or on the plain below.

And so it happened the Dr. C. C. Baldwin, Rev. Charles Hartwell, and Rev. F. S. Woodin went over the hills prospecting for a suitable place to build a sanitarium for mission use. They came to Kuliang and sat under the beautiful old cryptomeria that marks the Liong Chio village and as they ate their lunch discussed the feasibility of locating a sanitorium near. All three were favorably impressed with the attractions of Kuliang but before actually deciding, thought best to consult their wives. Mrs. Woodin was not favorably impressed because of the prevalence of malaria in the villages and at last Dr. Osgood cast the deciding vote in favor of the seashore; hence the American Board sanitorium was built at Sharp Peak in 1872, and for many years was the favorite summer resort of the mission families, as the M. E. M. [Methodist Episcopal Mission] and the C. M. S. [Church Missionary Society] soon after built sanitoriums near.

In the summer of 1886, Miss Newton and Miss Garretson looked about for quarters of their own. They found an unusually good potato hut and after repairing it slightly made it their home from 1887 to 1896.

It was in this potato hut that the first Kuliang Union Prayer Meetings were held. And also the first Kuliang church services.

Dr. W. H. Lacy's house was one of the earliest having been built about 1890, and the Smythe cottage a year later, and Rev. L. P. Peet's cottage the year following, 1892. From that time on the hillsides have been burrowed into with cottages and typhoon walls and the cottages number hundreds instead of tens.

[written by Martha]

*"Did I tell you that I sent for a basketball
and taught the boys how to play?"*

FOOCHOW, CHINA   FEBRUARY 1, 1902

Dear Mother,

Now it is vacation and I am not rushed to death on Sunday, so I think of the home folks more on that day perhaps than any other. You would hardly know me at present. Do you remember how I looked the time Ralph M. and I bumped heads? Well I got a hard bump yesterday playing basketball and have a bad looking face as a consequence. Did I tell you that I sent for a ball and taught the boys how to play? During this vacation the missionaries of Ponasang and the City and a few of the Methodists play twice a week. It is great fun. Old and young turn out and as none of them have played the game it is mostly fun and exercise combined.

Miss Chittenden has returned and Miss Hartwell has gone to Pagoda Anchorage so we are the same in number as before. Mr. and Mrs. Hinman of Shaowu are taking the place of Mr. and Mrs. Hartwell, so that leaves the Hinmans and Miss C. and I in the house. There are two kitchens and two dining rooms so Miss C. and I are going to keep house ourselves. She is blonde, about my size and a pleasant lady, five years older than I but looks five years younger. She speaks the Foochow beautifully so goes into the work without needing so much time to study as I do.

*Miss Pepoon, Miss Chittenden, and Miss Hartwell
with Chinese mother and family.*

This is the week the Chinese send their household gods up to heaven and get new kitchen gods for the next year. Miss C. and I vow that we will set up our kitchen gods at the same time, but instead of paper we will have some substantial ones.

It is Chinese New Year season and the streets are a sight to behold. They are thronged with beggars. Usually they have a big dab of red paint on their forehead and little streaks of it down their faces to imitate blood and great coils of something like celluloid sticking out of each nostril. Their long hair is sticking out about "seven thousand ways for Sunday", and they are clothed in the filthiest of rags, and carry long knives with them. Some have a gong and beat it. These beggars go about at this time and frighten women to make them give them money. Miss Brown and I went shopping the other day on curio street and a few began to follow us but as we did not stampede they left us. The lepers are out in full force. [There were an estimated 7,000 lepers in Foochow at this time.] Usually not many are out to be seen but now they are out begging, and more abject specimens of humanity cannot be imagined. At this time we ride when we go through the principle streets.

I was over to the Graceys' yesterday and they have been having the most terrible time with the gripe [influenza]. This week I had to get a waist [blouse] made, as they were to have a swell dinner. I am having a pale blue silk with white satin collar and belt. We have a fine tailor and he only costs 12½ cents a day.

Love from,   Martha

**"Think of a country where there are no orphan homes,
asylums, poorhouses, or charities!"**

[partial letter]

The past week I have been busy getting things in shape for housekeeping during term. Yesterday I had a great time. I had two men whitewash the walls (the houses are plastered), three washing windows, two scrubbing, two carrying the last shipment from Ponasang, one ironing, one cooking, two tailors, one teacher to help give my orders, an old woman to watch that things were not stolen, and two men working to file off my iron bed which is mismatched. Very important isn't it? It takes a regiment to do as much as one could do at home.

I had another big time on my birthday. We got a boat to go to Pagoda Anchorage and stay over night and see the Hubbards. I get on famously because I hire outside coolies and then one of our men to watch each thing. It costs more but saves a lot of yelling and fussing.

I must close now as I am going out to Black Rock Hill to get a woman to take her boy back and care for him. She hates one and loves the other, so she just cast out this little chap and told him to hustle, so Miss Hartwell found him and put him in school. He is a brave little fellow of about eight years but is mean from having to hustle. Think of a country where there are no orphan homes, asylums, poorhouses, or charities! And all the helpless without friends have to beg.

Good bye, with ever so much love from,   Martha

"They remarked that I was Miss Wiley, and was
so wise that I could teach men."

FOOCHOW, CHINA   MARCH 6, 1902

Dear Mother,

To-day I was escorted home in state by a couple of students. One walked in front and one behind and we pushed our way through the crowded streets. We met a lot of high toned young men dressed in most elegant clothes out for a horse back ride. They were evidently out to show their good clothes, but I was such a curiosity that they all stopped to have a look. They remarked that I was Miss Wiley, a teacher in the college, and was so wise that I could teach men.

I never was so busy in my life, but I get on pretty well by having Chinese do everything they can. One boy runs my typewriter a lot better than I can, but I do not care to have him copy my private letters, for their contents would be all over the City in an hour. He copies all my school work and in the summer waits on the table and I give him a dollar a month in silver, which would be a half dollar in gold. I have boys galore to help. I shall have to let my maid go home, as they are going to help replenish the earth, and when I have another woman, she will be a widow if I know myself.

To-morrow is feast of tombs, and we will have a holiday and won't I have a sleep! To-morrow everyone turns out and goes to the tombs of their ancestors to weep and howl and paste paper over them and offer sacrifices and have a great celebration all day, i.e. if they are heathen, and if they are Christian they perform about as we do on Decoration Day. The heathen began to-day to feast. There are a great many feast days in this land, as it is a necessity since there is no Sunday and people must play sometime or other.

To-day is a scorcher. I have been playing all forenoon so I must stop and write out my years report. I colored some clothes that had faded past recognition. An English lady told me of Maypole soap and I get it and just wash my clothes in the suds and it colors them very well and it does not fade as quickly as Diamond dye. If you ever want to color anything get some and try it.

I am going to send you enough money to get you a summer hat. I am afraid it is pretty late for it, but if you don't want it you can get a winter one in the fall. I got a pith hat in Hong Kong and look very swell in it. My other pith one looked dreadful. I gave it a kick up into the air and the tailor thought that was an indication that I did not want it, so he is wearing the old one. My ancestry must tell, as the good people of the port take me for an English lady, and now the English hat will make it all the worse.

Goodbye and ever so much love to all from, Martha

"Between her undue gravity and my levity, we could make a fair average."

Dear Mother,

We are wearing crepe on our door at present as the maid had a dress stolen and that is the next thing to a funeral in this part of the world. I suppose the mourning will continue until I relent and buy her one.

I get so cross sometimes that I would like to sail into the whole lot of servants and then I cool off and am thankful they are no worse, and wonder how I would live without them. It would take a foreigner his whole time just to get water ready to drink. Everything is a marvelous inconvenience. Labor is so cheap that no one tries to make things handy. If I keep house by myself I am going to send for a cook stove, but if I am with other people I will not bother about it. The cooking is all done with charcoal and it is wonderful what they do with their clumsy ovens. I never tell this cook from one month to another what to cook but if what he does prepare is not good he hears from me.

The married ladies go puttering around the kitchens trying to cook and I think that their food is not as good as when the cooks are left alone.

I think that I told you about my reception room. A man is coming to-day to bring me some ferns and palms for it.

I must tell you of a funeral which we celebrated a few days ago—I disgraced myself and giggled, to Miss Chittenden's great disgust. It is customary at heathen funerals to have a great sedan chair all decorated with red and the ancestral tablet of the "dear departed" in it and carried along before the coffin. An old Christian man died a few days ago and they were in a straight as to what should be done to appease the heathen relatives so that they could avoid the custom. So they propped the corpse up in bed and the son stood on one side and his wife on the other, holding the body up. Miss Chittenden took her camera and took a shot of him. She was so nervous about it that she did not get a very good picture and then she had to hurry and get it done for the funeral so she made a blue print 4-5 inches and they got a frame about three feet in diameter and put the little print in it and put it in the chair and carried it along in the red chair all by itself.

I had a special invitation to the funeral and when I arrived what did I see but that blue print in the chair all ready to head the procession and I laughed and laughed like I had hysterics it was so utterly funny. Miss C. had a face several yards long and I said to her that between her undue gravity and my levity, we could make a fair average. Fortunately I had a high coat collar and I went into that. I always act like a goose at the wrong time. I get so tickled.

I must stop this letter and get up and attend to business. I do not have headaches very often—much less often than I had at home but to-day I have a terror.

Love to all the family and much to yourself.

Your affectionate daughter, Martha

FOOCHOW, CHINA JUNE 7, 1902

Dear Sister,

I had been wondering why I had not received a letter from you in such a long time when Will's letter came and said you had Typhoid fever. I am always looking for something terrible to come through my letters and this time it came. I suppose that you are nearly well by this time. I am glad you went to the hospital where you could have needed care.

. . .

This is examination week and a busy time it is. I have all of the English classes of the institution to attend to. I have 12 of my own classes and then all those taught by Chinese, as we never have a Chinese examine.

Love from, Martha

"Here 12 large bookcases hold 1,200 volumes each of the Buddhist classics."

[unknown recipient]   APRIL 1902

A DAY IN KUSHAN MONASTERY

Knowing your interest in heathenism I venture to send you an account of an excursion into the very heart of it. Perhaps you remember my friend the Buddhist nun. One evening I climbed the steep flight of stone steps that leads to her temple on the top of "Nine Genie Hill" near our mission compound. It was almost April and I wished to invite her to the service of song on Easter Monday at the Heavenly Peace Church. She was most cordial and accepted my invitation with evident pleasure. In return she urged me to attend the initiation ceremonies at the Kushan Monastery, near Foochow.

On Easter Monday I waited for some time for the nun to come to my house but at last set off without her, thinking that her Buddhist scruples had outweighed her curiosity, but about two miles out I found her waiting by the roadside. As she was unable to keep pace with my chair coolies I lost her on the way. On arriving at the church she was offered a seat on the men's side of the church, which she declined. She was then sent to the women's side of the gallery, but as the women had never seen the head nun of the province in all her Buddhist regimentals she was mistaken for a man and ushered to the men's side again. This was too much for a person of her importance to endure and she left the church much offended.

On the day of the initiation Mr. and Mrs. Hinman, Mr. Jones, Miss Hartwell, and myself were ready to leave the compound by 7:30. The clouds were thick and lowering and a heavy rain seemed certain but the coolies were at hand and even urging us to be off, assuring us that the sun would soon burst out from behind the clouds. Our curiosity was fully equal to that of the chair-bearers and we started in defiance of threatening storms. You can easily picture the procession as you have joined similar ones when in Foochow. Mr. Hinman mounted his pony and led the procession while the chairs followed in single file. We were scarcely out of the Water Gate when the rain began to pour but our coolies trudged on uncomplainingly, and one of them was even amiable after falling headlong into the paddy. Since your experience with Foochow chair-bearers it may require considerable credulity to accept the last statement.

For an hour and a half we wound in and out among paddy fields dotted with hummocks. When the coolies were asked why these hummocks were made in the midst of flooded paddy fields they answered that, "dead men's bones lie underneath." Further questioning elicited the reply that the coolies could not be expected to furnish both the muscle and the brain for the party and that I might better resume my historical research with a teacher's assistance—advice, which I acted upon later. I was told that late in the seventeenth century the Japanese made forays into this province, and that the soldiers that fell in battle found here a watery grave.

At the foot of the mountain we rested under a fantastic arched gate-way while our bearers took tea. A prosperous beggar amused us greatly by the persistence with which he followed up each group of travellers. Soon we were again in motion and no longer picked our way along narrow footpaths.

A broad, stone-paved road worn smooth, by the feet of many zealous pilgrims, wound gently upward. Clusters of dwarf pines grew here and there on the rocky hillside and in the open places the red azaleas blossomed in all their spring-time.

In spite of the steady downpour the pilgrims laughed and chatted as they tripped along the beautiful mountain road. We too, left our chairs and entered into conversation with the company bound for the great monastery. Often we failed to come to an understanding with the visitors from far distant provinces but all were friendly and smiled pleasantly as we found our dialects differing.

At the end of four hours we were at the broad entrance gate of the monastery—"broad" in all senses of the word—through which the throngs of pilgrims were passing. The Buddhist nun had given me her card which I was to present on my arrival. On receipt of this she came down from the women's apartments and welcomed us most cordially, though relating how badly she had been treated at Easter time and telling how superior the vegetarians were in hospitality.

What pride she took in the establishment! It was pure joy to her to exhibit the beauties of the place to foreigners. Her old blue coat had been changed for a shiny black garment, in style very much like a college gown at home. Her hat was such a marvelous creation that it would baffle a Paris milliner to reproduce it.

She led and we followed to the top of the pavilion built to accommodate rich gentry and officials. There in the place of honor sat the idol Ka-ou, the patron saint of seamen. The story goes that during the Sung dynasty a girl of this province had a most remarkable dream. Her father and two brothers each manned a boat and with their crew fished on the neighboring coast. One night the sister dreamed that the boats were in danger and that she must fly to the rescue. She seized the prow of her father's boat with her teeth and that of each brother in her hands and was towing them all safely through the storm when she heard her mother's voice calling her. Being a filial daughter she was obliged to answer instantly and in so doing lost hold of her father's boat and it sank at once. In the morning she had hardly finished telling her dream when the news came that the father had gone down with his boat but that the brothers were safe. Of course it was at once seen that she was no ordinary mortal and after her death she was canonized by different emperors—"Queen of Heaven," "Holy Mother of Heaven above," and other titles to suit the fancy of the emperor. At one side of her sat the "Thousand Mile Eyes," who can see the distance of a thousand miles without the aid of glasses. On the opposite side sat the "Thousand Mile Ears" straining every nerve to keep up his reputation for good hearing. These three idols sit there and preside over the destiny of the fisher folks along the coast.

While up in this pavilion we had a good general view of the grounds. Temple rose above temple far up the mountain side and, from our point of view, left just enough of the mountain top visible to make a beautiful green cap above the flaming red of the temples. Here and there were aged banyans spreading out above sacred grottos; groups of feathery bamboos reflected their pale green tints in ponds swarming with sacred gold fish; shaggy pines stood like sentinels above rocks with century-old carvings of proverbs from the classics; rare shrubs bordered the walks through spacious courts, or stood in pots on the ornamental bridges that spanned tiny ponds. And most wonderful of all, the place was clean! No one can tell how much money has been invested in this great establishment for it has grown with the centuries.

You may form some idea of the immensity of the culinary department when 3,000 guests can be accommodated with dinner at one time and not disturb the serenity of the chef. As a student once said, "If you did not see the pigmies at work there you would surely think it the kitchen of a race of giants," so great are the cauldrons of steaming rice and vegetables.

It happened to be the priest's dinner time as we reached the kitchen and the nun hurried through the dining room to "hear" the men eat. The priests sat in rows of 50, each with three large bowls of good food before him, which was dispatched with evident relish—if the sound meant anything.

The abbot sat on a platform at one end of the dining room and viewed the ranks of eaters with visible satisfaction. Here we learned that this was his sixtieth birthday and that there would not be another such gala day at the monastery for ten more years. Just as we had filed by and offered our congratulations a bell clanged and all the priests arose and chanted several times and passed out.

From the dining room we turned to the library adjoining. Here 12 large bookcases hold 1,200 volumes each of the Buddhist classics. These classics are said to be transliterations from the Sanskrit. At the back of the library in a case containing a miniature shrine: three tiny idols (one of pure gold), a vial of Buddha's tears, and a tooth supposed to be Buddha's. The tooth is said to be one of the four secured in India by Kublai Khan. (Perhaps Marco Polo acted as agent in purchasing the teeth!) If Buddha's teeth were in proportion to the one on exhibit his mouth must have been about eight feet across!

Back of the shrine was a porcelain image, which was said to have sprung full grown from the ashes that had accumulated in the censers that stand before the images of the "Three Precious Ones," or Buddha (law and monkhood). It was well protected by a glass case or I think we might have found "made in Germany" somewhere upon it.

A goddess with hands sprouting out in all directions stood beside the porcelain image. Originally she had but one pair of hands but as the demand upon her grew more frequent she was obliged to increase the number. If missionaries could only increase their efficiency a hundred fold as did this goddess! Certainly we have not hands enough for all there is to be done.

The image of a skeleton sat grinning from a shelf near by. As a mortal man he had starved himself as a work of merit and now he is no longer mortal but a god, worshipped by poor who think that he can sympathize with them in their distress.

The skeleton reminded us that lunch was awaiting us in the guest house. Hardly were we seated at lunch when the nun came and urged us to hurry to the temple and see the priests worship the abbot. Considering the business at hand it was not strange that we did not respond very enthusiastically and at length arrived at the place just in time to see a long line of priests file out of a temple and the abbot disappear at the rear of a platform where he had seated himself to be worshipped.

Near the central temple is a bell tower in which sat a remarkably pious man—to his thinking. He had shaved the heads of the priests for 30 years and at last was given a higher position—a room in the belfry. He has been in the belfry nine years and has not uttered a word during that time. This is a purely voluntary work of merit. He has another method of laying up merit that is equally efficacious. His bed is about three feet square and there he tortures himself night after night trying to sleep in such a small space. Though he did not use his tongue his hands spoke most eloquently of the contribution.

While we were in the belfry the "unspeakable man" rang the great temple bell and immediately people poured out of all the temples, guest rooms, dining rooms and every other place where they had been stowed away, and the central court was a mass of people all stretching their necks to see something, no matter what. Soon the abbot, resplendent in bright yellow robe with turkey-red trimmings, holding the insignia of his office in his hands, came out of the temple closely followed by six priests scarcely less gorgeous in creations of yellow and blue.

It was a very picturesque crowd that met the abbot. There were Koreans with their hideous hats, Loo Choo islanders with their top-knots, Anamese, Siamese, natives of the 18 provinces, smiling little Japanese, and at last the boycotted Americans. After a great deal of curiosity it became evident that the abbot was going to have a photograph taken. He placed himself in the middle of a little stone bridge and grouped the six priests about him. On the steps of the bridge stood the monastery marshals whose duty it is to whip the unruly priests. As a background for the picture the remaining priests arranged themselves in terraces and made a very imposing appearance as they lined up 600 strong.

While the marshals were trying to drive back the crowd and we were trying to "snap" the abbot the nun excused herself and left us. Not long after, she appeared heading a long line of women under her tutelage. The humility enjoined upon Buddhists did not show in her as she marched to the chief place in the center of the group and arranged the women about her. Of these women, 80 had that morning had three round spots the size of a pea burned on their heads. Now they are regarded as fully initiated nuns, pledged to lifelong fidelity to Buddhism and entitled to all the prerogatives that fall to nuns of that religion.

Two hundred women were "vegetable grandmothers," that is they had pledged themselves to be vegetarians and to temple service, but had not received the sign upon their heads, hence were not considered nuns. One shy little "vegetable grandmother" of ten years ran shrieking from the frightful foreigners and the toothless old crone held up shrunken fingers to show that she was seventy four. Invariably they looked as though the vicissitudes of life had driven them to the only refuge where they could get free rice.

While the abbot and his gaudy company were being photographed, the clouds lifted and for the first time during the day the rain ceased, and just long enough for the photograph to be taken. The abbot with his train hurried under shelter and ascended flight after flight of stairs to the very highest temple. The nun returned and stationed us at the foot of the stairs that lead to the temple of the Three Precious Ones. Now was to be the grand ceremony of the day! This was what we had gathered from the four corners of the globe to witness! Everybody wanted to see and thought his neighbor had the best point of view and promptly jostled him out of it.

Now over 300 priests all in new yellow robes formed a double line from the foot of the stairs where we were standing to the temple where the initiation ceremony was to take place. Every one shouted to the person nearest to know what would happen next.

It sounded as though the 18 provinces were in rebellion and the rest of Asia were taking sides in the quarrel.

Just then the speechless old man in the belfry struck the ponderous bell and the mellow tones rang out above the din of human voices. No wonder that the old bell-ringer loved his bell! Unconsciously the throng was hushed. From above, a long line of priests with laudatory inscriptions began to move towards us. Then, files of priests bearing the ancient arms of China came next, followed by the mammoth umbrella of imperial yellow, which the Empress-Dowager had presented to the abbot a few weeks previously. Smoking sticks of incense in great bronze censers filled the air with fragrance.

Down went the head of each devout priest until it touched the floor. It was a very solemn moment for of all the odors "the smell of incense is most religious." But dreadful! The illusion was all gone when we saw the fat old abbot following the last censer and knew that this was done to worship him for on this day he "was greater than a Viceroy." His gay robe fluttered in the gusts of wind as he strode through the lines of kneeling priests, and his coarse face beamed with satisfaction as he sniffed the incense offered to him as though to a god.

After him came the 280 priests who were to receive the last rite of priesthood. Some were old men with sin-hardened faces and others fresh-looking boys, perhaps 14 years old. Each had been freshly shaved and rows of little rings about the size of a pea had been drawn on the heads of the candidates. As soon as the priests had passed the nun they called to us to "fall in." The thousands of spectators did likewise and the result was such a crush that it was a wonder that many were not seriously injured. The nun had her shiny black robe rent and the others were hurled headlong down the temple steps. In the door of the temple was the customary high door sill—over 18 inches high—and as the crowd surged against the entrance there were many who measured their length against the walls or on the floor inside. We showed the "superiority of our race" by getting in without accident.

As the priests entered the temple to "receive the sign" every bell on the grounds clashed; every drum was beaten its loudest; the wooden fish sent up their hollow echoes; the priests chanting added to the din; but above even this noise could be distinguished the thin shrieks of the nuns and the "vegetable grandmothers."

Those who were to "receive the sign" arranged themselves at little tables on which stood lighted tapers. Two priests stood by each kneeling candidate and placed conical bits of charcoal on the circles marked on the head.

The first of the number that attracted my attention was a wicked-looking man past middle age who chanted the formula most lustily while the priests were arranging the charcoal but when they took the tapers and lighted the cones he groaned and wriggled about although he had chosen but three—the least number of spots.

A small boy opposite had 12 circles marked on his head and while they were being burned down, down through the flesh and drops of oil were oozing out he made no attempt to get away from the attendant priests, though the streaming tears showed the pain he was suffering. Others knelt as though hypnotized and seemed hardly conscious of their surroundings.

After some minutes the 280 rose fully authorized to enjoy the privileges of priests of Buddha. They shook the ashes from their faces and knelt to the priests who had rendered them this great service. As we stood watching, the nun shouted to us that, "by Buddha's grace the rite was painless." A coolie nearby asked how she explained the boy's tears. She turned on him sharply and said that she knew from experience that it did not hurt but if he doubted the fact he might have his own head burned to see for himself.

Suddenly the bells ceased ringing, the drums were silent and the chanting softened to a mere hum. Out of the temple marched 280 men entitled to beg for a living. The great event was ended! Buddhists from all parts of Eastern Asia had assembled to participate in the meritorious rite. Now that it was over the crowds dispersed until 4 o'clock worship.

All the while the rain came down in such torrents that we decided to start home at once, though it would have been a sight well worth seeing to have stayed and watched a thousand priests and nuns go through the Buddhist ritual. So just as we were leaving the grounds the silent man in the belfry was calling the faithful to prayers.

Our sedans were laden with beautiful red azaleas picked by the chair-coolies. The hills were washed clean by the constant downpour and little waterfalls were tumbling down over the massive rocks that cropped out of the red soil. Clouds spread out below us and covered the valley with a soft grey veil.

What a full day and how weary we were! But not too weary to think aloud our thoughts.

"What a force for good or evil those priests would be if they were only educated, wide-awake men instead of the lazy fellows that most of them are!"

"Heathenism in its very gayest most attractive aspect" thought another of the party.

"The awful sadness in the striving that ends in nothing better than a seared scalp and the privilege of respectable begging," stated another.

We reached our compound just as the college bell was ringing the students to prayers. How good to be home! What can be more different than our light-shedding and life-giving Gospel and their stultifying forms? All their gaiety and fantastic display seemed but a mask to hide the dreadful sham beneath.

Two weeks later I went to the home of the nun on the "Nine Genii Hill" and found that she had returned from the monastery just the day before. In response to my rap she called out, "Blessed Buddha! Who is it?"

"Peace! Peace!" I responded. "It is your foreign friend."

How changed she was! Her jolly round face was thin and her cheeks hollow. "Are you not ill?" I questioned.

"Oh, no!" was the reply. "You see it is quite natural that I should be tired out. I am the head of all the nuns and 'vegetable grandmothers' in this part of China and, of course, I had set them to an example of piety. Hence, I arose at 6:30 A.M. each day and led my company of over two hundred women to the temple where we worshipped Buddha for three hours. Midday we again worshipped and in the evening the long service lasted until 10:30."

"Suppose that the women do not wish to worship so zealously. What do you do then?"

"Whip them! What else could I do?"—and indeed what else could she do with such women?

"Now I suppose you will rest for a time?"

"Only for a short time and then I must be off to Burma to solicit contributions."

"And for what purpose may I ask?"

"I must support myself, burn incense before the idols, and do alms" was the reply.

Then I went the rounds with her and saw this energetic little nun light the evening incense before supplicating "mothers," frowning devils, the grinning Buddhas and wished that her energy might be directed to a worthy cause. Our conversation on the little balcony ended as many another with her had ended.

"Oh, yes! The Jesus doctrine is very good. It would be almost as good as Buddhism if you would only become vegetarians."

Martha

Buddhist nun in everyday costume

"Kipling says this is the land where 'there ain't no ten commandments.'"

FOOCHOW, CHINA   OCTOBER 1, 1902

Dear sister Belle and family,

Your good letter came a day or two ago while I was in the basement looking over the newly arrived Boston boxes. This time I did not have anything to sort but books. I run the book business of the institution, it takes a great deal of time and thought, to be so far away from the supplies and yet keep in stock enough books for a couple of hundred boys. And that is not the worst of it all, for we try to give them the books at actual cost and that involves changing the price in gold into silver at whatever the rate is and then as they pay for the books in subsidiary coin, that must be reckoned also, since a large dollar is worth all the way from 30 to 100 cash more than a similar amount in small money. Then there is the revenue to consider in gold and reduce into silver, and the cooleyage. To go through this process twice a year is all that my patience will stand. When I sell books at the beginning of each term I always have a Chinese teacher who is an expert to look over every bit of it before it is accepted or else I would be minus at least a third of it on account of the quantities of counterfeit money. When Mr. Peet takes in the tuitions he has an expert from the Chinese bank come and weigh it all. You see there are some advantages in living in a civilized country when it comes to doing business.

Kipling says this is the land where "there ain't no Ten Commandments" and he knows what he is talking about. Whenever I go to Pagoda I think more strongly than ever on the subject. There is a large foreign customs and arsenal at that place and it is a perfect terror what goes on among the foreigners. No wonder that the Chinese call us "foreign devils" if they only come in contact with the worst of the foreign element! I have begun to wonder how much religion and how much environment has to do with ones conduct and I am beginning to think that if a man comes out here and behaves himself he is a number one man.

October 10 —— All the well people in China will be up on the hills flying kites to-day, as this is the ninth of the ninth month.

Last night we had to expel a boy and that is always enough to make a person sick. We put in so much time and labor on them that when they get along where they might amount to something they kick up their heels and away they must go.

For a long time there has been profane and vile writing found around and no one could tell where it came from and at last this boy was found in the act of doing some of the writing, hence his sudden departure.

I presume every one of us has been up in no complimentary terms on the walls of the halls. This was a boy we never would have suspected at all.

Martha

"I added that the pathway of life was full of trouble whether you travel it single or double."

FOOCHOW, CHINA   JANUARY 4, 1903

Dear Sister,

New Year's Day Mrs. Peet gave a dinner to the Senior Class and they came at 5 o'clock and I instructed them in the art of ping-pong and they took to it so lively that they would hardly stop for supper at six. They went through the agony of a foreign meal and, poor fellows, I do not think they had half what they wanted, for they were afraid to eat. After supper they wanted to play some more and at the end they wanted to know if it would be all right for them to have a ping-pong contest at their class day exercises and I said that I thought it was a very original idea and met with my heartiest approval.

After that Mr. Gardner gave a magic lantern show and a few Chinese gentlemen who had been educated in England and America were present. They could speak English without the least trace of an accent. I think that educated Chinese get the language better than any other nationality. At least I have never heard any other foreigner speak English so well.

Miss Hartwell gave me a pretty little watercolor sketch of Singapore, which she had made herself. Gee Whiz gave me a bushel of oranges from his own orchard. Mrs. Pastor Lau gave me a sword made of cash, which will keep off all the evil spirits which may happen to come into my room, if I hang it opposite my bed. A student gave me a collar, which his wife embroidered, and some Chinese girls embroidered another almost like it for me. Another student gave me three little carved monkeys.

The waist you sent me will be fine for the spring wear. I will be glad to have that white belt as I use it with many white dresses in the spring and summer. The gingham will do very well for dresses as any thing in colors does not do for every day wear as it soon fades.

I stocked the missionaries with ping-pong for Christmas and am going to give the graduates a set. That is a nice present and its cheapness recommends it to me. The cabinet maker will make the racquets for five cents a set and a bit of course netting makes a good net and add a couple of balls and the thing is complete for 15 cents. When the first sets came out here they cost ten dollars.

These cold days it would make you laugh to see the shirt tails displayed. There are any where from one to eight on an individual. The longest and dirtiest is nearest the skin and then they vary in dirt and length until the outside one is fairly clean.

This morning the preacher preached a sermon to parents and told them to be clean and thus to set a good example to the children and not to let the bed bugs drive them out of the house, but to get rid of the bugs and to wash their bodies and change their clothes at least once a week.

I am about to lose Gee Whiz as he is looking for another position where he can get more pay. He told me that his family cost him so much to live that his present salary was insufficient. He said "this marrying business is a great bother" and I added that the pathway of life was full of trouble whether you travel it single or double. He said that he thought it was undoubtedly harder for the double team. I told him that his happiness had been increased so many fold that he could stand a little additional trouble. His little wife also says that it is very troublesome to get married so it must be. I shall miss the little man now that he wants to get away. He said that he also wanted to get away where he did not have so many friends as he had to make so many presents when people got married or when they died that it took half his salary. I sympathize with him on that as I begrudge the money that goes into wedding presents as every student who gets married gives me an invitation.

Last night I was invited to one of the pupils wedding feasts and I did not intend to go but at the eleventh hour here came two of the boys to escort me there and I went stumbling along through the rain and entered the mansion and was the only foreigner at the feast. The young man had a handkerchief spread out at the place where I was to eat and there were two little plates for my benefit, since being a foreigner I was not supposed to know anything about chopsticks; but I used the chopsticks to their great amusement. The women were all at one end of the house and the men at the other. The bride sat at one of the women's tables and never spoke a word or smiled once, as that would be dreadful. I said to her that I did not expect to get married, as I never could keep from talking two whole days. And to keep from eating that long was quite too much for me and I made a face over it and exclaimed to see if I could make her laugh. There was the faintest little smile began but she had a handkerchief of enormous size and screened her face.

I found out afterward that it was very rude of me not to have some money along to pay for my supper, but it went against my Americanism to have to eat what I did not want and then have to pay for it besides.

I have an invitation to attend a very small wedding next week. The invitations are engraved and set out in foreign style and almost all the missionaries are invited and the wedding is to be in the church. The young man is a graduate of the college and is now a teacher in the Tung Wen in Amoy. The bride is a sister of one of the students. Her trousseau is said to be fearful and wonderful. She is reported to have 17 pairs of embroidered shoes. Why she stopped at 17 is a mystery to me. I would have any way gone on to two dozen. The bride was sold for several hundred dollars. The Chinese say that the Christians are worse than the heathen to demand great sums for the daughters and it looks so.

Miss Chittenden has arrived within the last few minutes and the air is vocal with the three of us. I stop and talk between words.

Yours with love,   Martha

> ### *"The white ants had eaten the rafters out and just left*
> ### *a thin coat of paint on the outside of each."*

KULIANG   FOOCHOW, CHINA   JUNE 24, 1903

Dear Mother,

This year I tried to get up the mountain earlier than I got away last year but it did not pay as I had to hurry so that I was too tired to live when I got up here and my servants were sick and we were a sorry lot the first day. To add to the misery the white ants had eaten the rafters out and just left the thin coat of paint on the outside of each, on the floor of the second storey. The men who do the repairing told me that the house was in good order and all ready for occupancy but as the servants began to wash the ceilings they found that at least half of the cross timbers were perfectly hollow.

Monday I sent out and got a lot of men and then the washing began in earnest. I had to have every square inch of house scrubbed for the mildew and mold were hanging down in the most luxuriant growth. I just went about and saw that everyone was at work and toward night things were pretty well in shape.

The rain is pouring down and I am glad that I am in a cozy place. There is a heavy fog up here most of the time and the air is so damp that everything molds unless there is the utmost care to keep them dry. What an effort it is just to live!

There is a P.O. now at Kuliang and we can send our mail down by that. The steamer goes out tomorrow and I want this to catch it. Love to all the relatives and much to yourself.

Your daughter,   Martha Wiley

> ### *"He explained that our brains were so soft that*
> ### *they were easily melted and that mine*
> ### *were especially susceptible."*

[partial letter]

KULIANG   FOOCHOW, CHINA   AUGUST 15, 1903

Ladies Missionary Society,
Ahtanum Cong'l Church
Ahtanum, Wash., U.S.A.

Dear friends of the society,

These days of tropical heat find me at the little mountain resort where many missionaries spend the summer to escape the oppressive heat of the cities.

I wish I could show you our little stone cottage snuggled among the dwarf pines and bamboos at the head of a ravine where tigers are said to prowl at night, though I have never seen any until they were rendered harmless by some Chinese hunter.

A month after I came to the mountain I was obliged to go to the City on business, as there were many odds and ends of work that needed to be adjusted at once. First I must find out if it is possible to hire chair-bearers, and engage them for the trip. The cook is supposed to manage all those matters and from the noises in the servants' quarters it appeared that a miniature Boxer Rebellion was in process to settle the price. At length it was decided that three men would carry me into the City for 50 cents each. We agreed to start at 5 A.M. and at that early hour I had finished my breakfast and insisted on getting off at once but the bearers had decided in the night that they needed more pay, and Labor and Capital contended for some five minutes, and Labor came out ahead and the price was raised.

Now I thought we would surely be off, but no such good fortune awaited, as they said they would not carry a chair with a cover. Here was a dilemma indeed, as it would be quite impossible to go in the heat without a cover. Again the cook came to my rescue and told the men that foreigner's brains were peculiar and not like the Chinese brains. He explained that our brains were so soft that they were easily melted and that mine were especially susceptible to the sun and that if I went without the cover I would probably die in my chair and it would make them a great deal of trouble. They did not seem to think that it would be any trouble, for me to die in my chair. After an hour of this we started on our way. The beautiful scenery soon made one forget such a small matter as an hour's talk with unruly coolies.

When we finally arrived we entered the City through the East Gate. Soldiers are stationed above supposedly as a guard, but what they guard has never been determined. At night the great gate is closed and all traffic is supposed to stop but a price of ten cents is sufficient to induce the "incorruptible" Chinese soldier to admit friend and foe alike.

Near this gate is the leper colony. The lepers of the City have their sleeping places here and in the morning the "head man" of the lepers sends out his company of beggars and they go to all parts of the City to beg and return at night and divide the spoils. Never a wedding or a funeral nor an idol procession but this head leper must be consulted and bought off, or at the time the procession is passing out of the house a company of the most loathsome will swoop down and demand extortionate sums of money or they will seize the interested party with their terrible hands. Needless to say they usually get what they wish and for that reason they are very bold. At this gate there is a temple where the souls of executed criminals are supposed to be confined by the idol called "City King." One of my teachers, who is Christian, said that no money could tempt him to enter that place at night and in the day time it was not safe as there were often heard quarrels among the spirits.

. . .

"Seven of the 12 women have unbound their feet."

FOOCHOW, CHINA   SEPTEMBER 9, 1903

Miss M.D. Wingate

Chicago, Ill.

It is a great pleasure to write of the work done by the new Bible woman during the past year. She, Caik Ung Sing, has a quality rarely to be found among the women, that is enthusiasm. She has been earnest and enthusiastic in all that she undertakes and hence has accomplished much for the women of the class. She first studied in one of Miss Hartwell's station classes and later in Miss Woodhull's training school.

The little school-room off the chapel has been crowded with the 12 women who compose the class. Seven of the 12 women had bound feet but during the past term all have unbound them—a most remarkable incident as often even the professing Christians are unwilling to sacrifice the "golden lilies."

Caik Ung Sing had unbound her own feet not many years ago and understood how to loosen the bandages without causing too severe pain. She personally visited the women in their homes and taught them how to remove the little shoes and strengthen the weak muscles. It was surely a work of patience and love for there were mothers-in-law and brothers-in-law and husbands and sons to be encountered, but she worked on in spite of opposition and at last brought me seven pairs of dirty little shoes, anything in appearance but "golden lilies"—as a proof, she said, that the women were really earnest in their desire to obey the truth as far as they knew it.

When we think of how much the Chinese admire those little feet and the "beautiful swaying motion" of the bound-footed woman as they walk, we will understand that this was a very real sacrifice on the part of the women and means most diligent work on the part of the Bible woman.

Each woman has her own interesting history but it would require too much of details to tell you of them all.

Very truly,   Martha Wiley

[Note: Foot binding is the practice of breaking the toes and arch of the foot (usually started between the ages of two and five when the foot is not fully developed and bones are softer) to ensure a woman's chances of marriage and to increase the ability of a lower-class woman to marry into a wealthy family. The toes are folded under and the arch broken and toes folded toward the heel. Bandages are wrapped consecutively tighter over a period of time, to achieve the desired foot size of three inches, with continuous care needed to avoid infections.

Men enjoyed the assurance of the woman's dependence on her husband. Foot binding resulted in lifelong physical disabilities and, later, (after the practice was banned), a previously bound-footed woman found difficulty in performing labor-intensive jobs that were the only available work for middle and lower-class women.]

Bible woman

"And the coffins stand in the parlor for ten or twenty years."

FOOCHOW, CHINA   NOVEMBER 20, 1903

Dear Mother,

I fear that the letter that I last wrote was rather difficult to read as my machine was in bad shape, and is yet. It is still suffering from the effects of the typhoon.

One of our senior class has been called away on a very sad duty. His father is a poor man who works some rice fields for some other man. He and his older son were at work when a vagabond came along and went to cutting down the rice and on their telling him to stop he took out the big knife he carried and struck the father dead and the son was badly cut up trying to help his father. The student had to go home to see to the funeral. But according to the law the officer must be informed and come to the place and inspect the body before it can be moved. The boy sent a letter to the proper official, but when it was handed to the man who keeps the gate he remarked that if it was sent to the officer he himself must be given a fee of $20—otherwise he would not take it to the officer. This went on for two days and the officer had not learned about the murder for the boy could not possibly raise the sum. At last Mr. Peet found out how things were going and went to make a call on the officer and while there incidentally told him of the affair and he sent for the letter and the culprit who had kept it was standing in the room with the letter in his pocket in order that if Mr. Peet should tell he would have it ready. Then it took two days more for the officer to get out to the village and all this time the corpse was lying in the field and the boy watching it. The thief said he would wait and kill the boy, too, so it was a task that many an American boy might have been afraid to undertake.

Now that the boy has his father in a coffin it remains to have him buried. It takes quite a sum to properly bury a coffin and often the coffins stand in the parlor for ten or 20 years until some descendant gets enough money and then he has a high time feasting the coffin and its friends. The Christians are beginning to understand that is not quite hygienic to have a corpse in the dwelling rooms and they usually come to get the foreigner to help bury the coffin at once. All around Foochow can be found rows of coffins waiting to be stowed away in the earth and the children have fine times playing over them and women sitting on them to sew.

One day, during our week of meetings, we foreigners went off to East Gate to see some land that the mission wants to buy and while there we took our afternoon tea on the grave of a Mandarin. He had been a grand man in his time 50 years ago but he fell into disfavor and the Emperor cut off his head. It proved that the accusations against him were false and the Emperor on learning this tried to make reparation for the wrong by having a head made of gold to bury with the body that the soul would not be obliged to wander headless through all eternity. To prevent thieves from stealing the gold head there were seven tombs made—one at each gate—thinking that the thieves would not take the trouble to dig into all of them to get the gold.

He had been a military Mandarin and had two great stone horses on each side of this tomb.

I hope the integrity of China may be preserved and that old China may never be dismembered by greedy nations. There are a good many things about these people, and they are not to be despised by any means.

from your Affectionate daughter,   Martha

"Hardly a foreigner has escaped dengue fever."

FOOCHOW, CHINA   NOVEMBER 3, 1905

Dear Nettie,

To-day is a fine bright day, like a May day at home. All the good people are at the union meeting and I am home to watch house. The last month we have been infested with sneak thieves to such an extent that it is dangerous to go off and leave the house even when locked. Whoever it is has a hobby for the Chinese things we have picked up, and he lets the foreign things alone, no doubt thinking that they would be more easily traced. The last thing that disappeared was a large vase from off our parlor table. I went out of the door and crossed a little covered walk to the house next to us and left a servant in the waiting room next to the front door that I had left. In a few minutes Miss Hartwell came in, missed the vase and no one had any idea where it had gone. We have two gate keepers and they said no strangers had come in.

Then one of the gate keepers left and the other one threatens to go because we went at them rather hard. It is like a reign of terror. Everyone goes around with a load of keys locking up each door as he goes through and suspecting everyone he meets. We have finally settled down to the feeling that some one of our servants is the guilty party and we are going to hold them responsible for any further losses. Mr. Hinman has a runner that is a swell fellow and his fees are a little low and we think that perhaps he is replenishing his depleted exchequer [royal or national treasury] this way.

In all my experience in China this fall has been the worst for foreigners. Hardly a foreigner has escaped dengue fever. This year it has been in a very violent form. About two weeks ago the leading man in the M. E. [Methodist Episcopal] Mission died of the dengue. Previously when one had dengue it was a joke and the others all "jollied him up" as though he had mumps or seasickness and the Chinese themselves called it the "great peace" sickness because they said no one ever died of it. This year it has been anything but a joke. This gentleman who died leaves a wife and four little children who will go back to America. They were lovely people and quite young—he was only 34 when he was taken. From the very first he was delirious and remained so except for a few minutes when he came to and said to his wife, "I am going home in the morning." The next morning at 6 o'clock he died and by six the same evening, he was in his grave. It is terrific to die out here in a hot climate. Within two hours a body is hardly fit to be seen, unless it is the rainy season.

Miss Hartwell had the dengue very badly and was very much frightened and I sent for the community doctor to come into the City and see her. She was very sick for two weeks and is not well yet, a month later, though she is at work again.

When I was at the Peak before going to the City, Dr. Gracey came down to stay over Sunday and he became so ill that he had to remain longer and about a week later I was coming home and all my bones ached and I was as wretched a specimen as ever went walking around.

Just sit down and push off a letter when you have time and I will appreciate it very much. Is your mother with you? If so give her my love to-day.

With very much love to the clan, and much to yourself,

affectionately, Martha

"In that little village on the hill there were 13 opium dens."

FOOCHOW, CHINA   APRIL 12, 1906

Dear Mother,

I suppose that you receive the occasional letters that I have sent you as well as those that I have written to others. I wish that I could tell you in detail all the strenuous times that we have had this spring.

I went up on the hills to stay for three days. The leading lady of the place acquired the habit of taking opium and so Mrs. Hinman and I thought that we would bring her down to the hospital and see if she could give it up. She is a Christian woman and the richest woman on the entire ridge, so her example is very telling one way or the other.

The morning after arriving we went up to the house where the lady lives and it was with considerable trepidation that we began to tell our errand. She made all sorts of excuses and at last she could think of nothing else, and we all hustled to get her off before she changed her mind, for opium fiends are most unreliable and it was not safe to wait. It was about 1 o'clock when the procession moved out of the house. Mrs. Hinman came down with her and I stayed on until the next morning. When I started down the hill there was such a dense fog that I could not see ten feet ahead of me, and the coolies would run into a tree almost before seeing it. The wind blew and it was really quite cold. I wrapped my steamer rug about me and wished that I had a fur coat. In about an hour we got to the foot of the hill and it was very hot. The road was so narrow that I was afraid to ride and so when I reached Sheep Slope I was dreadfully warm.

In the course of my exploring I came across a man who seemed to be unusually cordial and when I enquired who he was he turned out to be the father of one of my students. He invited me to his house, which looks like a walled city in the midst of a paddy field. He told me with great pride of his great possessions — 15 acres of paddy. He also told me of his family affairs. His wife died some years ago and his son who was 13 was married and the following year he had a son. So now the student in our school is 21 and he has a son seven years old. When I happen on those things they do make me disgusted with life.

To go back to the leading lady, she has been a case! It has kept the entire compound interested to hear about her. She smuggled in some opium pills and everyone thought she was getting on very well until the nurse found out what she was doing. Then they watched her closer than ever. For a few days she has had no drugs as far as we know. Last night she was quite crazy so it is probable she has had nothing smuggled in. It is so sad to go out in the country and see the acres and acres of poppies that are planted there and the people working in them. The curse of opium is ten times worse than drunkenness in our own land and everyone knows the woes caused by that. In that little village on the hill there were 13 opium dens.

. . .

A student was telling me the other day that his brother was so furiously angry because he had three girls in succession, that he sold one and the other was sent to a native foundling home where she would be sold off for evil purposes perhaps, and kept the eldest only. Another student here had seven sisters drowned before a son arrived. When this student was born there was great rejoicing in the family and the next girl was allowed to live.

Love from,   Martha

"She told me that if it were not for her baby
she would take opium and kill herself."

FOOCHOW, CHINA   OCTOBER 18, 1906

Dear Belle,

A few days ago I sent you a couple of dozen turn-over collars as you suggested that small things would sell better than large ones. They ought to sell for about 50 cents a piece to clear the expenses of the work and the duty and postage, and the linen. They are all handmade and it takes a woman a long time to make one. If you can dispose of them just send the money on to Anna and she will reckon with me. I should think that many of the people would like to get them for Christmas presents. This work keeps many of the poor Christian women from starving themselves or committing suicide in other ways. One woman who now does the best work on some patterns told me two or three years ago that if it were not for her baby she would take opium and kill herself and she meant it, too. Her husband had been an embroiderer of fine official garments and as a result of such close application to work he became blind and tried to hang himself. Shortly after, the married daughter and the husband got out of work and had starved for several days and so they hanged themselves in earnest. This woman had to have the officers come and take them down and bury them. A few days after, the woman had twins and one of them died, and several other tragedies took place, so you do not wonder that she wanted to die. Now she earns enough by her work to make an honest living and the family seems to be fairly happy again. All these poor Christians have just about such a tale of woe. There is little mercy for the widows out of Christian lands. The tender mercies of the heathen are cruel. So you see what sort of people make the collars and what a work of charity it is to get them a little work.

Love to all the relatives,

Your affectionate sister—Martha Wiley

FOOCHOW, CHINA   NOVEMBER 24, 1906

Dear Belle,

I think that I have written you that it is settled that I am to start for home about the middle of March so I will get to America next summer. I do not know just what is before me there but I hope that I can spend a good share of my time at home.

    I have all my things cleared up and so it will not be much work to store my things for home going and pack the rest. Usually when anyone goes home there are a good many of the women who come and stand around and wait to see what is left that will fall to them. I fear there will be little left, as I have always had so little room that I have cleared up every little while.

Love and Merry Christmas to all, from,   Martha

FOOCHOW, CHINA   DECEMBER 23, 1906

Dear Wallace,

It is Christmas time and I must send you a letter. Enclosed you will find a picture which you will recognize as myself. I have never had a picture of your baby. I would like to see if my namesake is anything like her auntie. It is to be hoped that she will be quite an improvement. If you have not sent a photo already I fear that it will be too late after receiving this letter as I will be leaving for Shanghai by the middle of March as my steamer leaves Shanghai the 23rd of March.

    Dr. Stryker will start with me but I fear that she will not be willing to stop off at Palestine as I wish to do. It is not certain whether the Gardner children will continue on with her or stop off with me. It is harder to tear up and leave than one would think. Seven years in this station has sort of rooted me here and when I begin to plan there is this thing and that and this person and that to be planned for before I go.

    I'm putting in a picture of the little son of one of the bible women. He is a nice little chap and works in the press setting type for a part of his school expenses and I have been supplying the rest. Now that I am to go home and my expenses will increase, and my salary diminish, I do not know what to do with my boy unless some good Samaritan is willing to do something for him. I'm wondering if you would like to make a Christmas present of enough to keep him through next year. Ten dollars will keep him in school with what he earns for a whole year.

Affectionately,   Martha

"It was one of the wildest meanest scrambles I was ever in."

[unknown recipient] STEAMER FUNGSHUN MARCH 16, 1907

First of all you must know that I am really off and then I must go back and tell you that I got off under very interesting circumstances. It is the custom for the Chinese to escort out of the City anyone in whom they are interested, if that person plans to be gone any length of time and so that was my pleasure.

The students planned to give me a farewell party. Thursday evening was the time they finally decided upon and the seniors planned to read some essays and came to me to drill them so that they would be a credit to me at my last appearance. At the end one of the teachers presented me with a pair of long scrolls with laudatory characters and in making the presentation he said that I had so many admirable virtues that I began to think that the scrolls must be meant for someone else after all, but in the course of time I found that they were mine.

March 18 —— Next morning, which was Friday Mr. Peet announced that I was to start for Pagoda Anchorage. Then the boys got out their firecrackers and prepared for the holiday. After an early dinner I went out to the front door and there I found about three hundred of the students and Christians lined up and I had to go through the line and make a farewell speech to each one.

This over, the firecracker fusillade went off and down the street and for a mile nothing could be heard but the noise. All the people ran to the doors and lined up to see what "great man" was going by.

Toward the end of the trip to the wharf a rain shower came down but when I reached the boat there was left about a hundred to say good bye and have more firecrackers in evidence. We pushed off in the sampan and as far down the river as I could see the boys were waving their handkerchiefs to me.

Miss Hartwell and I reached Pagoda Anchorage and went over to Mrs. Hubbard's, reaching there about 5 P.M. just before a bad squall. Dr. Stryker and the Gardner boys, who are also going, waited to come down on the houseboat and got caught in the squall and had a very hard time getting on the boat.

It was a common joke that I was not able to eat or sleep because of the thoughts of going home. Seven years is a long time to be in one place without getting out of the province and no wonder I was excited.

This morning about half past ten we reached Shanghai and there were so many rice vessels at the wharf that we had to anchor out in the middle of the stream and the little sampans all came round the boat in a swarm and then began the disembarking which was a sight found nowhere else. It was one of the wildest meanest scrambles I was ever in. The coolies were like so many vultures, sometimes 20 of them would be pulling at one of us trying to get the baggage and there was nothing for it but to whack them right soundly.

Mr. Beard was there to help us off or we would have had a much worse time if such had been possible. Finally we got our things ashore and there the mob came on again and the fighting, screaming and whacking was done all over again. The ricksha men and the wheelbarrow men both wanted our patronage, and to show that they were bona fide licensed coolies they would whirl around and show the numbers on their coats.

We had to watch the wheelbarrows all the time in spite of the fact that we had the licenses of the men or they would have perhaps disappeared. We got to Mr. Evans' Missionary home in time to get ready for tiffin [lunch] and for me to write two pages of this letter. After dinner we went out to explore and first went to the M. E. Publishing House to find our way to the R.R. station as we want to go to Soochow, then back to the Bund [causeway] to see about our time of sailing, and then to do some shopping and make some purchases for friends.

There were squads of sailors riding around through the city in rickshas and having a jolly good time. I suppose that all the nations of the world are represented here. The great, tall old Sikhs with their red turbans add very much to the picturesque effect. Well dressed Chinese police fill in the gaps, but the Chinese police are never allowed to become very numerous for fear that if any uprising should take place, as actually happened two years ago, the Chinese would side with the native population against the foreigners.

What a joy it was to be where we could be drawn by horses! For the first time in seven years I rode in a carriage! Dr. Stryker and the boys and I got so tired after our walk to the station and around town that we bargained for a carriage to use for two hours and that was to include a ride on the Bund in the French Concession. The mafu, as the driver is called, whipped up his old horse and in 15 minutes we had arrived at the French concession but there he had to stop for he had no license and that made another discussion as to price.

Ladies of all nationalities are seen riding on the Bund in the afternoon. From the poor bound-footed old Chinese woman to the most elegantly attired French lady, all are represented.

I wonder what sort of mental picture you have of Shanghai. I also always had a very dim sort of picture in my mind before I actually saw the place.

[letter continues]

"So I lie down in the arms of Ramses II in the shadow of his huge head and fell asleep."

SHANGHAI, CHINA   MARCH 19, 1907

Tuesday had been such a lovely day that we decided to get up early on Wednesday and go to Soochow. We had time to visit the Soochow University, Woman's hospital, Men's hospital, and Girls' school before it was time to go for the 4:50 train. How the wind blew and the rain poured! We were well drabbled before we got out of the waiting room on to the train.

The passengers were interesting and we carried on quite a conversation though we could not speak the Soochow dialect. We could make a few characters with our fingers and they could do the same and by signs for the rest we were able to elicit considerable information from the people. The women and men all had American cigarettes and smoked incessantly. One sickly looking boy smoked three an hour. The women prided themselves on the foreign cigarettes and holders.

The tombs are the features of the landscape. All over this great flat province little hummocks come up out of the mud and an unsophisticated traveler would not associate them with graves at all. The dead reign there truly and take up at least a fourth of the land, thus depriving the people of much that might be cultivated. They are very different from the beautiful stone Omega graves on the slopes of Foochow. Then here and there over the fields are unburied coffins, some uncovered and some with a little roof of tiles over them.

April 3 —— To-day we are about 20 miles out in the Bay of Bengal. The drunken ruffians that got on at Fonang continue to drink and make so that it distresses every one on board that does not do the same. At the table the women yell and laugh just like the men. The deck steward is fiercer than ever. It does seem queer to have these German stewards after seeing nobody but Chinese in that capacity for so long. The man who does our cabin work also waits on our table and is the leader of the band. When he gets his regimentals on and beats time for the band we would hardly recognize our cabin steward.

April 4 —— Many passengers are sick with the heat. We are 577 miles out from Penang.

April 5 —— I've been busy all day getting mail ready for Colombo.

April 6 —— Early in the morning we began to sight land and soon the little fishing boats were everywhere about and picturesque they were. The porpoises leapt out of the water for several feet and the children on board were all very much excited about them. The first sight of Ceylon [Sri Lanka] is not at all charming. We were at first too far away to see the beautiful coconut groves and when we entered the harbor the breakwater shut out everything else. About 10 o'clock we entered the harbor of Colombo and anchored a long way out from shore. The German mail steamers are all coal here and so the stewards all try to get the passengers off and out of the way, so great were the tales of what we would suffer if we stayed on board. Of course we did not want to stay on board but you would have thought so to hear them tell us how much better it was to get off.

Dr. Stryker and I were wild to get off for we wanted to get to the bank before the office hours were over as we had had such bad luck at the three ports just passed. We (and the boys) rushed down on the first boat and got ashore first of all and the porter of Bristol Hotel took us to the bank, which was very near the hotel and we got there just in time to get our money. You would have laughed to see those elegant English cashiers there.

A native boy in the bank uniform put our letters of credit under the cashier's hand then dipped a pen into the ink and gave it to the foreigner who wrote the necessary amount and then the native took up a blotter and blotted what was written and folded up the paper and it went from one hand to another until it reached its destination, and the cashier yawned as though the exertion was too much for him. I thought that this individual had been ill and was just convalescing, but on going into another department I noticed that all the foreigners did the same. One man brightened up a bit when he found that we had been more or less acquainted in Foochow, but it was too much of an effort for him to talk much or use too many words so I escaped before any damage was done to him. This is the hot season and perhaps they were all tired out just with the effort of existing.

Armed with some money the next thing was to get something to eat and then see the sights, so we went to the Bristol Hotel and asked for lunch in the café. It was so lovely there that we did not want to leave. With beautiful palms and ferns and fountains and electric fans and cool ices it was luxury untold for the sum of about 15 cents. But at last we had to be off and see what there was left as the other people from the steamer were all racing past in all sorts of vehicles from rickshas to automobiles. Dr. Stryker inclined to the automobile ride but I was too much taken with the joy of getting in a carriage and taking my time that I had my way and it was the sensible thing, too. The two boys went with us and so we were just the right size for a carriage.

Such a lovely afternoon we had! I do not know when I have enjoyed myself so much. We drove along the Galle Face road with beautiful residences and trees and gardens on one side and on the other the surf was beating up and the spray blowing into our faces. We went out to Mount Lavinia, which is seven miles out from the hotel and then went down by the sea while the horse rested. Natives would climb a tree and bring down a coconut for anything you would give them. We went through such beautiful groves of the different fruits of Ceylon but the most delightful of all were the palm groves.

But the jewel shops are what most tourists rush to. What beautiful gems of all kinds are displayed for the benefit of the tourists! It is hard to keep from coveting when looking at all those choice jewels.

We spent an hour or two in the city after returning from our drive and then came on board the steamer for dinner.

The stewards would not let us open the port holes because of the coal dust so most of the passengers that did not stay ashore took their chairs up on the top deck and spent the night. Dr. Stryker and I sat up there and enjoyed it very much as the assistant purser came along and seemed inclined to talk and we got him started and he told us yarns about every quarter of the globe.

I went down and opened the porthole, as it was unbearable with it shut. The steward said the ship would be through coaling at 3 A.M. and the hose would be turned on to wash down the ship and we would be drenched. But I said that I would rather be drenched than suffocated and woke up every ten minutes dreaming that the hose had begun to pour water into our cabin. As a matter of fact the ship did not finish coaling until the next morning about ten and the hose was not turned on our part of the ship but the passengers who went on the top deck were soaked with water about daybreak, and in the scurry to get down on the lower deck one woman was badly hurt. Such is the veracity of mankind! We cannot believe much that is told us.

Sunday morning was a sight to wonder at. All the peddlers in town were aboard and the fruit dealers and men with eatables were around the steamer in their small boats. The Far East passengers decked themselves out in jewels and since that time you can scarcely find a man or woman of that class who is not wearing from six to ten rings with all the stones named in the dictionary adorning their persons. Those coffee planters all seem to have money to throw away.

The three priests aboard are having a lovely time since these fellows got aboard, for every little while one of them calls the "holy fathers" up to the bar and they all have a drink together and then they have a smoke to finish. It is very evident as the bar is in line with the ladies' saloon.

Sunday was a day of buying and selling and drinking and in the evening the band played on the second class deck and most of the selections were drinking songs.

April 8 —— We are now on our way to Aden and will be about seven days without seeing land — between these two ports is just about like crossing the Atlantic.

It was worth one's time just to watch the amusing things that went on. In the afternoon I was on deck to see how the ladies suddenly became interested in the gentlemen that they had previously ignored because they were afraid of being "wall-flowers." I saw so many comical little traps laid for introductions that I was sorry when night came. I must say the Americans cannot do one thing well and that is to dance! They think they can but they cannot compare with the Germans. All the Far East Germans had several glasses of beer and some whiskey to prepare them for the hard work that was before them and they did dance! I do not see how they did do it with all the liquor on board but they did and did it well. It seems that the more cultivated people become the more is required to make them happy. The third class with its squeaky old accordion had double the fun that these first and second class people had. Some of the first class passengers came over to the second to have a little rest from the first, as there are a number of ladies in the first that are rivals as to who can be most popular and have the largest following. Is it not silly with people whom they shall never see again! I would be too unambitious for such short triumphs.

One poor old stack of bones got on at Colombo and she has been the amusement of everyone since as she evidently is living in the hopes of a Mr. Somebody coming along and she is not going to be caught napping when he does happen on the scene. We poor missionaries seem to be as abnormal a class to these people as they are to us.

April 12 —— We were near the island of Socotra a good part of the day skirting the coast of Africa in sight of shore. It was so clear that we could see Cape Guardafui when passing. From the shores the mountains seem quite high.

April 13 —— This morning at 6:30 the boat stopped and of course that awoke me and I found that we were at Aden, on the shore of southern Arabia. The place from the shore looks dreary and bleak. The hills are serrated in appearance and probably three or four hundred feet high. There had been no rain in three years but to-day when we arrived it was cloudy and in an hour or two the rain was pouring! Arabs come on with baskets, ostrich feathers, and sharks' teeth to sell, and as everywhere, postcards. I had just concluded a bargain for some cards—they are my extravagance—when the deck steward came along and drove the boy overboard and he went over like a rat. I am still in possession of the cards but how to pay for them is a question, as he did not leave his address.

April 14 —— In the Red Sea with no land to be seen on either side, the waves the largest that we have seen since we reached Shanghai. But the ship does not roll at all even though it is rough and I have not heard of anyone that dared to be seasick.

One of the passengers led a short service—the first that we have had on board. This is quite different from the English steamers where it is the rule of the company that the captain shall read the service if there is no clergyman to do so.

April 17 —— In the night we had passed the upper end of the Gulf of Suez and at 6 A.M. the stewards routed us all out to meet the doctor from Suez in the dining saloon. At seven we collected to have him look at us and see that we did not have the plague.

When we got on deck we found that we were anchored at an island of about 50 acres that had been formed by the dredging of the canal. This is connected with Suez—the town—by a stone pier about two miles long. On this pier is a steam railway and a donkey drive, etc.

After a few hours stay at the Port, we started into the Canal. As usual the band was playing and it was as lively as such a wretched place could be. On we went by Suez and it was a great pleasure to see the city as it is spread out along the canal. It is precisely such a place as you see pictured over and over again in views of eastern cities.

There are about 15,000 inhabitants in the place but they are largely Arabs. An ancient fresh water canal flows into the sea at this place. It is supposed to date from the time of Ramses II. As we followed the canal there was a fringe of vegetation all along the Egyptian side owing to the fresh water canal so near, but on the Arabian side there was hardly a spear of grass.

April 21 —— In the afternoon Leon [Gardner] and I went for a stroll along the hill that skirts the pyramids and saw acres of tombs with human bones scattered over the ground and old mummy wrappings in all states. It was really horrible to see the remains of the ancient builders of the pyramids scattered around in that shape when the work that they had done was still preserved. Leon picked up some beads that had been dug out and has quite a string of the real antiquities.

Then we came back and took a look at the openings of all the pyramids and decided that we wanted to enter. After supper the dragoman [interpreter or guide] said that he would take us. He got that wire that the men are always trying to get us to invest in and we waded along through the sand to the entrance. It was really gruesome when the time came. The Arab dragoman went ahead with his flowing robes of black and white and then we waded along in the sand by the light of the moon with a guard behind with a great stick in his hand—to make a show no doubt.

At the mouth of the tomb we sat down and decided who should go in first. I was not very happy about going down in that dungeon but I had to go or lose my face so he lighted the candle and we went slipping and sprawling down those little passages. One place the Arab went flat on his back and the candle went out and the bats flew and made noise with their wings. How my heart went pitty-pat! It was frightful while it lasted but in a very short time we were there in the first chamber of the little pyramid—that is the third pyramid. From this we reached a tomb chamber in the shape of a gothic arch. This the dragoman lighted up with the ever present magnesium and there I stood in wonder looking at the interior of the grand pyramid! The dragoman dug his hands on each side of the passage and stuck his toes in the rough red granite while I seized him by his two shoulders and held on for dear life until we slid into the tomb chamber proper. This was of massive hewn stones in what seemed by the light a large place. There was nothing there but a part of the queen's sarcophagus. While off of it are six little chambers that belonged to the children of the king. We stayed only about five minutes as the air was stifling and the bats numerous, then we climbed up again, sometimes bumping our heads and in one place crawling through a very narrow place blocked up with stone.

When we emerged from that hot air we were met by a very cold blast from the outer air. There sat the guard and Miss Byerly and the two boys and it was a good sight to see—better than the pyramids. The moon was shining up overhead so we could see the far outline of the sand dunes of the Libyan Desert.

When the dragoman had rested a bit, he took his beloved magnesium wire and a candle and then led the boys down. They came back all excited with the novelty of it all. Then we went to see the tombs of the earliest builders of the pyramids, which are in pretty good shape. In these places there were great shafts where the mummies were thrown, and the odor is simply dreadful. Then we saw the great ruins of the ovens where the builders had their food prepared.

But the finest thing of all was the temple of the sphinx. All the Arabs call it the "sphincus" and we have to burst out laughing when we hear the word. We went down to the entrance and found the door open. I had been over the place for three evenings but I had not seen those ruins as they were covered with sand. After passing through a long entrance of pillars we came to the temple proper. Such massive columns! And strange to say there are no hieroglyphics on them. The floors are of alabaster and the pillars of granite. There is no use of taking up more of your time with a lengthy description. But it was as wonderful to me as though I were the first to see these things.

Monday was a day par excellence! What a day I had of it! Abdul Salam il Cabri routed us out early and told us it was time to be off for a ride to Sakkara to see the wonders there, and though it was lovely to get a sleep after these days of strenuous sight-seeing, we rubbed our still dusty eyes and hurried out to breakfast and then by that time the camels had come and the donkey and the horse, and the men were putting on the saddles. Those cross camels growled all the time and the keepers had a time getting the saddles adjusted. Miss Byerly had Brandy to ride, Leon had Ramses the 3rd and my camel was Ramses the 2nd. Ray [Gardner] started out on the donkey and the swell dragoman, decked out like a sheik, took the lead on a lovely Arabian horse. How that horse danced and ran! He was such a big horse that I longed to ride him but I dared not ask the gorgeous dragoman.

We ambled and trotted along and shrieked with laughter at the fun of it for a mile or two, and then it was getting hot and the desert more dusty and the camels were more grumpy and it was not so nice. Half way there, Ray took my camel and I took the donkey. I thought that I was conferring a favor on him by letting him ride the camel but I soon found that I had received the favor, for the donkey was so much nicer than the camel. The donkey boy told me to ride like a gentleman and I did. The other members of the party laughed until they nearly rolled off their camels at the sight.

After two and a half hours of hard riding we came to Sakkara. It was hard to believe that this had been a great and wonderful city and that nothing but ruins were left now, standing in the sand dunes bare and deserted.

I will not have time to write about the many pyramids and who built them, but the step pyramid was the most wonderful. It was built by Unas the last king of the fifth dynasty and has the form of a flight of steps but cannot be ascended with ease or rather no one but the Arabs can ascend its steep sides. Before we reached this place I had tired of my donkey, and the dragoman was walking with me when I was offered a nice horse to ride around the pyramid. I think that it was not intended that I should accept but I did and got on that fine horse, a graceful colt, and rode round that pyramid. I will tell you frankly that if I had not been "riding like a gentleman" I should have gone over his head for he danced and jumped in the most approved Arab style. But the men said that I was clever and offered me the horse again to ride to the places near. We sat down under the shadow of one of the great rocks of the pyramid and ate our lunch and the donkey boy brought us water from a little Nile and we were so thirsty that we drank it even though it was almost as thick as milk.

I shall never forget how I went racing round that old 5th dynasty pyramid on a sheik's horse. You will think that I have turned Arab myself to hear these tales. Really they are not so big as the telling makes them. From there we went to Mariette's house. This is nothing much, but is interesting only as being the place where the explorer and excavator Mariette lived while doing his work.

The tomb of Unas was very fine. A passage runs down by a stairway and from this to the tomb. The walls of Unas' tomb were covered with beautiful hieroglyphics, colored with blue and as fresh and beautiful as when made. The scenes of daily life were all depicted there. The sarcophagus is still in the tomb but the mummy we met later in the museum.

The arched roof was like a little chapel—the whole seemed a really beautiful place and would not have been bad to be put away in. There were small chambers for the little children of the royal family and places for the statuettes. The hieroglyphics are the oldest Egyptian religious text known—so Baedeker says. The king's sarcophagus is of granite and the others of alabaster.

The Apis tombs were truly wonderful—I rode the prancing Arab steed up to the sandy path that leads down to the door of the tombs. In the long gallery we saw 24 colossal sarcophagi of the Apis gods. All are now empty. The 24 chambers were cut out of rock along each side of the principal gallery. Each chamber is 20 feet high, and the sarcophagi are of red granite or limestone 13x7x11 ft. each cut from a solid stone.

No doubt those huge old mummies were dragged by toiling thousands to the place and put in the sarcophagi worthy of kings—and now not a mummy is to be seen there. The natives say that the Romans destroyed them.

Tall palms were just in bloom and the air was sweet with the fragrance of the mingled palms and sweet clover.

We stopped at the shadoof [a pole with bucket and counterweight used for raising water] and drank of the thick water and I decided nothing more could kill me if the water did not. To think that the glorious city of Memphis had come to ruins was sad. Where streets a half day's journey in length had been were now only a few mounds and had we not been told, would never have recognized that they were ruins.

A little beyond the village of Mit Rahineh (Memphis), Ramses went steaming up the road at eight miles an hour until we came to a mud wall enclosure. Here he kneeled and I got off and entered and went up a little stairway until I stood alone—what do you think? Ramses II. There lay the mighty Ramses fallen. His colossus' 42 ft. of limestone in length—is a wonderful piece of carving. His face, in spite of its size, was beautiful and the expression sweet.

From there I walked on a little to another statue of Ramses II of red granite. While at the others I saw a company of tourists pass. I thought that all had gone by so I lie down on the arm of Ramses II in the shadow of his huge head and fell asleep. The Arab who led my donkey climbed onto the other arm where I could not see him and also had a sleep. After half an hour two Germans came riding up on donkeys and I awoke and pulled off my helmet to find these two men gazing not at Ramses but at me and they were having as much fun as I. They rode on laughing.

I met many tourists on donkeys but I went alone in state on my camel with the lone Arab. Some English looked at me so hard that I had to laugh outright.

We left the city and came back to the tent, but the boys stopped at Ghizels Gardens. The howling dervishes were in full blast. All Mena village, turned out to dance. They lined up and began their dancing, twirling, and grunting. Our sweet dragoman took it all seriously and said that when he got rid of us he would do some artistic dancing.

April 25 —— Down Abbas St. past the British and the Egyptian barracks we soon came to a sycamore tree that had fallen and some branches were dead but a few had green leaves on them. This is the spot where Mary is said to have rested with Jesus. A little chapel marks the spot and has above the door "Holy family exiles in Egypt."

About 4 P.M., we went flying over the bridge of the Great Nile before it would close and caught the tram for Giza. We went wandering around the pyramids and found the excavators just unearthing a newly found sarcophagus of the family of Chefren of the second [fourth] dynasty. It was quite a sight to see a sarcophagus really unearthed and dragged up a few feet.

April 26 —— Made memorable by a climb to the top of the great pyramid. Two Arabs half led and half dragged me up. But the ascent was nothing to the coming down.

On top Ray took our photographs. Our old Arab came up and said, "What will you do for me if I sing Daisy, Daisy Bell for you?" I told him that if I heard that on top of this pyramid I would certainly jump off. What a glorious panorama spread out before me. The Nile bounded by the Libyan Desert on one side and the Arabian on the other and the green strip dotted with little villages. The barley fields were ripe and the clover was ready to cut. All Cairo spread out before me. I had never thought to see this.

My limbs were all a tremble when I came down. We paid 50 cents for the ticket to go up and 50 cents for the two Arabs who dragged me along.

The stones are about as high as my waist and 400 ft. of them are rather trying.

The Arabs have a word quite unique—that is to "Mark Twain." I asked what "Mark Twain," meant and my guide said that in the past tourists came and offered a pound to an Arab who could get up and down first. Often an Arab would slip and he would land at the foot of the pyramid in pulp.

Two years ago a French gentleman and lady offered a guinea to the first and ten shillings to the second who went up the great pyramid and down again. My guide came down first and the other man slipped on the second ledge of the descent and bounded from stone to stone until he landed in a shapeless mass.

An Englishman got drunk and swore he could go up and down alone. He was within a few feet of the top when he came down in a hundred pieces. So the government seems to have banned the practice of Mark Twaining and the offense is punished by long imprisonment. I stopped once and the guide's fingers clenched my arm until every finger showed in blue the next morning. Still it is not bad.

The second pyramid has a cap on the top of the signal casing and only the Arabs can reach the top. Some tourists paid our dragoman to climb it and when he got to the top part rain fell and he had to sit up there and sing Daisy Bell all night.

Be sure to write so that I shall hear from you in Scotland. Address c/o Mrs. James Howden, 19 Gasturk St., Govan Hill, Glasgow.

Love to all, especially my namesake. I have some pretty beads for her,   Martha

"It does seem a holy place."

S.S. Teresa, Port Said   May 12, 1907

Dear Mother,

You will see by this heading where I am spending this Sunday. Well, I have been to Jerusalem. The two weeks there were the most instructive in my life. Every place is filled with interesting associations, but the few authentic ones connected with the life of Christ are most precious.

The site of the temple is authentic and though a mosque is on the spot, we can still see the great rock where Abraham offered Isaac and where Araunah had his threshing floor and where the Jews offered sacrifices so many years.

Down below, the double gate has been excavated and without doubt Jesus had often passed over those very stones when going up to the temple.

Then we climbed up to the place on the Mount of Olives and sat where Jesus did when he wept over the city. We wondered if He could be any more pleased when He looks down on the fanaticism and intolerance of the present city.

Then Gethsemane is the same—where He shed drops of blood in His agony. The judgment hall of Pilate has recently been identified and so we can stand on the old pavement and see perhaps the very spot where Christ was mocked and condemned. Down deep underneath is the prison with places hollowed from the solid rock where prisoners were bound. All around are bones and skulls dating from crusader times.

The Via Dolorosa leads out through St. Steven's Gate, but most people think that Jesus was led out of the Damascus Gate, and General Gordon found here a tomb which most people think answers every detail to make it the tomb in which Jesus was laid. There is Golgotha near, on a little hill outside the city wall and the garden spot, and the rock hewn tomb, unfinished.

I felt as I stood in the tomb that Jesus must have laid there. It is all in such perfect keeping with the bible narrative, and it is the only tomb found in or near Jerusalem with the tiny window into which disciples could look.

On the little hill above were huge rocks showing earthquake cleavage—until the Turks blasted them out four years ago.

There are many things that seem to prove that this is the real tomb of Joseph where he put Jesus. It does seem a holy place. Now an old man and a native Christian keep the place and let the grass and wildflowers grow among the trees, and the stone steps lead down to the tomb in two flights with trees on either side.

I hope never to have such an experience as the landing at Joffa. I do not know when I have been more frightened. Every instant I thought we would go headlong into the sea—the place is fully as bad as reputed to be. Every year pilgrims are drowned here. Now we are over the worst, and at Alexandria there is a fine landing. Whenever England has a hand in things, you may be sure that things are in decent order.

We do hope to get to Naples this week—I want to get home—it seems as though we have been travelling an age and yet it is just two months. I want to see you and the brothers and sisters and the children so much that I can hardly wait, though even when I get to America I will have to wait somewhere to have my eyes attended to. I have stood my trip much better than I anticipated when I started, for I was about used up then. A very nice lady is travelling with me, and the two boys about whom I wrote you.

Very much love to all the relatives and especially to yourself.

Affectionately,   Martha

"Evidence of what clan feuds could do."

BUNDORAN   COUNTY DONEGAL   IRELAND   JULY 11, 1907

Dear Wallace and Nettie,

It has been a long time since I have heard from either of you but I have learned from long experience to just keep writing and in the end you must reply in sheer self defense.

You see from the address where I am. This Scotland-Ireland trip is a great one. I went to the place where Jeannie's father and mother are buried. What a queer way they have of burying people here. The first one is put down ten feet or more and the next who dies is put down resting on the previous coffin. So our great uncle George and his wife Jane were buried in the same grave.

That cemetery was a beautiful little spot at Dunoon, but what a lot of mirth it would provoke in Americans to see the inscriptions. The epitaphs are more often than not simply a eulogy to the one who erected the stones. From the amount of *sympathy* put on the stone, the donors must think the recipients in a decided bad place.

Dunoon is a port of Brighton by the sea, pleasure bent and swarming with city people. It interested me very much from the history that took place on the spot. What a lot of cutting and slashing of people's heads there was in the good old days!

The castle is in ruins and just a rock with the remaining wall and foundation shows where Queen Mary spent many of her happiest days in Scotland. And the graves in the Yard of the old Kirk bear evidence of what clan feuds could do.

In this spot was the sight of Highland Mary's cottage. Her statue faces the water and looks over to Ayr—the home of "Robby Burns," her beloved.

We took the train to Greencock on the Firth. There at 8 P.M. took the *Thistle* for Ireland. In this latitude it is scarcely dark all night. I could see the isles and little towns perfectly well when I went to bed at 11 P.M. At 4:00 the next morning I got out to see Moville, the port of call for American bound steamers. From there on we sailed up Loch Foyle and

River Foyle. Saw the place where Annie Tufft [Martha's grandmother?] lived for a long time on the banks of the Foyle.

At 6 A.M. reached Londonderry. We were too far out to see the Giant's Causeway when we passed. At Londonderry, saw for the first time the famous Irish jaunting car. You climb up and sit down on a seat running lengthwise in the middle with your feet hanging over the side—then you hang on for dear life, and the wild Irishman who drives shows you a thing or two about getting into holes and getting out.

I want to see the estate at Bainbridge where our grandfather lived and some other generations before him. The place is now sold.

I've my ticket for the last Saturday in July—by *S.S. Mongolia*, Allan Line. Am booked to Buffalo via Montreal. So in two weeks and a day I will be on my way to "great America." I am longing to see you all and make the acquaintance of all the new babies.

It is so cold here that I am wearing all my winter clothes. How I shall live through next winter is a question, for I can't get on any more clothes. Get your furnaces in good order, for I'll need it.

Very much love to you both and to my namesake,   from Martha

"The most genuine admiration that I have seen in a man's eyes since the days when I was young and beautiful."

R.M.S. MONGOLIA   JULY 30, 1907

Dear Belle,

This is perhaps the last chapter of my wanderings.

We had a fine time seeing Londonderry. It is a queer old walled city, and withstood a siege by James II of England during some of the religious wars. In the old cathedral are many interesting relics, among them the hollow cannon ball that was shot into the town by the royal army when they wished to propose terms of peace. The proposals are inside the ball. A nice old verger by the name of Wylie showed us around the cathedral.

We had a fine sail out River Foyle, Lough Foyle by daylight, and then a good sleep until morning. We were to catch a train that met the boat at Greencock. Jeannie came to my cabin and told me it was "time to catch the train," but as I knew her habit of being too previous I took another nap and found myself at the landing before I was quite ready to get off. Poor Jeannie was dancing the Highland fling in her excitement—yet I got ready and had breakfast in the boat and waited half an hour on the train before we left Greencock.

On Saturday I went aboard the *Mongolia* about noon. Jeannie got me down there at 10 A.M. and the gates were not open until 12 o'clock, so we just had to stand around the sheds and wait.

Sunday was a horrid day—there was a driving rain and high wind and everybody sick and cross. Monday the storm was worse, but no rain. At breakfast I looked about and saw myself the only woman able to be out. I have sat through every meal. I always make that my rule, though I have not kept all my meals down.

This is the fourth day out and I am now on speaking terms with an old Canadian gentleman, a young man from Edinburgh, a Hindoo from Calcutta, and the ship's officers! The few men I've talked with think my brogue is American and ask me when I crossed over to Europe—or perhaps if this is as good passage as when I came over. "Oh", I reply, "I have never been on the Atlantic before". Then they conclude that I am English for they never dream of a lone maiden wandering around the globe as I have.

There will be very little of interest to write about on ship board as the days go by. We land at no ports, get no wireless cablegrams, and have just wind and sea.

I must go out and get some of the air that is going to waste and see if it stops my headache. The sea has always previously been a great delight, but not so this time.

August 1 —— It is very cold to-day—almost to the freezing point and a biting wind blowing. The passengers are huddled into the corners to get out of the blasts of wind.

For two days the fog was heavy and the fog horn blew all the time and the babies yelled at each blast of it. The captain says that we are nearing the ice tract and will soon be coming up with some icebergs.

One fellow crawled out yesterday and at the table told about "only one lady at breakfast on Monday—so they said." The people pointed me out to him, as I had been that heroic woman. He eyed me with the most genuine admiration that I have seen in a man's eyes since the days when I was young and beautiful.

August 7 —— Have been sitting out on the sea for two days on account of fog, so will be two days late reaching Montreal. That makes fourteen days across the "pond." Please let Mother and the others share this letter.

Much love to all,

Affectionately,   Martha

Shall mail this at Quebec so you will get it almost by the time I enter U.S. Will write again soon.

[Martha spends one month in Quebec sanitarium recovering from the effects of malaria.]

[During her time in the U.S., Martha receives an honorary M.A. degree from Whitman College. Speaking engagements require extensive travel. She eventually covers every state but Maine.]

Martha with Women's School

Manchu women in class—boy on upper step is teacher's son

TIMELINE 1911–1920

1911 — Overthrow of Manchu Dynasty
— Martha establishes East Gate School for Manchu orphans after the burning of the Manchu quarter
1912 — Republic of China (ROC) established
— Martha establishes industrial school in Maunchu quarter and also a Bible school with Miss Hartwell
— Trip to Great Wall, Mongolia, Korea, Manchuria, and Japan, visits tomb of Confucius
1913 — Sun Yat-sen establishes National People's Party (Kuomintang — KMT)
— Foochow College now teaches to high school level only
1914 — WWI begins
— Martha learning Mandarin dialect
1916 — Departs for U.S. to care for ailing mother
1917 — Donald Hsueh graduates Foochow College, attends Yenching University
1919 — Martha's mother dies
— Martha returns to China and devotes herself to the work for women

2

A NEW REPUBLIC

*"But for a girl to be born in the Tiger year is very bad luck, therefore
so many girls are thrown away in that period of the cycle."*

FOOCHOW, CHINA   MARCH 12, 1911

Dear Belle,

If you know how glad I am to get your letters and to hear how you are getting on and about mother, you would be glad to write.

I had to laugh to see the way Ahtanum folks keep on eating for entertainment. The grange is a new affair it seems. The street car is a great institution, is it not? How do you manage when you go to town for lectures? Do you run the auto over to Wiley City and then take the street car or do you make the round trip in your auto?

By this letter I will write the treasurer of Washington State branch and find out if the money that the Ahtanum Church has sent is being put in the general fund. Miss Hartwell has not received any of the money. Money so sent must be designated as a *special gift* to be sent to whatever person that you name. You had better send the next to me, as the end of this year Miss Hartwell will go home and I will handle the money anyway. So if you get the letter from the treasurer you will know that I asked her to write you.

I have got the East Gate School started. What tribulations there were getting things in order. It is a great piece of business to start anything new in China. And then when I had engaged a lovely girl, a graduate of Ponasang to teach, one day I received a letter with her name signed to it and the contents were that the girl would not teach. I sent a sharp letter back and then there was weeping and wailing. It seems that the girl had not written the letter, but the young man to whom she is betrothed had taken upon himself the duty of writing a letter without her permission, and stating that she could not teach. He was a proud fellow and did not want his betrothed to be a teacher. The girl had spunk enough to come along and is now teaching the school and 20 of the dearest little bits of girls are enrolled, so the school is starting off very well, indeed. I tremble to think that the fellow may want to marry the girl before long in order to make her stop teaching.

The teacher is a fine girl, and bright and pretty. When she was born, the midwife took her out on the street and was going to throw her away when the mother dragged herself out and came to the rescue. In China, the periods of twelve years all have names. For instance the first year is the Rat year, the next is the Horse year, the next the Cow year and the next the Tiger year, etc. until the period of twelve has been passed over and then the same thing is repeated again. My teacher was born in the Tiger year and that is what made it necessary to get rid of her. It is very hard for the girl to find a husband if she is born in the Tiger year, for that is the strongest animal and the king of beasts, and she will rule her husband. No one wants a wife who has an inclination to rule. A woman should be born in the Rat year and then she could marry a man who was born in the Cat year and all would be at peace. Or if the girl was born in the year of the Sheep, she should marry a man born in the Tiger year and that would be a lucky match. But for a *girl* to be born in the Tiger year is very bad luck, and no one wants such a person, therefore so many girls are thrown away in that period of the cycle. The little teacher was almost doomed to that fate. Then she had her feet bound when she was so young that she can remember crying with her feet as far back as her memory goes. When she entered Ponasang School for Girls she had to unbind her feet.

Martha

Foochow Girls School—Martha and Miss Pepoon

"Light up your cigarettes and dry us off with the smoke."

SHARP PEAK FOOCHOW, CHINA JULY 19, 1911

Dear Vina,

I wonder what you did the 4th of July! We had a picnic. All the people were invited to our lawn for tea and a program. The rain began to come down gently as it always does on the 4th of July and so the company assembled on my verandah and we had the picnic and program there and later it was pleasant on the lawn. Mr. Walker wrote a poem for the occasion. So many of our guests were English that we had to puff them up a little. Those who could sing sang; and as I could not sing I told a story. We had ice cream and everything but firecrackers. Since all of us had been reading the Lady's Home Journal, which you are kind enough to send, we thought it was incumbent on us to have a sane Fourth and so we disregarded the firecrackers.

There are a lot of young Englishmen at the telegraph house and with no company they make themselves very agreeable. We have invited them over here three or four times and they in turn invite us to play tennis. Last Thursday they invited us over to play tennis so Miss Walker and I went, and Miss Pepoon went as chaperone to these giddy girls and we had just finished one game when a sprinkle of rain began. The superintendant said that it was only a drop or two and to stand under the trees and it would pass over. So we huddled under the trees and the most drenching rains that I ever saw came down. The house boy ran out with two umbrellas and there we huddled—three men and three women under two umbrellas. The water was pouring down each one of us and we were soaking in a jiffy.

Just to be funny in this crisis I said, "Light up your cigarettes and dry us off with the smoke". I thought that any man would know that it was a joke but those Englishmen did not recognize the brand of joke and actually lighted their cigarettes and puffed away very diligently drying us off. We fairly screamed with laughter to see the performance and finally got home with a memorable occasion back of us. The typhoon will prevent our fun to-day. The bathing is fine and we go down most every day. Yesterday Miss Walker and Miss Meebold went down in the rain and had a fine time in the breakers. It was a little too thrilling for me. I am so afraid of the undertow that I do not go in when a storm is on hand.

Miss Meebold who came out with me is here this summer, and she is as happy as the day is long for she has become engaged to Mr. Christian, a new missionary from Oberlin. The public announcement has not been made but she has told me. In August she will go up to Kuliang where most of the Missionaries congregate for the summer and then there will be an announcement made. She and I were going to buy a cottage together but now of course she does not want to get into the deal with me so I think that I will take it anyway, for now it is almost impossible to get any place to stay unless you have a cottage of your own for the summer.

I am getting to be such a sleepy head this summer that I have a nap in the afternoons and then go for a sea bath and then come home and have supper and sleep again. But this will last only one month more and then I will have to be thinking of the fall term. I am beginning to study a while each day since my teacher has appeared.

Love to all,

from your sister [in-law],   Martha Wiley

"The city of Foochow was merely a black spot in the midst of a lake of water."

FOOCHOW, CHINA   OCTOBER 14, 1911

Dear Mrs. Umstead,

I fear that I have not done either my duty or my pleasure in corresponding with the Ladies Aid. Many times I have wished that there was time to sit down and have a chat with the ladies but then somebody would come or I would be obliged to go away on business and the days would go by.

The past summer I spent at the seaside and it was the best summer that we ever had there. Usually the glare of the sun on the water is very trying but this summer it was just cool enough to be comfortable and cloudy enough to prevent glare. This was due to the many typhoons on the coast. Every week or so the agents at the telegraph station would put up signals that a typhoon was en route but they did not strike in and do any damage while we were at the seashore. Miss Pepoon of Whitman College was there and it seemed as though the nice weather was just for her benefit as she was very tired and not at all well when she reached Foochow.

The 22nd of August I went to the mountain on business and then planned that a week later Miss Pepoon should follow with Miss Walker.

All this worked out very well and Miss Pepoon reached the mountain the day before a heavy typhoon reached us. It blew and rained for several days and then the sun came out and everyone thought that the storm had gone by. I came to the City to examine the boys who had studied in the summer schools and returned to Kuliang expecting to take Miss Pepoon back to the seashore.

The night that I arrived on the mountain another storm came down unexpectedly and for seven days and nights the wind and rain was so furious that we could not get about. Most all the houses were leaking and some pretty well unroofed and coal and wood gone. It was a pretty bad time. After seven days of bolted doors and windows, the rain stopped for a while and the plain below could be seen. It was a sheet of water. The city of Foochow was merely a black spot in the midst of a lake of water. The villages were smaller spots on the white surface of the water.

The first day that I could get away, Miss Pepoon and I started for the City. We found things in a bad state. Walls were blown down and leaves and trash blown over everything. Some of the buildings are very seriously damaged. We stayed over Sunday in the City and then started down to the Peak on a houseboat. We reached there at 9 o'clock in the evening and packed up by 12 and took the boat back to the City by daylight the next morning. The mildew and mold on my books was actually ¼ inch thick. The cockroaches had eaten holes in my best summer dress and the rain had come down through a hole on the organ and it would not even wheeze—as most organs do in this country. The servants had simply shut themselves up in their quarters and let things go to ruin.

Affectionately,   Martha

[Manchu quarter of Foochow destroyed by fire in revolution of 1911—the overthrow of the Manchu dynasty, the last dynasty before the Republic of China was formed.]

"Others say that he swallowed gold leaf and died of strangulation."

[partial letter]

General Song thought he would go over to the Chinese bank and get what money was on deposit to the credit of the provincial treasurer, but the president showed him a neat set of books instead and told him that money was on deposit at the Shanghai and Hong Kong bank. It is said that his soldiers are very restless because the last two or three months pay has not been given to them.

November 15 —— Wonderful stories are told of the great sum of money that was found in the treasurer's yamen that was taken by the rebels. The fact seems to be that there is little cash here sent from the south and that the revolutionists wish to quiet the people by making them believe that there is sufficient for all needs. All the sources of revenue are at present abolished.

Ngoi, former viceroy of Fukien, is appointed to proceed to Fukien and take possession in the name of the imperialists. He probably knows enough to have an attack of illness just before the time to start.

To-day I went with Mrs. Peet to the place where the Tartar general's taotai [official at the head of the civil and military affairs of a circuit.] and daughters had been hiding. We expected to help them get over to Nantai, but it seems that they had been warned the day before and gone through to Nantai.

November 16 —— A busy morning in the Manchu quarter—at 10:30 a blue jacket accompanied Miss Hartwell, Miss Perkins, and me to the parade ground to attend the memorial service for the soldiers slain in battle. All the dignitaries took off their caps and wept aloud before the tablets of the dead. No one followed the old custom of kow towing [to kneel and bow].

At the memorial service there were great heaps of paper money to be burned and paper horses to be sent up in smoke for the soldiers in the next world and all sorts of things that might be of benefit to them. The army lined up and presented arms before the tablets and bowed their heads. One Catholic and one Protestant Christian had been killed, so for them—instead of the tablets—there was a photo and name of the deceased.

To-day the Manchu quarter was again searched for hidden arms. No Manchus are allowed to leave their quarter of the city, and the Chinese who have no special business have been ordered to keep out of the Manchu district. Vagabonds are still trying to set fire to the houses. Tonight a man climbed up on the roof of one of the houses, but a sailor shot at him and he dropped and ran.

November 17 —— In the afternoon I went to visit some of the fine Tartar [Manchu] families. The family of the hiek-dai; or division commander, are fine looking people and very dignified and distinguished. The Manchus have been very little understood on account of their enforced exclusiveness. Any man who became a Christian had his stipend from the government cut off and was made to feel that he was generally out of favor. Now that any such fear is taken from the people, many of them say that they have long been favorable to Christianity, but did not dare to embrace a foreign religion before.

November 18 —— The story now is that the viceroy is not dead, but that another man was nearly dead and that his career was promptly finished for him, and he was put in the coffin in the viceroy's clothes and the official himself escaped. Others say that he swallowed gold leaf and died of strangulation. The Japanese were said to have been at the yamen day after day and that they might have aided the frightened viceroy to escape.

I took Miss Peters to the Tartar general's yamen. What was my surprise to see the most beautiful little park. There was a false hill of some size made of rock brought up from Sharp Peak, through which wound tiny paths. Little caves with stone seats opened up here and there. A soldier told us that one stone could be removed, and from the opening a subterranean passage led down to a cell under the little garden that was surrounded by a deep moat. The Chinese said that the officer's family fled to this place the first day of the battle.

November 19 —— All day spent in the Tartar quarter, where we had meetings in many of the houses. The Tartars are like different people in their cordiality. Everywhere we were urged to enter and "preach."

November 21 —— Mr. Peet has been written up in a venomous manner by the newspaper that purports to be the organ of the new government. He has demanded an apology and he awaits results.

The families of the treasurer and the Tartar general expect to start for Hong Kong to-day. I am glad they are gone, poor things! They have suffered terribly. As yet they do not know what has become of the Tartar general. The treasurer is afraid to tell them for fear all the women will commit suicide. He himself asked if he could get the body of the Tartar general and take it home for burial. He might get the coffin, but it is doubtful if the body is in it. In fact it is pretty nearly certain that it is not.

Chinese are to-day making a search of the Tartar houses trying to find guns. These repeated searches are making bad feelings on both sides.

November 23 —— The morning was spent with my new friends, the Manchus. This morning I gathered up a clinic for Dr. Kinnear. To-day was very hot and they were all very tired and cross before I got them home.

Makeshift hospital set up in Foochow College—Dr. Kinnear in center

November 24 —— In the evening the American consul came and told us that there was to be no more work in the Manchu quarter—that the Manchus had not given up those phantom guns and we were to stay out.

November 27 —— This morning General Song said that we might go on certain streets in the Tartar quarter, but not others, so we are free to do some work yet.

Martha

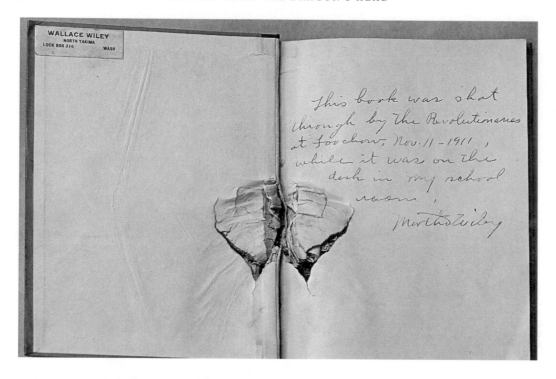

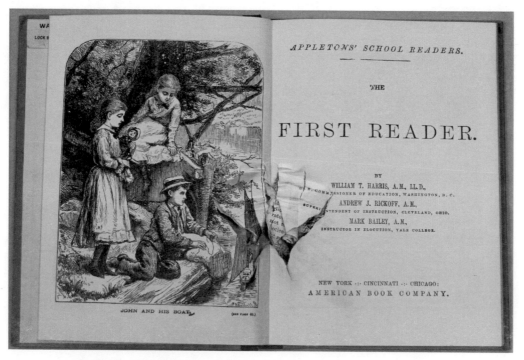

"*This book was shot through by the Revolutionaries at Foochow,
Nov. 11 – 1911, while it was on the desk in my school room.*"

—Martha Wiley

"I had the pleasure of meeting with Dr. Sun [Yat-sen]."

FOOCHOW, CHINA   APRIL 28, 1912

Dear Mother,

Last week we saw the wonderful Sun Yat Sen, on his way to Canton. Imagine my surprise to find that I knew his adopted daughter very well, in fact had travelled with her from San Francisco to Shanghai.

I had the pleasure of meeting and talking with Dr. Sun. He is a Congregationalist and was baptized by one of our missionaries in Hong Kong. He received his education in our American Board School in Honolulu. When he spoke in a mass meeting in the church on Sunday he spoke in Mandarin and one of our college boys interpreted. It would take a week to tell all about it.

Miss Pepoon and I expect to get off by the 1st of July. If the state of matters in the North permits we will go to Shantung, then to Peking, on to Korea and Manchuria and finish up our tour in Japan, and I will return by way of Formosa. Miss Pepoon is giving me this trip—I could not afford so great an expense myself. How glad I will be for an outing! For three months since the revolution I have hardly had a minute to myself, and such hundreds of poor after me!

We will have a fine time if matters settle down. The conditions here are fearful financially, but otherwise it is about as quiet as formerly.

With much love,

Your daughter,   Martha

"Two military executions took place this week and the heads were put up on the long bridge."

FOOCHOW, CHINA   MAY 16, 1912

Dear Vina,

Your good letter came to-day—as I have little time I am going to "down and at" answer. Things are humming in Foochow. Two military executions took place this week and the heads were put up on the long bridge. The brother-in-law of Mr. Peet's secretary was stabbed to death in his sedan chair on the street in broad daylight, and nothing done about it, as the Lieutenant General had ordered it. All the officers have tried to run away, they are so afraid of being killed by some assassin.

I have enough to keep me busy these days as I have started an industrial school in the Tartar quarter. Over 100 work there and about 40 eat there as well, and more than that live in the place. Eight women and eight boys graduate from the weaving department this month, and take their loom home and go to work, and more raw material comes in. It is a big business to keep this humming, but the foreman is a fine fellow and it goes on like clock work. Besides this, you would be pleased to see my women's school and girl's school in the Tartar quarter. About 150 study there. My teacher teaches a bible class of young men there daily. On Friday evening we have a prayer meeting. Sunday, preaching in two places with over 300 present—people who six months ago had never known the Gospel. Everywhere I go in the quarter I meet friends among the Tartars.

Best of all, I have rented a place and we are to have a Tartar church, and a reading room and a woman doctor to dispense twice a week. The girl orphans of the American Board are turned over to me and I have put them in the new school at East Gate, which the good people of Ahtanum partially built. There are 12 boys in private families on my list, 20 orphans in the industrial school, and 150 in the Christian Herald Orphanage. The correspondence to raise the money for all this has been enormous.

East Gate School—back row, center are Miss Pepoon, Miss Deahl, and Martha

Besides this I have the usual number of bible women and teachers and day schools, and teach four days in the college. Some days I wonder how I am to get through, but I have got on famously and was never in better health.

With very much love to all the Wileys,   from Martha

I am getting so proud of Wiley City. It must be booming.

FOOCHOW BIBLE WOMEN

By Martha Wiley

The Woman's Bible School (Miss Wiley is Principal) maintains a course covering eight years; it includes the studies required by the government, and in addition has a strong Bible course and instruction on homemaking, which includes all branches of housekeeping, all kinds of needlework, personal hygiene, and the care of children. Except for one paid servant, the cook, the women do all the work of the School, and many of them work in the garden as a means of self-help, providing vegetables for the School home.

Beginning with the fifth year, the students are given practical, Christian work, some for week-ends, some daily, others on Sunday. The greater number of students are widows, brought in from villages by Bible Women. The discouraged, the weary of life, those on their way to Buddhist nunneries, widows with children, find a welcome here. Frequently, educated men send their illiterate wives here for a time.

OUR GRADUATES

A number of our graduates have taken nurses' training and are scattered here and there, in hospitals, schools, and private practice. The women who go out for definite Christian work do the most conspicuous service.

But the Bible Women are only a small percentage of the stream of women who flow in and out of the school. Most of the women go back to their own homes and there they find themselves better equipped to make a home.

Foochow Bible Women with Martha and Edna Deahl

[previous letter is missing]

"We found ourselves in the walled park that is the tomb of Confucius."

JUNE 26, 1912

Dear friends all,

To go on with my story—after an early breakfast Miss Pepoon and I set out to see what we could see. We got a carriage and pair and had a Foochow speaking girl go with us to make the trip pleasanter.

First we rode out through the Tartar city. Such desolation can only be appreciated by seeing the place. Scarcely one brick was left on another in all the quarter. What had been the spacious yamen of the Tartar General was completely obliterated and the place could only be determined by the fragments of red painted wall. The stories of how the blood ran in the streets could not be doubted. How glad we were that the revolution and conflict between the Manchus and Chinese ended in a less sanguinary manner in Foochow. It was bad enough, to be sure, but incomparably less horrible.

From here we went out to the tomb of one of the kings of the Ming dynasty—supposed to have been the first. We crossed the city and gained an idea of the wonderful size of the wall, and of the enclosed area. You cannot believe that you are in a walled city when there are fields and orchards many acres in size to pass through—but it is true and after a time we got through the last of the gates and on the country road to the tomb, which is a wooden hillock with ornamental gates in front enclosing the entire grounds. I climbed the point behind the tumulus and looked over on Purple Mountain, where the batteries of revolutionaries were planted, which did such deadly work in the Tartar city. Not a sign of life was evident, and no evidence of so recent an occupation by the Chinese troops.

Every other person on the streets is in uniform and squads of soldiers go about singing their war songs, which are rather blood curdling judging by the sound. The week before that everything was under military control because of the recent mutiny and looting, and only three days before had the restraint been removed and the people allowed to move about freely. A few other sights were enjoyed but nothing to me was so impressive as going about and seeing the city in a general way—not in detail. There was a subdued and fearful atmosphere, which could be felt even by one who did not know the language. It will be many a day before the people forget the death and destruction that has been before their eyes for months. I hope that the end of it has come for the city of Nanking.

The new Pukan-Tientsin Railroad opened up to passenger traffic June 21st, and we want to take the trip on that road starting tomorrow. We asked a Dr. Macklin of the Christian Mission to tell us about the route. He had come down the line the week before, but all that he could tell us was the hardships, and he added that if we were relatives he would forbid our going. He said that the road was swarming with soldiers and the cars with their riding back and forth, and that there was no place to stay at night and nothing to eat. That he almost perished of hunger did not appeal to the sympathy of the heathen who controlled the road. Last of all he was rampant and we will surely get, if we go. Still, as a climax, he was charged two 3rd class fares to sit in a car where all the Chinese paid one 3rd class fare.

Miss Pepoon says that she will do what I say, so in the morning I will do what pops into my head. Somehow, I believe the good doctor might have managed better.

June 27 —— The "die is cast." We go by the P.T.R.R. and are on the train. This morning at breakfast the M. E. ladies were so concerned that they offered to send a "boy" with us until after we had been to the grave of Confucius. We accepted him and he hired a carriage and put us and our "six pieces" in and we drove down for an hour and a half to a place opposite Pukan. Here he hired a boat while I bought $3.50 worth of tinned goods. Then we scrambled into a sampan and a queer old coolie ferried us across. This is the connection between Nanking and the R.R.

When the employees were asked why the company had no ferry the answer was, "If anybody wants to sit in our cars they may plan to get on them". We found that because of the poor accommodations only third class tickets were sold. The "boy" whom we named "Thomas Cook," got our tickets and we went aboard the best car we could find. A very well dressed Chinese man went by and looked at us closely. We looked very nice, for Miss Pepoon had on a black China silk and I a dark blue–which we got especially for this trip and they were fresh and nice.

When we started, along came the swell man and said that we were in a 2nd class car and must pay two third fares, just as he held up the doctor. The conductor came with him and said the elegant youth was "train inspector." I knew that in the station only 3rd class tickets were sold, and told him so. He said, no matter, we had to pay or go to another car. I told him that we would go so we went to another car and he let our servant sit in the good car along with our "six pieces." When I saw this, Miss Pepoon and I returned to our seats and asked to see the tickets of the traveling Chinese. All were third class. Again came the conductor for a fare. It looked as though I would weaken when a fine Chinese heard the racket and came from another car and whispered in English the one word, "squeeze." Then my courage came back and I told him to get me a 2nd class ticket and I would pay for it. He could not get it of course, so we sat with the other 3rd class people instead of in the baggage car. Along the way we changed conductors and we saw no more of the "inspector," except his green hat, and he caught a car for Pukan.

The terminus, Pukan, looks like some frontier railway station in America. The English have built this section of the P.T.R.R.

We travelled along merrily after the squeeze episode was over. The boy Thomas prepared our supper out of the $3.50 basket, made a pot of tea, bought some eggs and fruit, and we had a fine time. All of a sudden the train stopped and the conductor said that we would tie up for the night. Where to go was the question. There were no inns, so we asked for the use of the car for the night. The conductor was a big fat jolly Chinese and was very proud to have two such fine ladies to look after. He did all in his power to make us comfortable. We piled our baggage between the seats and put down our bedding and slept very well for a while, but Miss Pepoon fought mosquitoes until she prayed to get rid of them, and then they came over to me.

June 28 —— Early in the morning the jolly conductor came to us to tell us that the train we were on would return to Pukan and we would have to get off. It was then only 5 o'clock. We got off and sat down blinking at the early sun wondering what next to do. We had to wait until 2 o'clock to start. The station master saw us and asked us to his room, and the boy got breakfast for us on his stove, and we wrote letters until 9 o'clock, and then we spied a house about a mile away that looked foreign, so we set out for the place. It was the home of the engineer in charge of the railroad construction, and his wife and daughters were very glad to have us stay for lunch.

Only three days before, a band of soldiers had come through, looting the town of Bung Bu, and the family had to board a car and flee, but they soon got back. Bung Bu was the scene of an episode during revolutionary days, when general Cang, the Manchu General, fled from Nanking, took possession of the cars that he needed, and set out for the north. A party of the enemy put some rapid fire guns on the station platform and intended to fire into the train as it pulled into the station. But the general heard of the plans and stopped the train two miles down the road. He then sent a couple thousand veterans up to the station on foot, and they caught and killed and hanged, upon the trees around the station, all the heads. Then the train came up and they went aboard and proceeded north.

After tiffin Miss Pepoon went back to the station on a hand car, but I walked past all those poplars that had been so decorated, and even in the broad daylight it made me feel creepy. We got aboard with Thomas Cook and had all of the yesterday experience over again. The conductor did not care to lend us a car either for the night, but the superintendant happened along and Thomas Cook and I went back to his car and asked him for a car for the night. He himself came and selected three 1st class compartments in an unused car that was brought along, so we have fine quarters for Thomas and ourselves until 5 o'clock tomorrow.

We are now at Su Chow Fu, the place where General Cang stopped his train and decided to stay. Poor old man! The revolutionaries try to get him to become loyal to the new government, but he says they are all schoolboys and cannot run a government. Soldiers fairly swarm about the train and railway. There will be another day with new experiences—so good night.

June 29 —— Last night in our first class car we found there was no light, so we went out to the mud village for a candle. There was sufficient heat without planning for that. Thomas Cook also got us two raw eggs to take before we went to bed—he understands foreigners so well. The time table said that we would have to wait for some time even after we left our palace car, so we left Thomas and started for the walled city, to see if General Cang would invite us to have breakfast with him, but Thomas had discovered that the time had changed the day before and just as we thought we saw an orderly in the distance, along came Thomas on the fast run to get us back on the train. We ran pell-mell and reached the station and dashed into our car and—sat there an hour!

Later —— We reached Yen Chow Fu from Su Chow Fu at 1:30 P.M. There is no station yet but a little two room Chinese house where the station master lived. Thomas dumped off our six pieces and we sat down on them and wondered what next. I spied a man who looked as though he could speak English and called out good morning and looked my pleasantest. He could speak English and was delighted to do so. He proved to be the station master and he had the two room house. He invited us over and we were might glad to go and have tea, for Thomas had not got a very good breakfast for us, as the bread had spoiled and we could not get rice.

This young man was fine. He hired wheelbarrows for us and stored our six pieces and we set out for a trip of 45 li [a Chinese unit of distance equal to about 0.6 kilometers or 0.4 miles]. Thomas and the little baggage we needed went on one wheelbarrow and Miss Pepoon and I on another while one man pulled and another man pushed each unicycle. Such squawking and unearthly noises can be made by nothing else than a Shantung wheelbarrow. The day was hot, the road dusty, and bumps were many. Occasionally Thomas got out the teapot from his wheelbarrow and got hot water and made tea to wash down the dust. You might suppose that we were unhappy, but not so. This was most interesting—fine crops of cotton, alfalfa, corn, melons and fruit orchards covered the plain, and at short intervals on each side were either avenues or clumps of pine that led to wonderful mounds that are tombs of the learned followers of Confucius. This Chinese "Appian Way" was to me fully as interesting as the "Appian Way" at Rome.

By and by as evening came on, we neared the yellow roofs of the walled city of Chu Fow. In 551 B.C. Confucius was born, and in his travels over the state of Lu, now Shantung province, he doubtless went over these same roads, and here his tomb is—the Mecca of literati of the nation. Our wheelbarrow men spurred up a little and we came to the end of a long avenue of cypress trees, so old that they are twisted and gnarled and interlaced most fantastically. Through this we approached a great gateway guarded by stone lions, and through this gateway was another long avenue of cypress trees ending with an even grander gate. Through the great arches we wandered and found ourselves in the walled park that is the tomb of Confucius. We stood lost in admiration and in enjoyment of the simple beauty. There was not one inharmonious touch to mar the perfect, quiet grandeur of this resting place of China's greatest sage. The walled enclosure is a park full of beautiful evergreen trees and grassy hillocks with unbeaten paths leading to the unpretentious graves of the disciples of the "Master."

"Spirit Lane"—a grand stone walk, cool and moist because of the leafy arch of cypress trees, leads up to the tomb proper of the great man. The plain grassy knoll with massive stone slab is a fitting monument to the man who has perpetuated himself in the hearts of more people than any other known man. There is dignity and serenity in the broad avenues of cypress trees, in the plain slab of stone, in the grassy hillocks and the stately arches over the gateways that, give to a visitor a new respect for China. This great man, first in the hearts of the Chinese, was not a warrior bent on conquest but a sage—a teacher of righteousness.

Approach to Confucius' grave

The darkness had fallen but still we lingered, loath to leave the still sweet air of the graves and the moist avenues with the flickering shade of the stirring tree tops. But our wheelbarrow men were not in a sentimental mood and could not people the dusk with the ghosts of time honored sages, nor imagine the "master" strolling up the avenues followed by his 12 intimates and his 72 disciples, and his 3,000 pupils. They could picture some pretty scenes in an inn half a mile away, so we had to mount our wheelbarrows and proceed. Thomas said the price was too high and we ought not to pay it. The proprietor of the inn wanted a dollar Mexican [silver] for his two spare rooms and space in the court for the wheelbarrows. Thomas beat him down to 80 cents, on our furnishing a candle to light us to bed, and paying 20 cents for hot water for tea.

I put up the mosquito nets, and oil paper on the beds and plenty of insect powder on the paper, got our candle lighted up and then got inside of the net and tried to write. Thomas got a can of beans out of the pack and in the course of time we had tea, tinned beans, and crackers for supper after such a strenuous day—we longed for the flesh pots of Foochow and told Thomas so. He went out in the dark and bought a dozen eggs, and a raw egg each consoled us while we lay wide awake most of the night. The beds were not hard for they were soft pine; neither did we suffer from cold; the insect powder was warranted to keep off intruders; and a mosquito net completed the outfit—yet we were so unreasonable that we would not sleep. Hence we got up early and set out to see the Confucian temples—this was on June 30th.

We roused up the watchman and entered while the dew was yet on the grass and trees and the crowds had not yet gathered. The temple area is truly beautiful, with its courts of stately trees, stone slabs of great height, temples with their variety of color, and birds of many kinds calling from the pine tops. Confucian temples stand all over China, but this one had a special interest. Ten majestic pillars guard the front, each carved inches deep in the solid stone. Slightly behind, is the temple erected to the wife of Confucius.

We left the place most reluctantly. But Thomas insisted on our getting started early. We had a breakfast of raw eggs, the rest of the beans and some crackers and set out at 8:00 A.M. and then returned to Yen Chow in two hours less time than it took to go. This was a very hard trip for Miss Pepoon, but she was plucky. We stopped at a nearby village and Thomas got a pot of tea and we finished the crackers. We carried our own tea pot and tea leaves and were surprised that the natives boiled corn leaves for tea and have hard tack instead of rice. We could buy no rice in the villages. The station master was glad to see us and we had tea with him and got our "six pieces," and Thomas bought tickets for us to Tai An and one for himself back to Pukan. The trains departed at the same time and we waved farewell to him from the window of our 2nd class car—the first time we had purchased 2nd class tickets on this line.

Of course we could have got on very well without him, but it was easier and more respectable and not very expensive—as all Thomas cost for a week's travel, board and wages was about $9 gold.

With love to all,   Martha

*"The girls are so anxious to study that they objected
to the summer vacation."*

Foochow, China   September 6, 1912

Dear Belle,

Your letter asking me to send a letter in time for your great meeting of the Society just reached me after I arrived at Foochow this fall which accounts for my not having written the letter.

You also asked me to write you about the money for the school. I have the school all up and going. Miss Pepoon gave me the last hundred for it and it is booming. The girls are so anxious to study that they objected to the summer vacation and so the teacher went on with the school all summer when she was entitled to a month's vacation.

Head of Girl's School, who was once an orphan himself, his wife, who was also an orphan and now a teacher, with the castaway girl they adopted.

But if you have any money to send for the work in the Tartar quarter I would love to have it. The people are committing suicide and other things worse because they are hungry and there is nothing. I have a couple hundred of them at work and could give more of them work if I had the original capital to put them to weaving. It takes $10 to start a man or woman into work. That buys the original material. I begin to pay them just as soon as they work—exactly what they earn. If you think this is easy, change your mind. Of all the scrapes I ever got into, this is the hardest to manage. I can tell you all about the difficulties of the weaving business, but it is a good business proposition, for the workers can soon earn their living. I hate to go on the street for there are dozens of people after me for help.

I wish I had time to tell you all about the affair that I got into the very day I got back from the north. The governor is an enemy to Christianity and I fear that our troubles as a mission have just begun under this new government. The old government let us alone but the new one tries to investigate every move and checkmate us. It is almost impossible to buy land now, and to rent to a foreigner is greatly condemned.

I wonder what will become of the country. Only last week the Chinese dailies printed that all the powers except the U.S. are trying to divide China. I have not got the foreign papers yet and wonder if that is really the case.

Last week all the southern end of the province was in a rebellion against the officers.

They are a bad lot, fully as bad as the old. How could they be better when they come of the same stock and have the same training in corruption?

When I came back, I was four days on the sea with a typhoon raging. The house was in bad shape when I got here and I just got everything all cleaned up fine ready for the opening of the college. Then the day before yesterday another typhoon came up and things are as bad as ever. The coolies tell me that part of the dormitory has blown down but I have not been out to see the damage. This fall is to be a very busy one, but I will get through it some way. The poor are always with me. While I am sitting here writing there is a man at my door begging me to help him with a little money to buy a coffin for his old mother who died last night. She was a member of one of the City churches and had been terribly poor. The son is pretty well gone with consumption. This is a miserable country at present, especially this province. Since I went north, I have come to the conclusion that the people here are the most poverty stricken in the country. They have gradually become so since Formosa was taken by the Japanese.

I have to go down to the orphanage and see that all the kids are clean and no creatures on them. I had to spank a woman the other day to make her work and she went to work and doubled her output of weaving. The others looked aghast, and then they got down to business too.

This life here is like watching a tragedy all the time. I am so glad that I had such a fine summer or I would not be so ready to tackle all that is before me now.

Love to all the family,   Martha

"It is enough to make a stone weep."

FOOCHOW, CHINA   OCTOBER 16, 1912

Dear Belle and Norman,

I wrote you only a few days ago telling of the excited state of the City and the surrounding country. Foochow City has become more quiet, but only yesterday the governor sent a new regiment of soldiers to quiet a district two days march to the south.

The distress among the Tartar people here is beyond my powers of describing. The 200 that I plan work for were getting along fairly well with the dollar a month from the government, when a proclamation of the governor was posted saying that they would get no more aid from the government. We are in duty, bound to help out the Christians here. The day before yesterday I could not help a man to food, and last night he killed himself. The night before, two others did the same. It is enough to make a stone weep to see the little children starving and their big scared eyes looking at the foreigner and hoping for food.

Sunday 85 Tartars were baptized. Some of the women have been three days without food other than a little gruel, and yet they had not said a word! The communion bread was the first taste of solid food that ten of them had taken in two days!

This summer I got $100 for my cottage rent at Kuliang, and I am buying $3 a day in sweet potatoes for this month, and adding a small portion each day to the food of the working people—they are in terrible need. This will hold out a month. Can you send me $100? If you could see these children and starving women you would sacrifice anything to send it. If they can be helped over this winter I can get them placed, and start them to work, but I cannot do it at once. It takes time. Most of them are too weak to earn much, and the weaving requires strength. I thought that personally you would like to give this $100 as your Christmas gift. Norman has always been good to help, and this money is terribly needed. I would not ask if there was any way to avoid it.

I have given all I have. If you give this, send me a cable with just my name and I will understand, and go on with the supplementary food from November 15th - December 15th. Perhaps by that time I can beg somebody else for $100 through January, and by that time they can be earning. This plant costs a lot to run and we raise all the money by letter writing. But your gift is special to save those from absolute starvation who are not able to earn anything yet.

Friday, five women ran into the house to escape from the brutal soldiers, to whom their poverty stricken husbands were selling them. The things that these women endure would make your blood curdle. Suicides are every day occurrences. You may not like to read this awful letter, but I am living in this state of things, and these decent women are *enduring* it. Please send me a cable as soon as you decide, for I cannot keep up this help much longer—we have been a month, without aid.

'I enclose cable'—that will be sufficient words if you send $100 gold. If someone else could send $100, just add the word 'two' and I will understand. I wish that some of those old farmers would donate the value of a cow to these destitute women and children, but do not wait for them if you can send the $100.

Send the draft on Hong Kong and Shanghai Banking Corporation, by registered letter. If I get the cable I will get the bank here to advance the money until the draft comes. I hate to bother you but the case is so desperate, I know you will want to help.

Love from,   Martha

FOOCHOW, CHINA   DECEMBER 16, 1912

Dear Belle,

Your letter came by last mail and I was glad to hear that all are well—for when the cold weather comes I am always worried for Mother, and I hope that she will be prevailed upon to go home with you for the winter. It is too cold for an old person to be getting up and taking cold while making fires. I trust that, long before this reaches you, you will have got her already located for the winter in your comfortable house.

I think that I told you I was going to Canton at the end of January to attend the "All

China Conference." I think that it will be a great treat. I have never been there and it will also give me an opportunity to meet all the prominent people of China—that is, all the prominent foreigners. The trip down there and back is awful, as the coast is so rough that everyone is sure to be seasick. However, I can afford to be seasick for four days for the sake of the benefits and pleasure.

Affectionately, Martha

[Note: no letters for 1913]

[In 1913, Foochow College shifted to high school status.]

"My mandarin teacher is first assistant to the coffin staff."

FOOCHOW, CHINA MARCH 24, 1914

Dear Mother,

I wonder what you are doing to-day. Perhaps one of those terrible March winds are blowing and the dust flying! To-day is very warm here and every one has blossomed out in white. I have got on my summer clothes too, so you know it is hot.

My Mandarin teacher is first assistant to the coffin staff and has been chasing off to funerals two days in succession and I have missed my study time. I fear that I will not graduate very soon in Mandarin at this rate. I can stammer along at it but it is not so natural as the Foochow dialect.

I hope that you have stayed with the relatives somewhere this winter and have not been alone.

With love to all and much to yourself,

Affectionately, Martha Wiley

"I teach a class of medical students each day for half an hour."

FOOCHOW, CHINA APRIL 11, 1914

Dear Mother,

This term I am doing a good bit of Bible class teaching outside of regular college work. I teach a class of medical students each day for half an hour. Besides this I have an average of one class a day of other regular school work and evangelistic work that I do. I still keep up on the religious end of the Manchu work and also the charity.

Miss Hartwell simply took over the industrial school, which was in pretty good shape with the men all trained to do the work, so she did not relieve me of very much. She has so many irons in the fire that she cannot give time to anyone.

[page missing]

Bible women at Martha's home for a refresher course—Catherine Lin, far left.
(Note Martha's gray hair from her bout with malaria.)

"That Tango business is a new one to me."

FOOCHOW, CHINA   APRIL 19, 1914

Dear Belle,

I have been full of business this spring. I want to get the Manchu church provided for and in shape before I leave for home and so have done a good deal of writing for money. This week I got a cable from Chicago saying that someone was sending $800 for purchase of the house that we are now using as a church. Permanent funds have also been secured for the preacher and the Bible woman. So things are gradually getting into shape for my furlough.

We still keep up the charity for the Manchus. I have raised $90 a month for these three years, but now it is cut down to $30, as a good many have got something to do and can care for the old people and children, and the government is helping certain classes a little. I have the preacher buy 500 pounds of dried sweet potatoes each day and pass it out to the poorest in five pound packets.

It is very wonderful how money has come in for this. Occasionally I have to give the money myself but often there is someone who turns up with a little spare money for the sweet potatoes. This money business is very anxious work. My school work is a rest from it, for no one can get at me when I am in my classes from 8 until 12:30. If I get where I can step out without finding someone starving it will seem very strange to me.

Did you get my letter about the tea? I wrote about it but perhaps the letter did not reach you. Miss Deahl sends out tea and has the one who receives it, sell it for 25 cents a box and remit to her. She then uses the money for some of her work.

Miss Hartwell looks after the industrial school now. She is turning it into more of a girls' industrial. I had about an even number of men and women when I started it. The men are the better workers but the women need the work more. She has about 100 of the orphans living there.

Anna sent me a clipping showing the kinds of clothing that is worn at home. Some of those fierce costumes must be taken from the Orient. The split skirt effect is just like that of a Chinese man's garment. When I was in Shanghai I saw much of that style in hotels and receptions.

That Tango business is a new one to me. I wonder how much that has spread in the West. It is fierce out here, in the ports. When people out here get sporty they exceed the limits.

We think that we will hire another woman for the house and that will make four servants. I hate to get another but we seem to run down three, so after a family council we have decided on another. Our old Mrs. Seven will have a fit when she hears about it, but she is too weak to do all the running around that is required. This time we are to get a field woman who is strong and husky.

The plague is beginning early and last week a man and his wife and child all died of it just opposite our gate. Yesterday the doctors were called to a case just across the street from the hospital, and the child died while the doctors were there. I do hope that this will not be a terrible plague year. Last year was a cholera year. One thing follows another in quick succession. We have two old pussies and each have four kittens to support, so they keep the rats away from our house very well and we are probably not to have the plague.

I am not getting any new clothes this year but a couple of new dress skirts for school wear. Tell Nettie that I am much obliged for the dress that she sent me—it makes a very swell summer dress. This summer Miss Deahl and I will live together in the same house as last year and have the same servants. I rent out my cottage and take rooms in the other. That makes the house keeping a little cheaper.

This afternoon I went down to see a sick man and saw on his bed a crazy quilt that mother had made. I gave it to him when I went home eight years ago. He said that he liked that quilt very much. When his daughter died she was lying on that quilt, and he hoped that it would last until he died. There are places where the patches are worn off and the flour sack base is shining through, but that makes it all the more decorative.

With love to all the family,   Martha

Edna Deahl with kittens

**Woman's Board of Missions of the Interior
(CONGREGATIONAL)
ROOM 1315, 19 SOUTH LA SALLE STREET
TELEPHONE CENTRAL 1388
CHICAGO, May 13, 1914**

My dear Miss Wiley:

Your letters of much interest reached me some time ago, and I think I have replied, but I want to say just a word in regard to the $1,000 sent to you by Mr. and Mrs. Douglas Smith for the "Manchu Church." It gave me very much pleasure to have part in that proceeding even though it was only writing the cablegrams.

. . .

Hoping you are all in your usual good health,

Yours with very much love,   M. D. Wingate

"I am quite proud of my protégé."

[unknown recipient]   AUGUST 10, 1914

I had a great surprise to-day. Mrs. Kinnear is going to America this month and is getting all her business fixed up, so she sent me $100 for the Manchu Church debt. Miss Williams has sent me $325.00 for Donald and the Bible women, Miss Pepoon $41, Mr. Dudley $50. So I am making out, but personally I have some extra expenses this summer.

I am quite proud of my protégé [Donald]. He is a really a fine, clean-hearted lad. I think that his engagement is going to go through. He is quite warming up to the subject since I invited the girl to dinner before I left the City. Now he says that *he will ask her himself*—a very new thing in China.

To-day I am lonesome for all of you.

Lots of love,   Martha

[Note: Donald came into Martha's care, along with his younger brother (who is never mentioned by name), sometime after 1911, upon the death of his older brother David who was a teacher in Foochow College. David wrote on his deathbed, "Teacher [Martha] when I am gone, take care of my brother."]

"I do not want to stay out here when you really need me; there is only one mother."

FOOCHOW, CHINA   SEPTEMBER 1, 1914

Dear Mother,

My typewriter is all out of fix but still I think that it is a little more legible than my writing. I think some of the school boys got funny when I was not at home and put it out of order.

What a dreadful summer we have had as far as typhoons are concerned. There were 12 days of typhoons in July and more than that in August and this is September 1st with the worst wind of the season simply blowing things to pieces. For eight days it has been raging without coming to a climax, so I do not know how much longer it will last. To-day I had an engagement with a dentist and worked my way up the hill and had an old tooth pulled out, and then came home in a rain that went clear to my bones. Now I have a basket turned over a Chinese stove and all my things heaped on top drying out.

I expect to go down the mountain about the middle of September. School opens the 15th. Plague and cholera have been much less destructive this year than last. Perhaps this is because of the storms so much of the time.

Miss Hartwell came up to Foochow to get 40 of the orphanage boys and take them down to Sharp Peak where they will learn carpentry and masonry. To-day I had a note saying that she got down to Pagoda with the boat load of boys and this last typhoon struck, so she is stranded with all those boys on her hands and this awful storm raging. She will think more than ever that the storms are purely diabolical.

Vina said that you wanted to know when I was coming home. That depends altogether on you. If you are well enough for me to stay out the remainder of my term I will do so and then wind up all my business here and stay with you. If not, I will come any time that you think I ought to come. I do not want to stay out here when you really need me. There will always be many millions of Chinese left but there is only one mother, so I do not want to wait when I ought not.

I wish that I had a good home newspaper to get the war news. We are wild for news and can only get a few telegrams. We Americans get the German and Chinese, and the English people get the English, and often they will be exactly opposite. I cannot see why that is the case, but at any rate it leaves us nothing but our own conjectures, even after paying for a telegram.

With much love from,   Martha

FOOCHOW, CHINA   SEPTEMBER 4, 1914

Dear Anna,

I am enclosing a ten dollar bill for you to use if I owe you anything. If not you may get me a pair of lace shoes (not ties) and a pair of rubbers to match. The shoes you may get of light weight, as they will be winter shoes for "dress up."

Cholera broke out in the orphanage and a matron died of it. Miss Hartwell took the exposed parties to Sharp Peak. None of them took it.

These few days are spent in writing. My Mandarin teacher got a chance to go to Amoy and get $20 a month, so I bade him God speed and he left me at once. This keeps me from reading my usual three hours a day.

If it does not rain to-day I want to get out and walk. We are so cross that we could bite tacks.

Nana

*"I will have my 41st birthday. I am now
an old maid sure enough."*

SHARP PEAK, CHINA   FEBRUARY 10, 1915

Dear Belle,

I was very glad to get your letter a few days ago. What a lot of old people have passed away! It makes us begin to feel that we are now the old generation ourselves. I can hardly realize that within a few days I will have my 41st birthday. I am now an old maid sure enough. What a disgrace to the family, from a Chinese standpoint. However, if you could see my flock of Chinese you would think that I was not lacking in children.

I think that I have sold my Kuliang cottage. At least I have rented it for the summer and will sell it to the renter if he wants it. I hate to sell it. I have a sentimental affection for the place, but it is all expense and no income and it is uncertain each summer whether I will live in it or not. And especially I would not want it if I went home. So I am pretty sure I will be at Sharp Peak again this summer.

The last two years I have taught the senior class Bible I have taken up Daniel and Revelation, so this winter I am having a little book translated into Chinese for the use of the women, both into the Romanised and the colloquial character. That is why I have these two college students here with me.

Miss Hartwell was down here for two days but I hardly saw her. This morning she was up and off at 4 o'clock, and the rain was coming down and she had to walk that long way down to the boat over the slippery hills. Her chair coolies ran off and she is left to walk. Her energy never seems to fail, but as she gets older she gets more tempery. However, the Chinese seem to understand and like her just the same.

Love to all,   Martha

**"Poor old China has been so cut up, she has
done well just to survive."**

FOOCHOW, CHINA   FEBRUARY 16, 1915

Dear Wallace,

You would be about as surprised to get a letter from me, as I would be to hear from you. So I am going to surprise you, but do not let that shock you too much.

This week I am at Sharp Peak on the coast all by myself—that is, there are no foreigners with me. There are plenty of Chinese on the island. There are about 30 rooms in this sanitarium and at night when the wind howls and rattles all the windows it is very creepy, especially when the sea is roaring its worst. One night I had been reading a ghost story before I went to sleep and I woke up with a ghost right in sight. Fortunately I have one of those dry battery electric hand lanterns and I turned that on and found only my mosquito net waving in the breeze.

The coolie and the two school boys I have along, sleep off to one side of the servant's quarters. I came down here to write letters and get away from somebody's dinning all the time, and I have had a good time even though the storm has kept me in and the weather has been so cold that I have had to hug a hot water bottle.

Sunday was China's New Year's Day and I invited the Chinese of the island who wished to come and take tea and have Sunday School afterward.

There were about 50 that came of all kinds and descriptions. Day after tomorrow I will have to go back to the City and get to moving and opening school and a dozen other things.

The chair coolies have gone on a strike and will not carry foreigners without an exorbitant price. I have not done so much walking in a long time as I have done this year. I do not know what we will come to if they hold out much longer, but have an idea that we will give in to them.

Last week the vice consul gave a reception for the new consul that came—a Mr. Pontius—and it was great to see the Japanese consul steaming up in all his regimentals very early, and getting out soon, so that he would not meet the German consul. I wonder if they feared that one or the other would burst if he came in contact with his enemy.

All the people here are in great anxiety for fear that the Japanese are meditating some mean thrust at China. A German cable to-day says that Japan is waiting to get a slice off the coast of China. If she gets that she will include this province in her piece of the melon. Poor old China has been so cut up by factions and revolutionists that she has not the strength to fight anybody. She has done well just to survive.

General Li is taking back all the land in one quarter of the City that Miss Hartwell and others bought, as he is planning a great camp of soldiers inside the City, and he wants the barracks there. I have a piece of land there with a boys' school on it but he has not called for mine. I hope that my piece is just out of the line. My suspicions are that he wants what the foreigners have, and I bought mine through a Chinese and have had the deeds stamped in his name, so the general does not know that it is a foreigner running the place.

Miss Hartwell had any number of the poor at work there and it is a great pity that she has to hand it back to the general.

Love to Nettie and the children and your good self,

Affectionately,   Martha

"I think that he is a fake dentist and in reality a spy."

FOOCHOW, CHINA   APRIL 18, 1915

Dear Mother,

It is Sunday evening and the rain has been pouring down all day so I am staying at home and writing. You will be glad to know that after all these years the ladies have a house that is all their own. The house that we have is down in the Manchu Quarter on Water Gate Street, near the Ancient Fairy Bridge. You may remember that when we began work in the Manchu Quarter just after the revolution the governor lent us a house, which we tried to buy. He would not sell and took the house away out of pure meanness.

An old monk from Kushan Monastery came along and took a fancy to this street and decided that he would build a big house and rent it for industrial work. He selected as his site the place just opposite the one we wanted to buy. The governor was an idolater and a great friend of the monk so gave him the piece of land that was needed and writings to show that it was a perpetual lease. The monk built a big brick building two stories high, with two wings built of the ordinary plaster walls. We bought this from him for $4,400 and have spent about $1,000 to repair it. We have also bought more land on each side of the house and now we are getting things pretty well in shape. We moved down here the 6th of April.

Street opposite of Martha's Fairy Bridge home

We have had several hundred guests in the past week and all have had tea and cake and heard the Victrola and had a good time.

The upstairs rooms have white paint on all the woodwork and the ceilings are cream with white walls. The new matting is dark green and cream color and the tables and chairs are stained old oak. There is a long verandah on each side that serves as halls.

My study and bedroom connect with a little stairway and my store room is just across the verandah from the study. The place is convenient enough to live in, but it is a fright to get my school work done at this distance. It is about a mile from the college, and as the boys are not allowed out except twice a week, I have all the running to do if I want any of them to come. Sometimes I have three trips to make, morning, afternoon and evening. Naturally I am not as enthusiastic as the other two ladies. This morning I went over there for my S.S. [Sunday School] class and the rain came down in torrents and by the time I got back I was as wet as a rat.

This past week I have gone to the dentist every day to have an aching tooth treated. The dentist is a little Japanese man who has an office over the South Gate. Each time that I am there I think that he is a fake dentist and in reality a spy. At any rate I think that the fake part is correct. I made him wash up the things that he used, and he had what you would call a "tantrum." The second time that I went he had things cleaned up a little and he himself had on a clean coat, and the last time he put clean covers on the chair. I am getting him trained in a bit. He lets me see that he washes the instruments.

Affectionately,   Martha

"Rice will be at famine prices this fall."

FOOCHOW, CHINA   MAY 23, 1915

Dear Mother,

The rain has been pouring down for weeks and to-day it is just showing us what can be done along that line. There have been five floods the last month, and the crops in the valley are all washed out, and rice will be at famine prices this fall.

China has had so much worry with the Japanese question that the people are very discouraged. Yesterday I was at the Consulate and one of the interpreters shook his head over the matter and said that China had begun her reforms too late. To-day it is said that Russia has entered claims for Mongolia and Germany has made new demands.

It makes one so furious that the Europeans are killing off each other and begging the rest of the world to feed them while they do it.

Our new place is so large that now we must have more servants and more entertaining is required. We now have a cook, a gardener, a washer man, and two women. And it keeps them all humping so we have to add a gatekeeper to the staff. It is lucky that men are cheap or we would have to do the work ourselves. I look after the downstairs work and Miss Deahl takes the upstairs.

All the hospitals begin the inoculation of the plague serum tomorrow. There is quite a crusade against the plague this year, but the dread disease is creeping right along in the most crowded places and this damp weather is also very bad for it. If we could have a week of blistering hot sunshine it would prove the best check.

Yesterday I had the mason bring three or four bushels of lime and spread it out all over the attic floor so that the rats will stay away from the attic. Miss Hartwell has lime over her study and store room floor so that you cannot walk around without stirring up a dust. I have Jaye's fluid [toilet disinfectant] on all my floors. I have ordered lime for the floors of my schools. Tomorrow the plague will doubtless get a great setback as the Christians who can get enough money are preparing to be inoculated.

It never seems possible that I could get it. Diseases that would scare the life out of me at home do not get one at all excited out here. I was more fierce on the rats than on the plague because it seems to be so dirty to have them around.

Cook at front gate starting for market

The gardener is getting our flowers all fixed up. I wish that I had some garden seeds to plant. Do you suppose that Belle or Vina could send me some lettuce seed in an envelope when they write? Any other kind of seed that grows quickly, like radishes, I could use. When I return in the fall it will be time to plant most of the seeds. Near our house I have a school and there is a nice little piece of land that our gardener could use to plant foreign vegetables. This is the first time we have had enough land to plant a garden.

The other day a big centipede eight inches long crawled out from under the sitting room door and a woman present calmly got up and tramped it while I squealed. About a week later the mate came out of the same hole and you should have seen the battle that Miss Hartwell and the centipede had! She finally got him killed. They are very hard to kill as they run very fast and are so wiry.

I will close with love to all the tribe, and especially to your good self.

Affectionately,   Martha

FOOCHOW, CHINA   JUNE 6, 1915

Dear Mother,

Here it is Sunday again and I have not written the letters that I should. Last week I was inoculated for plague. All the foreigners and hundreds of natives had a dose of the plague serum and it made most of them pretty sick for two days and not feeling well for a week. It did not affect me so seriously, as I went on with my teaching, but Miss Hartwell went to bed with her spell of plague and Miss Deahl lay around for a week. It is given as a hypodermic and does not hurt any more than such needle pricks usually do, but when the poison begins to circulate in the blood the fever rises.

With lots of love to all the Wileys,

Affectionately, Martha

"Before he died he came to the house and gave his 11 year old son to me."

FOOCHOW, CHINA   NOVEMBER 25, 1915

Dear Mother,

Wednesday of this week we began the women's meetings, and these followed the book that I have just translated and have had printed. I had a thousand copies printed and more than half of them were sold the first week and there will be none of them left pretty soon. This book is on the study of Revelation, and as there is the most ignorance along these lines all the Christians workers wanted to read the book.

I am coming out in bad shape financially this year. Special gifts are dropping off and everything is so high and this house is so expensive and there are so many calls for money that I am afraid to look at my bank book when it is sent to me each month. War is making so much difference with all work. You used to say that we always had to live in such a "pinched" fashion. A missionary is in a chronic state of worry over finances.

Last week one of the college teachers died. About a week before he died he came to the house and gave his 11 year old boy to me. This was the last time that I saw the man. But as soon as he died I went over to the house just across the street to see how they were getting on with the funeral arrangements, and they said that he died in great peace of mind even though he was in great suffering, and he told them not to worry about him for he "had given his soul to God and his son to Miss Wiley and he was content to die." The boy thinks that he belongs to me and walked over to my house and led me to the funeral and stood by me while the sermon was going on, and he told me that he expected to be a good boy and not make me very much trouble. He is a cute little boy but as mischievous as any American that you ever saw. I suppose there is no help for it and I am elected to have another boy to look after.

Ding Goi [Donald] is doing well, but the most trouble of all the boys and girls that I look after. But perhaps because he is naughty sometimes he is my favorite.

With love to all the family,

Affectionately, Martha

[partial letter] 1915

My two special boys, Dai Tuang and Ding Goi are getting on fine and are the most promising lads in the school. Dai Tuang speaks English beautifully. He graduates this year and then will go into the Seminary and take a course in Theology. Ding Goi has had only three years of English, but in a year after Dai Tuang he will graduate from the Chinese course. He does not know what he will do yet. He is as smart as any boy need be. He is good in every branch of study, but he does get puffed up a little too much occasionally, because he is so smart and knows it.

I am so tired of that wicked war that I hate the sound of the word and am glad we hear but little of the details.

With love to all the tribe, but especially much to yourself,

Affectionately,   Martha

[1916 – Martha in U.S. to care for her ailing mother – returns to China in 1919.]

[newspaper clipping]

MRS. MARY WILEY DIES AT HER HOME

January 18, 1919
Resident Here 50 Years – She Leaves
Eight Children and 24 Grandchildren

Mrs. Mary Ann Wiley, for 50 years a resident of the Yakima valley, died at her home in the Ahtanum this morning. She lacked a month of being 78 years and had lived on the family homestead, which is now the site of Wiley City, since 1868. She was one of the oldest and best loved pioneers of the valley and leaves a host of friends and relatives to regret her loss.

She was born in Prescott, Canada, February 18, 1841, of Scotch-Irish parents. When 8 years old she moved to Illinois, going from there to Minnesota. In 1858 she was married to Hugh Wiley, at Winona, Minnesota.

They came west via New York, Panama, and San Francisco, reaching Salem, Oregon, in 1866, where they lived for two years.

In 1868 they moved to Yakima, where they homesteaded at Wiley City. In 1884 Mr. Wiley died, but Mrs. Wiley continued to live at the family home.

The funeral will be held Monday morning at 11:00 in her home.

. . .

"You will devote yourself to the work for women."

AMERICAN BOARD OF COMMISSIONERS
FOR FOREIGN MISSIONS
CONGRETIONAL HOUSE 14 BEACON STREET
BOSTON, MASSACHUSETTS

JUNE 13, 1919

R.F.D. #5
North Yakima, Washington

My dear Miss Wiley:

We have just closed another Candidates Conference and have the rush of its affairs added to our ordinary routine. For this reason I have been slow in reporting the action of the Prudential Committee at the meeting on May 27th, reappointing you to the Foochow Mission, your support to be provided by the W.B.M.I. [Women's Board of Missions of the Interior], and with the expectation that you will devote yourself to the work for women. This is in accord with the desire of the W.B.M.I., and we understand in accord with your own inclination, so that we hope it will be quite satisfactory to you. I am reporting the matter of your reappointment to Foochow, and am congratulating them — as we do ourselves — upon having so capable, faithful and long-time a worker restored to the Foochow Mission. You will take up with the Treasury Department in due time, I am sure, the matter of your booking and routing for your return to the field.

Permit me to add my sympathy in the event which clears the way for your return to China. Though I am sure you will be happy to go back, you will be having sorrow in your heart over the separation from your mother, which the close of her earthly life has brought and which thus sets you free. May comfort and courage be yours.

Sincerely yours,   M. E. Sturig

"China has signed the peace treaty.
I dread what may have been done."

S.S. KATORI MARU   SEPTEMBER 17, 1919

Dear Belle,

This is the 17th and we are approaching Yokohama to-day, probably by 5 P.M. The voyage has been very tiresome and I have felt well only one day of the trip.

Every day I would think of you folks eating tomatoes and peaches and then I would get a smell of fried potatoes and onions and that was enough for me to live on that day.

The worst is yet to come for I have five days from Kobe to Tientsin on a small boat and it makes me sick to think of it. It will be good to reach Foochow once again and stay there a while.

The Japanese are very courteous and obliging and the Katori was steady most of the time, but the sea was rough.

Most of the way was in fog but strange to say the air was clear along the Aleutians so that we had a fine view of the nearest islands. They stood out like ridges of solid rock.

Yesterday we went through a storm. "Wireless" tells us a cyclone swept the Japanese Islands destroying a lot of railways.

We have had one line saying that China had signed the peace treaty. I am crazy to know the rest, and yet I dread what may have been done.

It was certainly good of you and Norman to spend so much time in Seattle to see me.

Lots of love,   Martha

PEKING, CHINA   SEPTEMBER 30, 1919

Dear Anna,

It is good to be in China again! Tientsin is a very progressive city with tram cars and all modern conveniences. By the time we had got ashore and baggage looked after it was 12 o'clock and four of us rushed up to Mr. Grimes' house where one woman was acquainted. The servants made us up four beds in one room and we got to bed. But Tientsin uses Wilson's [Daylight Saving] time so we had to get up an hour earlier than the sun time, and as breakfast was at seven we were sleepy and tired after a month of pure laziness. At 9 o'clock we took the train to Peking.

Dr. Stryker called me out to go with her in her automobile to make some calls on Chinese friends, and then go to the Forbidden City to see the museum of Chinese antiquities. I had never seen this before and it certainly opened my eyes as to what wonders the Chinese had performed in days gone by. The grounds are wonderful with trees, moats, marble bridges, etc.—all a part of the Forbidden City. The collections are in some of the spacious palaces. It is truly wonderful.

Dr. Stryker came down in her auto for me and Donald was there. As I got my things out onto the platform someone from the rear caught me by the shoulder and I turned about and found Donald. He and Dr. Stryker and I had a long walk on the wall. The wall is fixed up as a wide boulevard for walking on. We can look over the whole city from the wall.

I will write you more if anything else is worth writing. People here are just as furious over the Shantung question [regarding peace treaty negotiations with Japan, asking for economic and residential concessions] as they can get. I will go on to Shanghai and take the first boat house to Foochow. The cholera is not so bad there.

Donald is the happiest little chap you ever saw. His English has not improved, but he is more manly and self-reliant, and every teacher says that he is a promising lad. His health is fairly good but he stoops too much. He is very good looking and very neat.

Lots of love to each and every one of you,

Affectionately,   Martha

Gospel sampan

*Country church built and maintained
by the women members—Foochow.*

TIMELINE 1921–1930

1921 —Chinese Communist Party (CCP) established—Mao Zedong a founding member
—Donald graduates Yenching University with B.A. degree, begins teaching at Foochow College

1922 —Donald and Catherine married
—Provincial revolution
—Donald and Catherine have son that dies—he lives eight weeks

1923 —Martha almost dies from pneumonia, three months in U.S. hospital to recover

1924 —Returns to China
—Donald in U.S., receives M.A. degree in education from University of Washington
—Donald and Catherine have second child—Ella or "Little Boat"

1925 —Sun Yat-sen dies
—Foochow under martial law

1926 —Donald and Catherine at Teachers College, Columbia University, New York City
—"Boat" dies
—Martha recovering from typhoid

1927 —Living under Russian Cheka (Bolshevism)
—Martha is a refugee in Formosa (seven months)

1927 —Donald and Catherine's third child is born in U.S.—Mabelle
—Donald becomes the first Chinese principal of Foochow College at the age of 32

1928 —Martha returns to Foochow

1929 —Donald and Catherine lose another child

1930 —Donald and Catherine lose another child

3

FOCUS ON EDUCATION

FOOCHOW, CHINA   JANUARY 18, 1920

Dear Jean,

Such a long time and no letter written to you! Christmas has passed and the nice things sent by the Achelpohl family helped to make many children and poor women happy.

Christmas Eve I had a party for women and children. Each child got a piece of red cloth, almost a yard, and a picture. The cloth was to make a "pocket," a very much needed garment. The women each got a towel and a picture. The cloth and towels were made in the Manchu Industrial School. After that they had songs and games and tea and cakes, and all went home happy.

The Bible women came for two hours Christmas day and they got enough grey cloth for a suit—this, also, was woven by the poor people.

Oh yes, the pictures were a joy. And the cut up pictures are very entertaining. Donald's ten year old brother was sick of fever and just getting well. He played for hours with the puzzle pictures. I am sure that there are dozens of things that I've forgotten to mention, but the people who got them have not forgotten.

To-day I am sitting on the upstairs verandah writing and the thrushes are singing in the trees. I can see cabbage, cauliflower and lettuce in the garden, and all sorts of flowers in bloom, and it still feels cold. We do not have fires in the houses very often. Wood is too expensive.

Lots of love to you dear girl,   Nana

"Politics were never more exciting than now."

FOOCHOW, CHINA   FEBRUARY 14, 1920

Dear Vina,

Your good letter arrived yesterday. It is good to hear about your home life, your sewing and cooking and social events. Every little while I read a story just to get in the atmosphere of a normal American home.

Yesterday was the day when the "Kitchen God" has molasses smeared over his mouth and then burned. He is supposed to ascend to heaven with a very sweet report of the families' affairs so that prosperity will attend them next year. The family stays at home with doors shut for this function and no stranger can go in. The spirit of a new "god" is supposed to come down. The family buys a picture of two old crones sitting side by side and pastes it up behind the stove and has a new "god" for the new year. We are very free from interruptions on that day.

By this mail I am sending you an account of the Japanese fracas here in Foochow. Now the opium situation is becoming truly perilous. The Japanese influence is causing the Governor who is accused of being pro-Japan, to force the planting of opium upon the farmers. Soldiers take poppy seeds to the district cities and sit around until the seeds are planted. This province is in a sad plight. China must have another revolution to throw off the yoke of militarism, which the masses hate. The student body is protesting even when beaten and imprisoned. The boycott that was laughed at is making Japan sit up and take notice. Politics were never more exciting than now.

Lots of love to all of you,   Martha

FOOCHOW, CHINA   FEBRUARY 28, 1920

Dear Belle,

The Woodhouse calendar says that it is February 28th or else I could scarce believe that it is so far on in the season. It seems a very short time since I left you folks standing on the wharf in Seattle.

Every day is filled up with something and so the time goes much faster than it did at home. Yesterday we had some photos of the children taken. I had one taken of Horace Dieu, your boy [the boy Belle is sponsoring], that I will send as soon as finished. It will be ready before the next letter. He is a handsome chap and very smart. He is just ready for high school when it opens next week.

This vacation Horace has been making wire netting for chicken pens and waiting on the table and doing anything that came up to earn some money for clothes. The $30 that you send will now only buy books and food. I am going to let him borrow the rest from the school, and then when he gets through he can pay it back to the school. When you began supporting him $30 a year was a great plenty but now for $30 gold we can get only $25 silver. Also the purchasing power of a dollar is much less. So I will use the $30 that you send to get the things that he cannot borrow money to get. Then, if he sticks to the school, it will show that he is really determined to get an education.

March 14 —— This letter has been sticking in the typewriter so long that the machine has rusted. Since I began the letter, the rain has hardly stopped for a day, but things have been humming just the same.

Since I wrote you last, the anniversary of mother's death has passed and her birthday. Strange I think of her much oftener now than when she was living! There is enough to talk about for a week, but my fingers are numb. Much love to all the family, and especially to yourself.

Your sister,   Martha

"Don't go in there."

FOOCHOW, CHINA   APRIL 25, 1920

Dear Anna,

I have just returned from a meeting and found that I was not sleepy, so will write a page or two. A week ago, Saturday and Sunday, I went to the village of Kang-cheng. It stormed fearfully and we could not stay in the church, as it was too wet, so we stayed in a village home. The lady of the house was getting a feast ready and cutting up fish. The family pig came in and she took her hands out of the fish bowl to slap the sides of the pig, then two cats jumped onto the table to get the fish. I dashed to the rescue and slipped on the mud floor and almost sat on a big dog that was on the bed. That dog had hated me at sight and was just waiting to get a chance at my leg, but I missed the bed and the dog missed me.

Thursday and Friday, I took a City Bible woman and we went to Au-iong-die, a dense suburb of the City where we have a church and a Bible woman who is not very hot on her job. We three had a short prayer meeting in the church and started from there to enter every door on the street. The resident Bible woman kept saying: "Don't go in there," but I was out "to thoroughly investigate" so we entered each door.

This is the "red-light" district, or in Chinese the "White-face" district, so called because bad women powder so white. All these streets, acres and acres, are a festering mass of houses of prostitution, opium dens, gambling joints, leper beggars, wine shops, idol prayer shops—even my abused nose had not smelled such smells as we met with. The City Bible woman stopped and tried to vomit sometimes.

We had two days of "investigating." Nearly all of the thousands of women are from the

South and are bought as babies and trained up to lives of sin. Seldom is a woman there because of her choice. A few were glad to listen to what we had to say.

One house was pointed out as a house where a family lived. We entered and found a woman with a family of girls. The next to the baby was a pretty child. The aunt told me that the mother gave that child to a prostitute when the child was three days old. When she was two years old the owners died, and so the parties owning the brothel were going to sell the child to another place when the aunt paid $10 Mex. [silver] and redeemed her.

A narrow door fronts the street and a little stairway about a foot and a half wide leads up to a tiny bedroom, where a poor woman spends her days and nights. The price of "guests" varies from a dime to two or three dollars in these places, but I went into one grand place where "guests" pay perhaps a hundred dollars a night, but the manager gets the money and the women get their food.

There is no way to start a "Door of Hope" work here, as there is no City government to back up the work as in Shanghai. We did not wonder that the Bible woman had little to show for her work in that place. It is almost useless to try to do anything in a place like that in China. In Chicago and New York, missions can flourish in such places, but conditions are very different here. The last pastor who worked here had three boys who went to the dogs.

I am going to begin to get the present pastor out of there as he has three boys and two girls and it is a sin to make them live there. The pastor is one of my old school boys.

April 26 —— A telegram came from the up country saying that a 40 foot flood was on the way down the river. This is a few feet above the ordinary and will give us a regular spring freshening about tomorrow night. The river is so wide and spreads out through such a network of canals that it takes a big lot of water to flood the plain.

Are you folks going anywhere this summer? I will go to Sharp Peak. Miss Hartwell has bought two boats and is going to have engines put in them to go up and down to Sharp Peak.

Lots of love from,   Nana

"For a few minutes peace fell on the house."

SUNDAY, MAY 30, 1920

Dear Anna,

Saturday P.M. was the Women's Missionary Union, of which I am the foreign president and Miss Ling is the Chinese. All morning I went around and reminded the women and got them out and we had a fine enthusiastic meeting. After that Miss Ling and I went across the river to visit a widow who gave $100 to the organization for missionary work. It was late when we got home and the gate woman came and told me on the quiet that while I was gone the cook and his wife had gone upstairs and taken my bath-tub to their room and given their child, just getting over the measles, a bath. It was such a piece of "gall" that I was mad.

I never spoke a word, but this morning I went out and called the woman and put some disinfectant in the tub and saw that she gave it a scrubbing. Then they were mad. The whole force was going to leave. The cook was wild. Miss Hartwell soon talked him down and proved that he was wrong—but he proved that he had never used the tub at all and the gate woman had *lied*. For a few minutes peace fell on the house. We finally finished our breakfast, when the best cat we have seemed to be turning up his toes. Some castor oil and fish helped him out.

I went on to church finally and found my squad of women missing, so walked back to the living rooms and there they were full force. Dai Luang's little girl was unconscious and no one could get her awake. So we got a ricksha and set out on the trot for home. Fortunately, Dr. Ling was home and brought her to, partially. Dr. Ling said that her attack was worms, but did not quite see why the child should be *unconscious*. A little later a woman who is in the school said that the child took sick with nausea as soon as she reached the church, and the pastor very kindly *gave her a dose of medicine*. He evidently gave her a compound of opium, and a little bit more of it would have caused a funeral to-day.

My nap this afternoon was not very restful. I'll go out in the garden and look at the vegetables. They have no moral nature, for which I am responsible. It is a comfort to have cats and a garden. We now have two mother cats with kittens and they are beauties. The tomato vines are loaded with green tomatoes. About July 1st I will go to Kuliang, and if the vegetables are yet green we will see nothing of them on our return.

May 31 —— Last night, as I was writing the last lines, two auto-trucks went by the house with a terrible commotion. Dr. Ling thought that the students had gotten into trouble, and I feared the soldiers. This morning it seems that more than ten ex-soldiers were seized and executed. It is said that they had on Japanese uniforms and had Japanese weapons seized. One body is still lying not far from our house. We live in a terrible world.

The other night at dusk, the woman servant went to the well, which touches our verandah, to draw water. When she picked up the well bucket, a big ropy something was wrapped around it and flopped up over her shoulder. You can imagine how she yelled. The cook ran out with a bottle of Joye's Fluid, a toilet disinfectant, and poured it on the snake, and then took a stick and killed it. He was so proud of himself that he carried it out on the street and showed it off. The snake was over four feet long. I do not know whether it was poisonous or not.

Love to all the family, Martha

"I have been helping some folks get engaged.
What do you think of that for an old maid?"

KULIANG, CHINA   AUGUST 31, 1920

Dear Belle,

I did not get up the mountain until the middle of July and then had to go down for a week, and now I am going down September 1st to see Donald off to Peking and do some repairs and get ready for the Bements who come from America, and the Walkers and Miss Burr who are on the way to Shaowu. We are, a sort of half way station where everybody likes to stop. There is scarcely a day that somebody is not here.

My Kuliang house is very central and many of the committees are here. So I have had little time to write or read or study up here on the mountain. Besides I have been helping some folks get engaged. What do you think of that for an "old maid"? If it goes through all right I will send you the particulars next time.

Thank you a thousand times for the draft that you sent. I think that it practically came from you, as the S.S. [Sunday School] could not do so much. Your boy and the S.S. boy are with me this summer as happy as they can be, here on the mountain running errands and washing house and waiting on the table, etc. In a few days they will be back in school again.

Write as often as you feel like it. I do not get many home letters.

Lots of love to you all,   Martha

"Her face and hands were dark purple and she could scarcely speak."

FOOCHOW, CHINA   NOVEMBER 25, 1920

Dear Vina,

To-day is Thanksgiving Day. You are probably eating turkey at this time. Miss Hartwell and I had our ordinary dinner. There was a big dinner in the compound at Peace Street, but we were not sure that we were invited so we did not go. I was glad to have an excuse not to go, so I just plan to say that we had no notice of a Mission dinner. It costs too much to have a big spread, and while the famine is so terrible in the North it seems a shame to stuff one's self with luxuries. I have many reasons to be grateful and thankful this day. One is that I got over the dengue fever so much more quickly than on former occasions. I had only ten days in bed and then a week or so to recuperate.

On the heels of my being laid up, Miss Lin—the girl that Donald became engaged to in the summer, took cholera. I urged her mother to bring her to the hospital and when she arrived her face and hands were dark purple and she could scarcely speak, with a temperature below normal, and other symptoms very bad. I feared that she would die as she had reached the stage when a collapse follows, but Dr. Dyer gave her three hypodermics and other treatments, and she pulled through and this morning came smiling into my room to spend Thanksgiving. It would have been a great loss to the mission if she had died, for she is the most gifted young woman that we have in our work.

Night before last we had two guests from Chicago. While we sat there talking a terrible thing happened in the Governor's Yamen about three or four blocks away. You know that in South China there have been troops upholding the Southern Government. Well, they agreed to surrender to General Li, our governor, and arranged with him to come to Foochow and hand over their authority to him. They came in on an afternoon boat, the four leading southern generals, and took a carriage to the General's Yamen, got out and handed their cards to the footman and he handed their cards to the colonel, and he bowed and smiled and motioned to the guard and four soldiers, seized General Hu and shot him through and through and dragged off the others. General Hu was the ranking Southern officer. Just on the other side of us, a colonel was murdered in his bed.

[partial letter]

"Donald will teach in Foochow College."

FOOCHOW, CHINA   APRIL 11, 1921

Dear Anna,

There has been much sickness in the compound, and with 40 women and over 20 children and the servants and all the hangers on, there is seldom a time when some of them are not sick. The cook had a very severe illness and just got back when the coolie and washer man took sick. His brother came to substitute for him, and just as I came in there was a tremendous blowing and snorting in the laundry, and I stepped in to find the new man blowing all the starch through his mouth to make it even. I dumped the whole thing out and gave him some good advice, which he will follow to the extent that I will watch him.

This week I have had a lonesome spell. I guess it was because I was thinking about Miss Hartwell being up in Washington State at Yakima. I hope that the Wileys will like her. She is really a good woman inside her fussy little ways, and she has worked like a slave the past seven years.

Yesterday I went to two villages in the afternoon and had Sunday School for the children. The Manchu Church is having a revival, but I am not in on that. It seems to be a men's revival and *they need it* to be sure.

I am glad that my work has changed, largely to women's work. The men are very different since they cut off their queues, and act more like men—they quarrel more.

Donald has finally settled what he will do next year. He is coming back to Foochow and will teach in Foochow College. He had several good offers of places in Peking, but I think probably his engagement was what brought him back. Miss Lin has used all her influence to get him into mission work, even though at a third of what he would get elsewhere. Foochow College would pay $40 Mex. a month and elsewhere he could get $120. Donald will stay in Peking for the summer so that he can use the library. His subjects will be psychology and economics. I can hardly believe that the little chap has grown up and has really done good work in both those subjects so that he had offers to teach them in the Christian Union University and the Government University in Peking. As soon as he returns he will have his small brother to look after. He is too much of a handful for me to manage.

April 12 —— The steamer did come in and I had a letter from my friend Miss Williams enclosing $50. That will change into $100 Mex. I was certainly glad to get it. She is a dear good woman and sometimes surprises me with help for some of my protégés. She is the one who has largely supported Donald. She says that she wants to send him a wedding present for $15 to buy something. [Miss Katherine and Miss Jane Williams were friends and financial supporters of Martha's work in China.]

April 14 —— Your box has just arrived and Bing-Ieng was here to see what was inside. He said that I would be ten years younger with so many fine things to wear. I pointed to my grey hair and he said that it was too bad that I could not do something for that affliction. The things are lovely. The voile dress will be very useful to me, both of them, in fact. I like the skirt very much. The pedometer was a great curio to Bing-Ieng. He will want to borrow it I am sure. Many thanks for each article and the making of them. I hope that when I send for things that you pay yourself out of the money that I have with you. If I have none let me know and I will send enough to cover the purchases that I make.

Lots of love to the Achelpohls,   Martha

"I wonder if the pedometer works better on such occasions."

APRIL 16, 1921

Dear William,

I have just sprinted down the street with ten thousand people watching my pedometer flop. This is how it happened.

To-day there is a popular demonstration, sort of anti-Japanese, and all the trades and industries are out full force parading. Tens of thousands are in the streets marching to the Governor's Yamen. Opposite our front gate is a factory, and the proprietor had baskets of strings of firecrackers to fire off every time a float or other interesting thing came along.

One firm hired a lot of horses and trapped them out with gay colors, and then hired a lot of poor little girls from their parents for 40 cents a day and decked them out with gay silks and streamers and painted faces. When the firecracker went off, the little sack of a girl on the first horse fell off, and before the wooden shoes of the crowd could get into action I was yelling for them to catch the horse and Dr. Ling and I were tearing down the street as fast as we could go. The girl was dragged about a block hanging by one foot to the stirrup. We got her into the doctor's and she was not seriously hurt but badly skinned. I wonder if the pedometer works better on such occasions.

Also I had to go over the river four miles and back to get a naughty orphan girl that is getting too modern. I have her now waiting my displeasure and I am sure that I do not know what to do with her.

The P.O. came. Next time please just send the ordinary bank draft such as you send to a person in America. Then I can cash it when exchange is good. It is very troublesome to cash a P.O. order, as the Chinese do not have a part in the international system.

Many thanks for the P.O. order and all the other favors.

Martha

"Donald is already working on a newspaper in Peking writing articles."

FOOCHOW, CHINA   MAY 9, 1921

Dear Anna,

I am not going to Shanghai this summer, as the famine has been so bad that the missions decided to postpone the "All China" Conference until next year. The money for expenses went into the famine fund. While I was in my room I had the inspiration to have the coolie clean my study, as I do not let him in here when I am away. The first thing he did was to pull a chunk out of the first page of this letter. You will see that I have pasted it together.

Ding Goi (Donald) will graduate the 14th of June. He is already working on a newspaper in Peking writing articles, and is making his expenses. I am glad, as he has been quite a drain on my salary in spite of the help that I have received. Belle's boy will have one more year after this term and then he will finish the Normal and will earn his own living. Your boy will require a good many years before he is independent.

Lots of love to all the family,   Martha Wiley

*"He was about four feet long and had every
appearance of being poisonous."*

FOOCHOW, CHINA   MAY 22, 1921

Dear Doris,

The other night about 10 o'clock we had a roaring row in the kitchen and what do you think was the occasion of the noise? A big snake made his way into the kitchen, and after the coolie had carried up bath water and all was shut up for the night, he went in to turn out the light and here was the snake. He was about four feet long and a reddish brown color. The head was small and pointed and had every appearance of being poisonous. The coolie thought that he had killed the snake, and he coiled him up on the lower verandah to show him off the next morning to all the servants and hangers–on. I went by on my way to school and the creature was wriggling. Very soon he would have been off. Ever since then I am careful as to where I walk.

Has your Aunt Belle written you that Miss Hartwell was out at her house? Miss Hartwell wrote me that she had a fine time at Wiley. All the folks took her in and made much of her, I think. She is really a good woman and a good friend to me, though she is what the Chinese call "fussy."

When you get time, write me of all your doings. I am still planning to have the calf of my leg eat the corn on my toes. You may tell your mother that, if she says that her corns hurt her!

Lots of love to all of you.

Your aunt,   Nana

*" 'Miss Wiley I can read! I can read! For all my life I have
waited to do this very thing and now I can read.' "*

FOOCHOW, CHINA   JUNE 29, 1921

Dear Anna,

I went up to the mountain for two days and put my house in order for the ladies who will be with me this summer. What terrible neuralgia I had during that time—the change from the heat to the wet cold—but nevertheless the house was in nice shape when I left it with little Miss Burr there. Miss Peters came the day after so I just missed her. Another lady will room with Miss Burr. Dr. Stryker will also come to Foochow so I will be crowded this summer. The two rooms are rented at $60 each and we all share the board. Dr. Stryker will be my guest so I will not charge her anything for room, just board.

[Note: In a letter dated August 28, 1921, Miss Burr describes Martha's summer residence: Jacob's Ladder is the long, winding, cobblestone, rough, narrow road leading to Miss Wiley's house from the Horse-shoe road which is the main thoroughfare around this mountain. We have enjoyed the cool spacious porch, easy chairs and the murmuring of wind among the pine and aged cryptomeria trees.]

When I got home I began examinations in the Women's School and on Monday of this week closed the term. I have had a very happy term and the women have done well and some of them are truly very dear little women. Many of them are wives of my old students. We do not appreciate the simple fact that we can read. One of these women stopped in the middle of a sentence and grabbed my hands and explained, "Miss Wiley I can read! I can read! For all my life I have waited to do this very thing and now I can read." A few days after, the husband came in. He said that he wanted to thank me for the progress that his wife had made, for she had written him two letters "with her own hand." He said that he had waited five years to get his mother's consent and then he finally had to bring her anyway without the consent.

[page missing]

"Young China is getting too smart."

KULIANG—FOOCHOW   JULY 31, 1921

Dear Doris,

I am writing this letter by hand as Miss Peters, the Methodist lady who took a room in my house, does not think it right to write letters on the typewriter on Sunday, so I must write with a pen. Do you not think that I am a very considerate land-lady?

Last night Dr. Stryker and I heard some noise in the yard and we got a lantern and went down among the trees and around the house hunting thieves. This morning we heard some of the same kind of noises just before daylight. I got up in my long white robe and my hair standing on end and that was enough to scare anyone. I looked down among the trees and there were ten or more Chinese in the yard stealing plums from the one tree. I stood on the stone railing and waved my arms and shouted, and those thieves looked up and saw this ghost and with one whoop they vaulted over the stone wall and ran for their lives. It was awfully funny. Then I put on a kimono and started down the hill after them, but just then my cook appeared and I turned the chase over to him.

I have been down to the City for a week and it has been very hot and very tiresome, and my face broke out with prickly heat until I am a beauty.

Donald will be back next week. He has an A.B. degree and is pretty happy about it. He and the girl he is engaged to are pretty clever. She got appointed as delegate to the Home Missionary Society at Peitaho, North China. She went from Foochow. He heard about it from her and he worked on a plan to go from the university, and they have had the time of their young lives up there at the convention together for two weeks. Young China is getting too smart.

Lots and lots of love to all the Achelpohls, and an extra hug to your dear self,   Nana

"If I had to have an operation out here I would just lie down and die without the farce of having an operation."

FOOCHOW, CHINA   OCTOBER 21, 1921

Dear Anna,

I am worried to death about Donald. Since he came south he has been getting thin and pallid and he himself is frightened for fear of tuberculosis. If anything should happen to that boy I would be most sorry—more than you could believe. Catherine Lin was here to supper last night, also Donald, and he told her that he had gone to a doctor for examination but had not got a statement of results. He also told her not to tell me for I would be frightened—but of course he had not got out of the house when she did tell me. They have made up their minds that they will be married in the winter if they can scrape up enough money.

Miss Lacy, a young woman just out for the Union Kindergarten died suddenly last week after an operation for appendicitis. If I had to have an operation out here I would just lie down and die without the farce of having an operation. She was the daughter of old missionaries and a fine girl.

October 26 —— Mr. Peet has been appointed Vice-Consul here at Foochow and already he looks like a new man. The Consul is off at Amoy and he is running the Consulate now.

Lots of love to all the Achelpohls from,   Nana

"I must tell you a little of Donald's wedding."

FOOCHOW, CHINA   JANUARY 29, 1922

Dear Belle,

I am shut in by a pouring rain and no one can get at me either.

I must tell you a little of Donald's wedding. Catherine Lin had a very pale pink silk dress, with little ribbon roses that she and her friend had made for the trimming. Those silk stockings that you sent just fit her, so she wore them. She had a dainty white veil that Mrs. Beach lent her. Her plain little face really looked sweet and pretty. Donald had a very dark blue coat with a black satin jacket, the regulation Chinese wedding costume. They were a good looking couple.

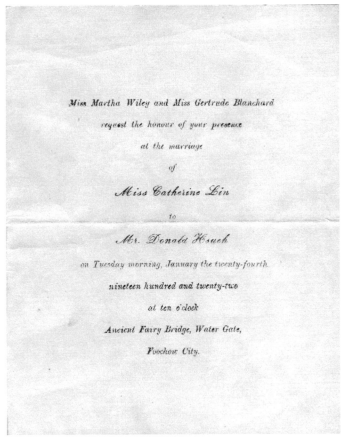

Wedding invitation

I had the large verandahs beautifully decorated with arches of bamboo and festoons of roses and banyan leaves. A man from the hills brought me five coolie loads of tall ferns—as high as your head—and baskets and baskets of "ground pine," a beautiful furry vine. We had poinsettias by the hundreds in our yard.

All the boys and girls from the schools were home on vacation and I set them to work. The house, large as it is, was two days decorated till it was a dream, and all for a trifle of money. It took some thinking to do it but I planned it long ago. The ceremony took place downstairs and the reception and refreshments upstairs. At 12 o'clock the couple started to my cottage on the hills for a week, and the rain has been coming down in torrents. They have had their honeymoon to them selves if that is what they wanted. There was a little shack, not better than a barn, adjoining our compound and I fixed that up and made it into a cozy little Chinese house that they are very proud of. Their bedroom is white and blue, a strange innovation for Chinese who want everything red, usually. Do you remember a blue trimmed towel that you gave me? I gave that to them for their dresser, so we are represented in the towel and stockings.

The cake was a beauty—my cook made it, and I never saw as pretty a wedding cake in

America as this one. Now the wedding is over, Catherine will come back and help me with woman's work and Ding Goi (Donald) goes on teaching in Foochow College, but they want to go to America for further study.

With much love to the two old folks,   Martha

Donald and Catherine Hsueh on their wedding day, January 24, 1922.

"I will go to Shanghai as delegate to the All China Conference."

MARCH 16, 1922

Dear Anna,

This is about the first sunny day in weeks and it makes me feel better already. We have had continuous rains for a long time and it was hard to get over the "grippe" with the weather so wet.

The Women's School is going on merrily, with about 40 women and a dozen children. The little girl who was abducted and taken to a "bad-house" six or eight weeks ago was handed over to us last night. It took lots of running over to the police stations and still no track of the girl. Bing Ieng got a detective and set out to find which particular house the child was in. He tracked the suspected kidnapper to a place about four miles across the City. In the meantime – before the trial – the main witness, who was a woman, died of childbirth. Well, there was one thing after another that came up, but the girl is back here and her stupid father who was largely to blame will obey our rules in the future, I hope.

About the middle of April I will go to Shanghai as delegate to the All China Conference. I want to stay a week longer than the conference and "play." My vacation last year was a farce and I have not caught up yet.

March 24 —— A lot of things have been going on since last I tried to write and started this letter. But yesterday was the greatest ever. The American Minister to China came into port on the battleship *Albany* at 8 A.M. with his wife and daughter and at 10 o'clock the ladies of the party were entertained here. Mrs. Peet and Dr. Ling and Miss Blanchard and I gave the party. We invited 24 but had only 19 to dinner. There was a misunderstanding going on between the Governor and the Consul as to who was greatest, and so three ladies from the Governor's family failed us.

We had a great splurge with shark fins and birds' nests. The feast lasted from 1 P.M. to 3 P.M. This was our first great splurge since Donald was married. I do these stunts with mixed motives. One is to let such people see Mission work; one is to get in touch with the high class Chinese women in Foochow; and one to keep up prestige among your own fellow workers. The new people sometimes think that they are "it," but when we do a really fine stunt that they cannot come up to, it is good for their appreciation of the older ones.

Will you please get three pairs of shoes for me? One pair high shoes: lace, brown leather, very soft kid; one pair high shoes: black, lace, also very soft kid; one pair black lace shoes. If you get them a very comfortable fit for you, I can wear them. The shoes made here are unbearable.

Lots of love to Doris and Jean and William and to your good self,   Martha

P.S. Please send me a warm, wooly, winter sweater – big, for I am fat.

"Just as we got seated a rat dropped down into the water jar."

SHANGHAI, CHINA   APRIL 24, 1922

Dear Vina,

Sunday was Easter and a busy day. On top of that a letter came from Miss Hartwell saying that under certain conditions she would arrange for Donald and Catherine to go to America. These two were busy all day Sunday with Easter music and we planned to talk the matter over on Sunday evening. Just as we got seated a rat had dropped down into the water jar. That ended our discussion of America. Dr. Ling said it was a bubonic rat and we had to disinfect and clean up. Next morning the ceiling had to come out and lime was poured in and such scrubbing and disinfecting as you never saw. Then we had to be inoculated for plague, and in the P.M. I got my trunk packed.

Donald said that he would go with me to the steamer. We got rickshas and set out. It was 2 o'clock in the morning when we got to the steamer. I made Donald go home from the launch, so there was no one to help lug packages up those gang ways at night. Oh, the joys of foreign travel!

Thursday morning at 6:30 we reached Shanghai and the rain was pouring. I had a raging sick headache all of the voyage and all day Thursday. Friday I went to the Doweyite Church, where another of my former pupils is a preacher. I had Chinese dinner there and Mr. Lin set out to convert me to Zion. Faith healing is the strong point. He simply roars about the wickedness of taking medicine. I told him I was more of a faith healer advocate than he—for I believed that *all* healing was in the Lord's hands and according to His will. He said that I was simply using a suave way of evading the question. He made an engagement to come tomorrow evening and finish convincing me of all my errors.

The points that I have known from childhood he is *teaching me*. I let him teach me because he is certainly earnest, but an awful bore. For instance he wanted to know if I *tithed*. I said *no*, I *halved*. He stopped for a few seconds and then said, "You are an exception."

"Oh no!" I said, "You simply are not acquainted with the inside facts." If he can get over his awful conceit and censoriousness he will be a usable man.

Much love to all—the old folks and the young folks.

Affectionately,   Martha

"I am told that our letters are now censored."

FOOCHOW, CHINA   OCTOBER 5, 1922

Dear Nettie,

You probably think that I am a very poor correspondent, but there are times when it seems impossible to get to letter writing. We are now in the throes of a provincial revolution. Thousands of Chinese are fleeing from the City carrying all their worldly goods.

There are 50 blue-jackets in the City to protect us and we are told—that is, Miss Blanchard and I—to go to Tai-bing-ga, the larger compound for protection, when things start to moving. The Southern troops are moving in from the north of the province and are now within two days of the City. The governor's troops are an uncertain quantity and they may go over to the invaders or they may fight for the governor or they may mutiny and loot. It is the latter that we fear, for if they begin looting we are within three or four blocks of the barracks. They have done looting and they like it—the Governor has been a strong ruler up to date but he is losing his nerve now, it is said, and does not want to fight.

People are coming here and they think that this will be safe for it is American property but looters are no respecters of property or flags.

I told my school women that any one who was afraid and wanted to go home for the week might do so and there was a grand rush for the country. In two hours there was not a woman in the school except the teachers. I am on the run most of the time getting people placed. Just now I am waiting for dinner and then will go across the river to the orphanage and fix up some wards for the fleeing city people who are more or less dependant upon me. The manager is a regular "fraid cat" and has a fit every time I send a new party.

We more often act from principle, but most Chinese act from policy. It is not good policy to receive anybody. If they favor the North then the southern soldiers may make it hot for those who receive them—and the contrary is true—and as no one knows how the battle will result, it is just sticking on the fence for most people of any prominence. This morning a friend of a former minister of the navy wanted to get rooms in the orphanage for his family, and the superintendent was scared to death as this man is in both the North and South.

Yesterday the American Consul called together the Americans and had a discussion as to the measures to be taken and so we are just following his orders.

October 10 —— I wonder if you read anything about our doings in the American papers. Perhaps it is not of enough importance compared with the world affairs but it seems very important to us. Fighting is still going on up the river, but the troops that were expected in the City every minute never reached here. Contrary to all expectations, the governor's troops have repulsed the southern army. Most of the Fukinese are glad that it turned out so, for now they will have temporary relief from the soldiers' looting.

It is said that a load of soldiers came in from the North by steamer to-day. Every day boat loads of wounded are brought into the military hospital right near us. Our compound is so near the center of things that we see and hear a good deal of the movements.

As matters stand now, Governor Li is victorious and the southern troops are retreating up the river. Yet we cannot be sure of that, for the southern general has previously let the northern general think that he was retreating and then surrounded the army and taken the northerners prisoners. The southern army is also expecting reinforcements from the South and the North. Wu Pei Fu of northern fame will help the Governor, and Chang Tso Ling who was defeated at Tientsin will aid the southern army. Admiral Sah is said to be sitting down at the Anchorage with his commission of Civil Governor in his pocket, but has not dared to land. These military tuchuns are just like the old Persian satraps must have been—they get a place as military autocrat and hold it until a greater rogue pushes them out.

My school is still absent and my fellow worker went to the country so I am monarch of all that is here. I spent too many weary weeks and months helping to gather up money for this compound to give it up very lightly.

The cook and I had three flag poles put up and a good sized flag at the top of each. We also had all the dozen gates in the walls braced and all in the compound had to go in and out of one. We had each door marked in both English and Chinese and also all the valuable papers transferred elsewhere for safety. Then we were getting ready all the tubs and jars full of water to put out fires if it got to be the fashion to set houses on fire in order to rob, as it did during the revolution.

My fellow worker does not like the cook but he is my main help in the rush of these busy days when every one is trying to get help and find ways of planning. Yesterday, three of the Chinese banks failed and closed their doors, and the Provincial Bank resumed payment after the government had squeezed a million dollars from the Chamber of Commerce, and when the bank resumed payment on Sunday it handed out only five dollars to each creditor! Don't you think that that was surely insult added to injury?

I am told that our letters are now censored so I cannot write everything that I might or the letter would never get to you. As it is I think that I will send this batch by the English P.O.

While all are gone I am getting the place in pretty good order, so that if my school reassembles I will be ready for steady work—but I fear that the women will not come back—those from the country.

October 16 —— This has been such a strenuous week that I have not had a chance to finish my letter. The Southern troops defeated the Northern, and the advance guard entered the City on Thursday. They were the most war-worn looking fellows that you can imagine. They had no uniforms and their clothes were old and ragged and dirty and they wore big straw hats, at least a good many did, and they looked anything but military-like as to clothes—but yet they had the strut of conquerors as they defiled along the narrow street to the hill above our compound. The Governor's troops were cut off from supplies and news and one division came to the West Gate and did not know that the day previous the Southern army had entered, so that made the second day of fighting at the City gates. Before the first day's battle took place, the Governor and his brother and the Provincial Treasurer fled to the foreign community. The Governor went to the Japanese bank and the American Consulate, and a few hours later Admiral Sah took them to the Arsenal down the river to be guarded.

There is still firing here and there in the distance but I do not know what it means. Perhaps the governor's remaining soldiers are fighting their way to the City and do not yet know of the retreat of the Northerners.

The governor's soldiers were all well armed and clothed and big lusty men who could have fought the Southerners to a finish but they had no cause to fight for. They wanted to get home and they did not care who became the next military autocrat if they could get home.

There has been no actual fighting in the City except just outside the West Gate and the South Gate. The loss of life perhaps mounts up to several thousands, but nobody can be sure. The hospitals are pretty well crowded now with the wounded, and there are lots of bodies still unburied on the hills around the West Gate.

When the Southern soldiers got into the City, they went up and down the streets knocking down the doors of houses of the Northern people and telling the people they had a free hand at looting. That has been going on for three or four days now. Yesterday it was going on full blast in these streets of the Manchu Quarter where we live. Soldiers pounded on our doors but when they found out a foreigner lived here they went on. There is still a good deal of street fighting on account of the plunder.

This place has been pretty well filled with refugees—those who fear the looting—but the large compound at the college is like the steerage on a steamer. The neighbors have simply swarmed in.

Love to all from,   Martha

***"I am weary of sitting on top of a volcano
with my suitcase in my hand."***

FOOCHOW, CHINA   OCTOBER 21, 1922

Dear Belle,

We are still up in the air as to what is happening to us and what will happen to the City. There are three factions here all wanting the power, and the fourth will be here in few days if his army can make it over land.

The night that the Southern generals got into the City they had a regular Belshazzar carousel within four hours of the time they got in. They made a great feast and called in squads of prostitutes and they did not get through until the second night of their revelry. The old Governor was a military despot, but I think he could not have been worse than these fellows that are in the yamens at present.

Admiral Sah is a man of decency and integrity, but his marines are too few to fight the Southern army and besides he does not want to fight. He wants to conciliate the triangle and get them together on terms. We are still ready to grab our handbags and run at any minute. This morning I got a letter from the Consul saying that in case looting began and the soldiers were turned loose on the City, then we were to get out at once, and in case we could not get out, to send word to the Consulate. I had to laugh at that, for in case I could not get out you may be sure that not one of my servants could venture out.

This week it was reported that, if the Chamber of Commerce did not come up with $150,000 that the Southern general would turn his soldiers loose on the City and loot and get six months of arrears in pay. The Chamber of Commerce was bled white by the Governor before he left, by threatening to turn the Northern soldiers loose on the City if almost a million dollars were not paid in.

Personally I do not expect to have to leave the City but if these villains begin to loot you will find this child sprinting out the grand boulevard to the foreign settlement. The Southerners are nearly all brigands and robbers and vagabonds that have been picked up and put into good fighting shape by the minority of regular soldiers.

Our Chinese W. J. Bryan, in other words Sun Yat Sen, is said to be the instigator of all of this. Others say that General Hu Ciong De is on this trip to get revenge, for all of his family were put to death by General Chong, who whipped Sun Yat Sen and drove him out of Canton Province. Still others think that the numerous and cruel executions of Governor Li made him many enemies, and that caused the turmoil.

At any rate, for months while the men in office were storing up their millions, the school teachers were unpaid, with the roads gone to ruin, and the banks closing, and taxes on every conceivable thing.

Prices are now at double what they were. It is very hard for the missionaries to come out square now and we economize much more than formerly, and it always seemed that we were at bedrock before.

Yesterday I went out to "Horse and Saddle Village" where I have a Bible woman stationed, and she was in the thick of the two days fighting. The village is in a little ravine in the hills north of the City, and the Northern men were on the hill and the Southern men on the other, and the firing went on back and forth and some shells dropped into the court. She and her small child wrapped up in their thickest quilts and crouched on the bed or under it. In houses along the way the roofs had been hit by shells and a few houses burned. The pigs and animals were taken for food, and the people in a rather terrified state.

October 22 —— It is Sunday to-day and very peaceful. The war seems to be at an end for the present and the generals had a great feast together yesterday.

When I packed up a trunk to send out of the City I packed my shoes and my papers and the rest was left. I do hope the rumpus is over. I am weary of sitting on top of a volcano with my suit case in my hand.

Lots of love to all of you in St. Charles, Martha

"The streets are almost deserted."

FOOCHOW, CHINA OCTOBER 30, 1922

Dear Anna,

We are continuing in the disturbed state as when I wrote you last. Business is stopped. All Chinese banks, pawn shops, stores—closed. The streets are almost deserted, except when a new scare comes on and more people rush out. We are tired to death of it all. There is more fighting up country and more wounded coming in, but we feel that the fighting will be outside the walls unless the several rival claimants for power finally get to each other's throats.

After this month there will be no more foreign P.O. in China, and immediately the Chinese P.O. has increased the price to 15 cents per letter instead of 10 cents.

Dr. Ling ran away to Shanghai, but when the house is full again we will have six women in all. Dr. Ling, Miss Blanchard, Miss Hartwell, Miss Chittenden, Miss Bosbyshell, and myself. I dread the crowd of them, but it will not be for over a year. I plan to go north next year if I can scrape up money enough.

Lots of love to all of you, including the new member of the family—the Buick. He probably takes the place of a son.

Martha

"Now that I am not going to die interest is flagging."

FOOCHOW, CHINA   DECEMBER 10, 1922

Dear Anna,

I will send you this letter, which is my unique experience—written in bed! Along in October there was a sudden change in temperature from 90 degrees-50 degrees, and I took a hard cold.

Dr. Kinnear first thought that I had bronchitis and pneumonia combined but it turns out that I have only an acute case of bronchitis, which requires that I stay in bed and keep well dosed with various drugs to loosen up my chest.

The first day that I was sick in bed I think I had over 50 calls, next day about half as many—now that I am not going to die interest is flagging. Catherine comes over all her spare time, but when I am sick she does much of my work.

Did I tell you that they lost their baby? We had two terrible months of anxiety here in the City. Donald took Catherine over to the Orphanage four miles out of the City, as we expected all the fighting to be in the City. Then the Northern troops fled, the Governor was seized, and so those fleeing troops went over to Nantai where the Orphanage is, and for two days and nights the soldiers threatened to loot and burn the whole district in which the refugees were, including the Orphanage.

Catherine took sick over there and Donald brought her back to the Mission hospital where she was getting on all right, when we had two days of fighting again and hundreds of wounded were carried into the hospital. Well, their little son arrived too soon and lived just eight days when he passed out of this troubled world. They called him "David Wiley Siek." [Siek is Foochow dialect; Hsueh is Mandarin dialect.] The name David is made up of two characters, one of which is my surname, and the other part of my name, Martha. They thought they had found a fine name for him. They sent me a note and I went to the hospital at 6 A.M. and the baby was dying. The doctor was working over him in the operating room and Donald and Catherine were weeping together.

We made a dainty little casket of white silk and put the doll-like baby in it and put rosebuds all around him. Donald carried in the casket and showed it to Catherine and then he and I closed it up and started out of East Gate—just us two. He got a man in the village to dig the grave along side of his brother David and then the little David was put away. Donald sat down then and cried a few minutes and then we hurried home, a walk of four miles or more. We could get no rickshas as the ricksha men had been seized, to carry shells for the soldiers.

I made a special point of burying this baby decently, because the heathen way is to take an infant of that age out to a dump heap [baby tower] and throw him away. Catherine cries about him now. They will probably have enough later, but this first one was very wonderful and very precious. This has been a ghastly autumn—everything going wrong when it did go, or else not going at all.

Lots of love from,   Martha

"One bullet splintered a groove in the oar I was holding."

[letter from Leonard Christian]   FOOCHOW, CHINA   MARCH 6, 1923

Dear Friends:

We are back again in our station at Foochow, with the opening days of a new term upon us, but before plunging into work, I want to share with you one of the most exciting experiences that Agnes and I have passed through thus far during our thirteen years in missionary service.

For some time we have had it in our mind to visit Agnes' sister in the new station at Kienning, recently opened by the Shaowu Mission, and everything seemed to favor our making the trip during China New Year vacation this year. After consultation with the American Consul, and permission to leave port granted by the Mission, we started on the long journey over the 500 rapids of the river Min to Shaowu. The trip was taken in a "sparrow" boat, and required ten days of hard work on the part of our three boatmen to cover the 250 miles. At Shaowu we were met by Louise Meebold, Agnes' sister, and after a pleasant visit with friends in Shaowu, we started with Miss Meebold on the 100 mile journey across country to Kienningsien. On the fourth day, after crossing a snowy-topped mountain, we dropped down into the fertile valley that follows the waters of a branch of the Min to the large walled city of Kienning.

On February 27th we started on our homeward trip through some of the wildest country to be found in Fukien. In the first two days we shot over 158 rapids, passed through wonderful gorges, with snow-clad mountains towering 5,000 feet above us. On the afternoon of February 28th we beached our boat in front of the large walled town of Tsiong-lok, where there is quite a promising work being carried on by the American Board.

Next morning. March 1st, I awakened at 6 o'clock and roused the boatmen: but they were not keen to start so early because a heavy mist made it difficult to see for any distance. By repeated urging I got them under way by 7 o'clock. The old "buccaneer" as I had named our headman, was rowing in the stern; I was getting my morning exercises on the forward oar, while the "buccaneer's" assistant was preparing the morning meal. There was not a boat astir, nor a sound to be heard as we slipped down stream through the mist. Suddenly excited voices broke the stillness, and through the mist I saw three men rush from the tall jungle grass on the left bank of the river, and come to a halt on the shore. They raised their guns and fired straight at us, loaded and fired again, all the while yelling at us to come ashore. Although the boatman obeyed and was heading inshore they continued to load and fire. One bullet splintered a groove in the oar I was holding, a little below where I held my hand. A boat full of armed men, as if from nowhere, pulled out from under the bank and made for us. Hardly had the nose of our boat grated on the sand when a number of these bandits leaped over the side of the boat brandishing knives and swords. Two men seized me, and tried to wrench off my ring. As it did not come easy they took a knife and would have cut off my finger if I had not pulled it away and taken off the ring for them. Agnes was still in bed when we were first hailed, but jumped up immediately when I shouted that we were being fired upon. One ruffian seized her hand, and took both her rings, and then proceeded to roll up and take away the blankets and other bedding. After taking my ring, four men bound my hands tightly behind my back with grass rope, and held me on the bank while they searched Agnes for money that might be concealed on her person. Meanwhile others were inside the boat, looting in true bandit fashion. When they were satisfied with their search, they put us both and all the loot aboard the boat again, and ordered the boatman to row a little farther down the stream. Sitting there with my hands tied behind me, in the midst of our captors, I had a chance to pray with Agnes, and we encouraged each other.

When the new landing was reached, I was shoved and dragged ashore, and placed in the charge of five men who forced me to go with them. Some ten or more were left behind to ransack the boat. The men rushed me up the bank, across rice paddies, up a pair of stone steps, into a village, through the street of the village and past the temple at its entrance. Here one of the priests was sweeping the temple floor, and was warned to say nothing of what was going on. I could not understand his answer, but easily guessed that he assured them he saw nothing. Once outside the village, the bandits lead the way up a mountain trail, with steps cut into the hard red clay. Several rushed ahead, one held onto the rope that tied my hands, while another brought up the rear. The cords on my hands cut in and cut off circulation, so I asked the fellow who held the cord if he wouldn't loosen my hands a bit. His answer was a poke in the back, and a rough command to hurry my steps. After climbing for about 15 minutes they called a halt, and I was given a chance to catch my breath. Several hundred feet more of climbing brought us to a level path, where we halted for some time. Much of my time was spent in prayer that no harm should come to Agnes, who was on the boat with the remainder of the band.

While we waited for the remainder of the band to join us, one of the men who spoke a rather mixed Foochow, informed me that I was being held for two thousand dollars ransom. I made it plain to him that I was a stranger in these parts, and could not produce such a sum, whereupon one of the bandits nearby leveled his gun at me, and another followed by waving his sword to show how my head would be taken off if I did not come across. Neither of these threats scared me, for I remembered the number of times missionaries have been threatened in the same way. This opening of conversation gave me a chance to tell them who we were, and what was our purpose in coming to China. They listened to all I had to say, but made no comment.

In about half an hour some ten others joined us, bringing with them all the loot they had taken from our boat, and that was practically everything of value. It included our bedding, clothing, shoes, camping outfit, rings and a small gold watch entrusted to us by Miss Funk, and a big collection of miscellaneous articles, many of them with considerable sentimental value attached. One tall chap joined our group with Agnes' velvet turban on over his cap. It was a sight to make one laugh under other circumstances, but just then it sent a pang through me. Seeing I was without a hat he came over, and placed the turban on my head. Then the band went to looking over the goods they had taken.

Several articles that they found in my handbag they brought to me to find out their value or use. They wanted to know what my fountain pen was for, what was inside the little spring tape measure, and whether or not certain articles were gold. I was surprised to find that after a short conference they decided to loosen my hands, which was a great relief, as my right hand had grown cold and was without feeling. When they had looked over all the articles in my handbag, they dumped most of them back in again, gave me the bag, and to my amazement told me to go. I needed no urging, and had already descended a hundred feet or so, when they called me back. My heart sank, for I thought they had changed their minds; but evidently they wanted to give the rest of the band a chance to get away. Ten minutes later they handed me a lantern, and said I would need it on the boat. On my second release I fairly flew down the mountain trail, and then to the boat to find Agnes in the front. I called to her from a distance, and when she saw me she broke down and wept—and so did I. Agnes then told me all that had happened in my absence from the boat.

After I was taken away into the mountains five of the bandits took possession of the boat. They searched it thoroughly for money and valuables. It was unbelievable to them that we had no money with us so they searched everything, even running their arms through the baskets of rice. When they had bagged everything of value they talked with Agnes about the matter of ransom. They demanded $3,000 or they would shoot me. Agnes told them that she could not get the money up here, but it might be arranged for in Foochow, and asked for an address to which to send the money. They tried to insist that they must have the money right away, but finally left the boat.

After my return we started down to Yankeo where we arrived early in the afternoon. That night we were put up in an empty room of the Yankeo Hospital, and the Christians there vied with one another in showing us every kindness. None of them were people personally acquainted with us, but they surely treated us just like their own folks.

The next night we struck the Methodist Mission at Yenping for board and lodging and were furnished with food and bedding for the rest of our journey to Foochow, and arrived home without any further mishap.

Yours most sincerely,   Leonard J. Christian

"General Uong's soldiers went out and began seizing men on the street."

FOOCHOW, CHINA   APRIL 17, 1923

Dear Anna,

On Wednesday a week ago General Song, underling of Wu Pei Fu, arrived with an army reputed to be 20,000 strong. He asked General Uong, who is commander here if he was North or South in sympathy. Of course he answered "North." Then General Song told him to prove it by getting out at once and going to Ing-hok and other places to drive out the south. To "get out" he needed 2,000 load bearers. Uong's soldiers went out and began seizing men on the street—and going into private homes and dragging them out. The brother of a carpenter that I employ got dragged out and has already been beaten along the street with a load on him.

. . .

Love to your good self,   Nana

"I have been wandering through the Valley of Death."

FOOCHOW, CHINA   MAY 23, 1923

Dear Belle and others,

Since I last wrote any of you I have been wandering through the Valley of Death. My suffering was so keen that I begged the Lord to let me die. Sometimes it seemed the doors above were almost ready to open for me, when the great floods of prayers would shut them. I did not want to come back.

If I am able to travel, I will sail for Seattle end of May or in June. So will soon be with you—some time in July for a few months.

This is my only letter in many weeks.

Love from,   Martha

"I had no choice in the matter and was 'bundled off' pell-mell."

WILEY P.O., YAKIMA, WN.   OCTOBER 3, 1923

Dear Miss Williams,

You will see that I am again in the good home land, reaching Seattle July 27th, as my last dealings with pneumonia brought me out the loser.

Since reaching the U.S. I have gained every day and will soon be back to my normal health. It was very inconvenient to leave my work in Foochow, but I had no choice in the matter and was "bundled off" pell-mell.

Last week I was in Seattle, and "The Women's Class" agreed to give our boy Donald a scholarship in the State University (of Seattle, Wn.), which is $200 gold per year; and a very good family are to take him into their home. He will make the plunge first and if he thinks advisable Catherine will come later. This is their own plan and they are determined to come to U.S., so I have helped them to find a place, even though I discouraged their venture.

The last letter that I received told of Donald almost losing his life trying to save a girl teacher's life. The girl was Catherine's guest and at midnight in the midst of a deluge of rain went out and jumped into the "well" (perhaps it was a cistern). Donald heard a noise and thought that a thief had come in, and in searching found the girl in the well. He went down to save her and in the struggle she almost drowned him. Finally a coolie got them both out. The girl was drowned and Donald completely exhausted.

Catherine has full charge of my work while I'm away. This was voted to her by the Mission, so it shows how much she is thought of by the members of the Mission. All that I fear is that she will find it quite too heavy a burden for her.

Donald will not plan to reach U.S. until May of 1924, then enter the summer term, working for an M.A. degree.

With love,   Martha Wiley

[Note: Martha returns to China]

S. S. PRESIDENT GRANT
M. M. JENSEN, COMMANDER
En Route to Yokohama
Dinner

RELISHES
1 Canape of Cheese   2 India Relish   3 Celery en Branche
4 Stuffed Olives   5 Salted Mixed Nuts   6 Sweet Gherkins

SOUP
7 Chicken a la Reine   8 Consomme Victoria

FISH
9 Poached Sea Bass, Egg Sauce

BOILED
10 New England Dinner

COLD
11 Shoulder of Veal, Celery Sauce

ENTREES
12 Compote of Pigeon Macedoine
13 Braised Sweetbreads a la Francaise
14 Small Sweet Omelettes

ROASTS
15 Prime Ribs of Beef au Jus, Browned Sweet Potatoes
16 Leg of Mutton, Currant Jelly

VEGETABLES
17 Creamed Mashed Potatoes   18 Boiled Potatoes
19 Baked Egg Plant   20 Fresh String Beans

SALAD
21 Game, Mayonnaise Dressing

PASTRY & DESSERT
22 Steamed Suet Pudding, Lemon Sauce
23 Cherry Pie   24 Fresh Blackberry Pie
25 Wine Jelly   26 Pound Cake   27 Assorted Pastry
28 Neapolitan Ice Cream   29 Nabisco Wafers
30 Assorted Nuts and Raisins   31 Season Fresh Fruits
Cheese: 32 Edam   33 Swiss   34 Roquefort
35 After Dinner Mints   36 Cafe Noir

Saturday, Oct. 4, 1924.   G. M. Gordon, Chief Steward
CLOCKS RETARDED 42 MINUTES

ADMIRAL ORIENTAL LINE
Managing Agents
UNITED STATES SHIPPING BOARD
EMERGENCY FLEET CORPORATION

Ship's menu

"They get a vegetable diet, mostly of mustard greens for this pious service."

SUNDAY, NOVEMBER 30, 1924

Dear Belle and family,

This has been a busy day as all days are, whether in Wiley or Foochow. I was at a place called Au-ciu all forenoon, and this afternoon went to a place near where a lot of old women sit in a temple beating drums before a lot of fierce idols. They get a vegetable diet, mostly of mustard greens for this pious service.

I enclose a photo of Ella [Donald and Catherine's baby]. Her Chinese name is "Boat" so we call her "Little Boat," or sampan. This picture was taken to show you the shoes that you sent. I sent a copy to Anna also.

We have had wonderful weather until to-day, when the clouds thickened and I can scarcely get enough air out of the mist to breathe.

Love to all the family,   Martha

"I am bad enough to please anybody most of the time."

FOOCHOW, CHINA   JANUARY 25, 1925

Dear Anna,

Your letter came a few days ago. You did have some storm with ice settling over everything! It must have been beautiful to see the icicles hanging on everything.

The Board has made a new ruling that all missionaries must retire at 68 years of age and go to U.S. and the Board will give them enough, plus the personal income of the missionary, to make up $800 gold per year. Miss Hartwell has only three years more to reach the limit, but I think that she will be an exception. Mr. & Mrs. Hubbard retire this winter, going home March 4th. Don't worry about my being too good! I am bad enough to please anybody most of the time.

Everything seemed so hopeless when I got back this time that I was homesick and cross. When I got over the "flu" things looked normal again. The W.B.M.I. has promised me a helper this year. Now I am alone in this work. Miss Hartwell and Miss Chittenden are engrossed in the industrial work and do not touch the women's work except as it comes into their school plan. I do not know how I could get on without Catherine and little "Boat". Boat is eight months old to-day. When Catherine carries her to the head of the stairs she looks around for me then laughs aloud and kicks and plays. She is very little trouble now.

Now I must go to church and also find a job for my teacher's son. When I saw Dr. Bement this week she asked me about the cost of living in U.S. I said that I could not tell very well as I sponged on my sisters. She replied: "Believe me, when I go to my relations they sponge on me. I stay across the continent." You folks certainly did more for me than you ought. I will not need any clothes until I go back except for some shoe strings — long ones, black, small size for high shoes.

Lots of love to you all,   Martha

"The boys all went on a strike and stabbed some of the teachers."

FOOCHOW, CHINA   FEBRUARY 27, 1925

Dear Anna,

On Tuesday the 10th of February we had a party of five tables of ten each, and Mr. & Mrs. Hubbard were given a little farewell.

On Friday Miss Hartwell went to Diong-loh where the Hubbards were living, and she and Mr. & Mrs. Hubbard all started down to Sharp Peak on Saturday morning. Mrs. Hubbard felt badly so she turned back and decided not to go to Sharp Peak. Mr. Hubbard and Miss Hartwell took the boat and went on.

Mrs. Hubbard went to her house and went upstairs and lay down, and the servant called Miss Nutting, and she got the Chinese doctor from the Mission hospital, but Mrs. Hubbard died at 9 A.M.

After Mr. Hubbard was notified we got rickshas and went to Southside, four miles away to where Mr. Brand, a man who makes coffins, lives. The Brands and I went on by motor boat, with the coffin, to Diong-loh and had a bad time getting to the town as the tide had run out. From the landing we walked a half hour to the house.

I helped find things and prepare the body to put in the coffin. Though Mr. Brand is called an undertaker, he is just a man who has coffins made and conducts funerals (free of cost on his part) for foreigners. Mrs. Hubbard had been dead just 24 hours when we began and it was too long for a body to be left with no disinfectants. We had a hard time to get enough disinfectant to wash our hands thoroughly.

About 11 A.M., we were through and the body in the coffin and lovely roses all about her. She looked very lovely. At 1:30 we went to the church in the village and the coffin was opened and the Chinese looked upon her. Then after a short service, we went to the boat and came up to Foochow. No launch or motor boat will carry a coffin, so we had to get a big ferry boat and have a motor boat tow it up. We got up to the City late in the evening and took the coffin to our Mission compound, and next day we had a service at Ponasang for the Chinese, and then a beautiful English service, and Mrs. Hubbard was laid to rest in the American Cemetery. Mr. & Mrs. Hubbard had been missionaries here over 40 years before retiring.

February 28 —— The M. E. school for boys all went on a strike and stabbed some of the teachers. The report is that the next will be the English Mission School and the third Foochow College. The very devil seems to be in the people. This is the anti-Christian movement that you have read about, mixed up with the "Red Society" or Bolshevism. Even the women are too independent to be decent. Three years' time has produced a tremendous upheaval in China. There is now so little of the hope and buoyancy of even five years ago. We all long for better times, economically and otherwise.

This year I have been very comfortable. We have had enough wood to burn on our own "farm." With the trees that I cut down and the timber from repairs, I kept a fire in my room and so did not have such a cold year. Wood is very scarce and worth its weight in paper money, as the pirates are so bad that the boats cannot bring down rice or wood.

My room has been the camp ground for everyone who felt that wood was expensive and the weather cold. "Little Boat" has spent her time here and makes a fuss when she has to go home. We have five cats and a monkey. The monkey was given to us by a former student—now a salt official in West China. When he went off he took a slave girl and so none of his family would care for the monkey, and he sent the old chap over to Miss Hartwell and me. We can't get anybody to accept him as a gift. "Little Sister," my coolie, takes care of him and tries to teach him some tricks, but he is too old.

Do you realize that I have had a birthday? I am getting on the down hill grade, and I am not sorry. Life gets more and more difficult.

Love to all from,   Martha

"I am planning to go to Alaska to work in the fish canning company this summer."

[letter from Donald]   4633 21 N.E. SEATTLE, WASHINGTON   APRIL 7TH, 1925

Dear Mrs. Woodhouse [Belle]:

I am planning to go to Alaska to work in the fish canning company this summer. I hope to earn enough money in two or three months in order to continue my study next year beginning from next autumn quarter.

Catherine's teacher, Miss Dornblaser, from Springfield, Ohio, has asked Catherine to come and everything has been planned for her. I expect to meet her in Seattle before I leave for Alaska, that is, the middle of June. I hope Catherine can leave Foochow in May. Of course your sister [Martha] will miss her very much but I think she will be a greater help to your sister after she has had good training in this country. I also expect to go back to China next summer 1926.

Baby Ella has to stay at home. She will have her grandmother, Catherine's mother to take care of her for a year.

>   With love to yourself—from Donald Hsueh

"The young generation are fast becoming Anarchists and Nihilists."

Dear Anna,

Thursday evening one of the students in the school was suddenly attacked with Bubonic plague. She was at her classes all day and at supper, but while sitting in the evening service she became deathly sick and ran over to our house. We sent her to the hospital immediately, and the doctors said that she had plague and gave her a hypo and sent her home. The nurse that we have in the house went with her.

Then Miss Hartwell went over to South Side and bought ten bottles of serum and we were inoculated that evening. I came home, and the coolie and I carried out the patient's things and disinfected the bedroom. Then the women in the school helped me wash the floors and walks of that building with disinfectant. Next morning the students and I gave the whole building a thorough washing with disinfectant, and in the P.M. we had the whole school inoculated.

What a terrible place China is now! The student class has gone crazy. The Russian Bolshevism has got into the young generation, and they are fast becoming Anarchists and Nihilists. Not long since, they threw pistols into a mission school and threatened the students if they did not strike. Yesterday all the students in Foochow College walked out. To-day the students are going along the streets parading and bawling out their songs, making fools of themselves—for there is no issue at stake with anybody, or anything.

China is absolutely without a government. What is worse there seems no prospect of any change for the better. Soldiers are increasing in number and in the spirit of the brigandry. People scarcely dare to travel on the launches now. Catherine went to the country to be gone three days and stayed five. We planned to send someone to hunt her up if she did not arrive the next day.

June 9 —— To-day was the climax to the students' nonsense. All the girls' schools were declared closed and the girls left for home. A general strike is declared for tomorrow when all servants walk out. The cook is trying to get things done up ahead so that he can walk out with a good conscience. I went to the foreign settlement and bought $40 worth of supplies so that if I have to cook and not go out on the street we can live out of tin cans, as anything else would spoil. As I came home, students were distributing posters with a cartoon of a foreigner and the inscription: "Mr. Foreigner, don't you want to go to heaven?"

And underneath was a cross with a foreigner nailed to it. Other posters had "Down with the foreigners!" And others, "Down with pastors and preachers!" It is an anti-Christian movement inspired by Bolshevists and originated in the Russian College in Shanghai, the Asiatic headquarters for Bolshevism and their propagandists.

Some of my women were on the street and the students yelled at them and called them "foreign slaves." I had fondly imagined that I was *their* slave.

The atmosphere is worse than the Boxer times if I remember well enough to compare. Then there were only a few fanatics raving. Now the "intelligenza" are digging a pit for their own destruction and that of others.

June 10 —— Last night a college student who has a wife in school told his wife to run to the rear of the house if she heard a noise as the students might throw some bombs into the school. Miss Hartwell got all her "valuable papers" into a trunk and told me to get them out if fire took place, then she went over to the Industrial School where Miss Chittenden is for the night and to-day. The Consul phoned us to close our doors and bar them and not open up for the whole day.

Now I am in this compound with the cook and the coolie and about 50 women and near half as many children "sitting tight" for the day. We will go on with our examinations, but we are not singing *aloud* and not studying aloud for the spies to hear us as they go around. It is only 6 o'clock and the students are to begin their parade this morning. It is going to be as hot as the hottest to-day, so the boys will not need to warm up much. I have nailed a white towel on the shutter to let the other compound know that all is serene. If matters get spicy I will take it down.

We will fill the water jars and get ready for a fire. I have done these stints several times and found it unnecessary and hope that this occasion will prove the same.

Some stabbing has been going on but not many cases. You have doubtless seen the account of the affair in Shanghai, which precipitated this nation wide uproar.

[The May Thirtieth Movement—a labor and anti-imperialist demonstration, turned riot, killing thirteen demonstrators.]

June 10, P.M. —— About 4 o'clock a terrible pounding on the front door of the Woman's School took place. The women and children all ran to the rear and I went up near enough to the door so that if a bomb came over it would get past me. The cook went out of our house door and around to a side street to see if a squad of students was trying to bomb us, and found one of the pastors standing there kicking and pounding and shaking—he was just ready to "throw a fit" for anger because nobody opened our barricaded door. There is *some* fun in the fracas.

June 12 —— What next! To-day I came back from school and found a cobra on the top step of my study. His ugly hooded head was unmistakable. He made no effort to run but puffed at me twice. It was such a surprise that I stopped to look before I uttered not one, *but several* elemental shrieks that brought the coolies on the run expecting to see me blown to pieces with a bomb. The snake ran under my study floor. The coolies guarded the hole with bamboo sticks and I went for a carpenter to tear up the floor. He refused to do so as he feared the snake would jump up in his face. The cook and I tore up the floor but could not poke out the cobra. Miss Hartwell was away, but she arrived and added her share of help by sending for a snake charmer to come and catch the snake. I could not see how big the snake was, for his body was partly hidden by weeds.

I think that this is about enough for one week—plague, inoculations, riots, and at last, a cobra.

Later —— Four snake killers came and told me to point out the snake and they would kill it! I pointed under my study but that was no help. One will come tomorrow and lie in wait at the same place and see if the cobra comes out. They said that a person lived about five minutes after a bite from such.

9 P.M. —— Soldiers are falling into lines of guards along our street. The cook said we were again under marshal law.

Old U.S.A. would seem good to me for a summer vacation.

13th —— All quiet.

Martha

[letter from Emily Hartwell]

Dear Miss Wiley, Have you received anything like this? I have just sent a copy to Consul Price. We are all quiet here. Some students came in to see whether we really were disbanded this A.M. I think they went out satisfied. This letter however was written today you see.

June 10, 1925

A Town in China

Dear Miss Hartwell:

Will you please let the boys and girls, carpenters and all your employees ceased from the work and to join the national action!

We would like to advice you that you cannot treat any Chinese like your own slaves, as they are not the production of the "Empire & Capital Plans".

Beware! The present condition is nearly to burst, but still we do not know yet which foreigner will meet it.

Be careful of my young people & then you are safe!

Yours revengely, A.S.S.C.M.

[letter from Emily Hartwell]   FOOCHOW   AUGUST 28, 1925

Dear Miss Wiley,

You will want to know about the typhoon just as I want to know how you got on at Sharp Peak. I hope Nong-muoi was back to help you, for if the storm was as bad for Sharp Peak as it was for Foochow you needed all your typhoon bars to help you out. Every one here says it is the worst typhoon they have ever seen.

Every fruit tree in Sa-mo-cang is down, but I shall have them put up again. Do-mi says they all went down in a previous typhoon. This is the worst he has ever known, as well as myself, I mean for Foochow. Sharp Peak must have been worse if you were as near the center of the typhoon. I am anxious to learn how Morrison and June and Hurd cottages stood the typhoon, as well as the sanitarium.

Very much love to you all,   Emily S. Hartwell

"Missionaries are having a testing time to see if they know what they are out in China for."

FOOCHOW, CHINA   SEPTEMBER 29, 1925

Dear Sister,

A notice on the Post Office bulletin board says that a mail is coming in to-day so I am looking for some mail. I wonder if you have got through this summer without getting sick yourself with all that you have to do.

These days are terrible days in China. It is a time when missionaries are having a testing time to see if they know what they are out in China for. The student union are dead set against the Bible being taught in the Mission schools and against the observance of Sunday in the Schools. Some of the foreigners want to cater to the demand and yield to the students, and some of us have fought like tigers on the other side.

Donald's baby is getting well again after her summer of dysentery [infection of the intestines] and is a very loveable and happy child. She gets out into the yard and shouts and laughs until I look out and notice her. She understands quite a bit of English, which the others think is a great joke. She is now 16 months old.

Much love to all of you from,   Martha

FOOCHOW, CHINA   MARCH 31, 1926

Dear Anna,

It seems a long time since I wrote you as so many things are crowding into life in Foochow at present.

Last night I rented my Kuliang cottage for $250 Mex., but I will have to put $50 repairs on it and also pay $50 for my room at Sharp Peak so I am not getting rich. I am trying hard to sell the property, as affairs are so uncertain in China. If I can get $2,500 Mex. I would take it, though I want $3,000. If things keep on going as they have been for the past three years, very soon there will be few missionaries in China.

Changes in mission policy and personnel are very swift and radical. In one year's time we have given over to the Chinese all control of churches, schools and hospitals—and some advocate the Chinese recalling missionaries on furlough, which is done in North China.

April 2 —— To-day is Good Friday. I am lonesome for all of you. The past year has been a "clipper." I have missed Catherine's help very much. The baby is well again. Catherine says I may change her name to "Helen," so we will call her Helen after this instead of "Ella."

Love to all,   Martha

"A husband and his parents sold a little
fifteen year old wife to a 'bad house.'"

FOOCHOW, CHINA   JUNE 10, 1926

Dear Anna,

I had to laugh at your emphasis on the "great comfort." Boat is a dear baby but she has been a "great care." For two weeks last month I took her to the hospital every day. It happened that I could get the trip in between classes.

. . .

This week I have "been to court." A husband and his parents sold a little fifteen year old wife (the daughter of a Christian) to a "bad house." They lied to the girl to get her there. When she found where she was, she could not get out. The first "guest" they brought her happened to live near her father's place, so the girl cried and begged this man to tell her father. He got four police and broke in the door and got the girl. She is very small and timid, and hid behind our chairs and cried while I was talking to the officials. The "court" ordered the husband and his parents arrested, but they can't be found. The decision as to who gets the girl remains unsettled.

With much love to the Achelpohls from,   Nana

"Three times has Miss Wiley snatched her from the jaws of death."

[letter from Emily Hartwell]   SHARP PEAK   AUGUST 26, 1926

Dear Donald and Catherine:

It is to express to you my own sorrow and sympathy in this affliction that has come to us all, that I write you. May the God of All Comfort be with you these days when you get the news. If you have seen Nga Geng-guong you may be somewhat prepared as he saw how weak your baby looked the day he left. Miss Armstrong also must have told you our great concern for your baby, and Miss Wiley has written you fully, so we feel you must have felt she was very frail. [Donald and Catherine were in the U.S. at this time.]

We are very sad for we all love her. Three times has Miss Wiley since she was left, snatched her from the jaws of death. At last Miss Wiley herself was barely saved by going to Kuliang and Miss Chittenden and I have both been ill in bed at Sharp Peak.

I promised dear Miss Wiley I would do all I could for your baby. While I was in bed at Foochow, when Dr. Dyer told me I must not see the baby as I had bronchitis and she might catch it, I worked three days to get the baby taken by her grandmother for Dr. Dyer to examine her thoroughly before Dr. Dyer left for Kuliang. Dr. Dyer said she was very weak, but not seriously ill with any disease at that time. She gave your baby some iron preparation and said she should take malt and cod liver oil, so I had Ga-io buy a bottle for her, which she liked and took each meal. I was disappointed because I wanted the baby to sleep in a cooler place than your house, and I tried to persuade the grandmother to bring her over to our house, but the grandmother excused herself saying she felt she could not leave your things.

Ga-io, Naung-muoi and nurse Jong all tried hard to persuade the grandmother to take the child to Dr. Lau if she was worse as Dr. Lau had pulled her through three times and understood her better than others who had not doctored her we felt. I say this because I want you to know that we tried to do everything that could be done.

. . .

Yours,   Emily S. Hartwell

"I shall eat my Thanksgiving dinner lying on my back."

                             FOOCHOW, CHINA   NOVEMBER 21, 1926

Dear Anna,

This is the ninth day I have been in the hospital again—flat on my back. Just now I have a piece of pasteboard and this paper "on my chest" while I try to write. I was losing one beat in every five when Dr. Lewis sent me here and I have not raised my head since. Yesterday he said that I got up to one beat in every 14 to 18 beats.

One of our boys, 20 years old, had Typhoid like mine and went to the Men's Hospital, and after he was quite well of the fever his heart began to act up and he died two weeks ago. Dr. Lewis thinks that I will pull through this all right, but he does not want to take chances. Since coming here I can sleep and eat, quite an advance, especially as to the sleeping question. If I could be propped up a little I could do lots of things, but I am as flat as the bed, excepting an inch or so of pillow. I will be flat until my heart gets back to normal—and one week more. After that I will creep up a pillow at a time. This is my first attempt at writing since I came, and my hand and arm seem weak.

This Mission Hospital charges missionaries only $3 Mex. a day. I have a private room and special nurse (Chinese) and am well taken care of. The American nurse drops in every day. I found that the Chinese nurse was a woman from my Woman's School some years ago, and she lays herself out to be good to me.

. . .

Donald and Catherine are both in Teachers College, Columbia University, New York City. They are staying at Inter-National House on Riverside Drive.

Before this reaches you Thanksgiving will be past, and perhaps Christmas. I shall eat my Thanksgiving dinner lying on my back and very likely my Christmas dinner the same.

Now I think I will rest my little paw.

Much love from,   Nana

"We foreigners have graduated from 'Devils' to 'Dogs.'"

FOOCHOW, CHINA   MARCH 13, 1927

D̲ear Anna,

It was good of you to want me to go home, but out here I can do a good day's work even if I have to be on my back. At home I would be a nuisance. I have a nurse hired by the year for now for $10 Mex. a month—$60 gold a year! She likes me and takes good care of me, even though now I need no care to speak of. She will also take the responsibility for the Woman's School sick off me.

March 19 —— When William has time to write a few lines I would like to know about the size of my annual income in the U.S. If I should have to leave here now I would be pretty short of cash until I was well enough to work.

Who would ever have imagined that our quiet, peaceful Foochow would turn into a hornet's nest? We are living under the Russian Cheka. Fifteen thousand Russian "advisors" came into South China in one squad. A Russian is right at the side of every official. On the 14, 15, 16th of this month, there came nearly being a civil war right here in Foochow, between pro-Russian and anti-Russian parties.

I sort of wished that they had precipitated a demonstration that would have lessened Russian influence. We foreigners have graduated from "Devils" to "Dogs." That is now our pet name. I have given only my side of what is going on. The women wept when I left the City for a few days, and the little woman from Cat's Head said that her "tears could not be restrained" when she heard how the foreigners were treated. The Christian women have certainly prayed hard for me to stick by them in their hard times.

Lots of love to all,   Martha

"So here she is on my hands and a pretty time I had getting her
into Japanese territory with no passport."

TAIHOKU, FORMOSA   APRIL 2, 1927

Dear Anna,

You will see by my address that I am again "refugeeing." On March 24th, the communist party staged a demonstration in Foochow, and took Pastor Ling buo-gi of the English Mission and put a yellow cap on his head with bad characters written on it, and then tied his hands behind his back and made him stand in the busy square, and let everyone ridicule him, and then paraded him through the streets.

On the heel of this, very sensational radio messages came, and so on Saturday when I went to the Consulate on business the Consul ordered me out of port. I could not get into the City until about dark. You can imagine what I had to do—a big house to close, servants to plan for, my protégés to provide for, my things to pack, the Woman's School to plan for. I decided to bring "Little Sister" [Martha's coolie] as I could not lug things up and down the gang planks. He had only Sunday to get a photograph taken and a passport. I sent him in the morning with full directions how to do and where to go.

About 2 o'clock he returned with no passport and I had to go four miles to get that done—then had my own passport to get visaed at two consulates, had to get bank accounts settled in two banks—had to get property deeds sorted and given to responsible parties to take in to be taxed—and a thousand other things. From Saturday evening to Monday morning I was some busy.

April 13 —— To continue—after a strenuous day I stayed all night at Mrs. Peet's. Monday the rain came down in torrents. My luggage had to be put on a launch at the City and sent to Pagoda Anchorage. At the latter place, my trunks were hauled up by ropes and in the hands of three men—I expected to see them fall into the river. Miss Hartwell went to Pagoda with Ga-io the cook. She ran up the plank as fast as her many coats would permit—for it was a fearfully cold day—and held a cabin for me. My various pieces of baggage were counted and the men paid. By that time it was only a few minutes until the boat would hoist anchor and start. Miss Hartwell left the boat and went on shore.

In a few minutes here came a girl (Chinese) with a letter and a cheque. Miss Hartwell was wishing her on to me. She had been joining the riots and one party was ready to seize her, and the other party was willing to pay her for her activities. It was not healthy for this precious orphan in Foochow. There was no way to plan but to bring her along. So here she is on my hands and a pretty time I had getting her into Japanese territory with no passport. But this is another story.

Mr. McClure of the Shaowu Mission came to meet me, and we carried the things into the customs and finally got them through and from the Keelung customs to the Station. Here we did have a time buying tickets and expressing baggage all by using signs. "Little Sister" was more of a liability than an asset, except that he could lug things when I could make him shut up. My baggage was rolled and dropped and pounded and kicked around in that station until everything was broken that could be broken. At last we got on the train for Tai-peh, or Taihoku as the Japanese call it. By dark we reached a Japanese house rented by the Shaowu missionary ladies, and we dumped our things down there and were glad of a mat on the floor.

We have at last found a doll house, and just a week after my arrival we moved our baggage and ourselves into the tiniest house I have ever lived in. It is a real Japanese house, and mats all over the floor. We were told to keep the mats clean and not walk on them with shoes. The whole house is about as big as my bedroom in Foochow.

The outside dimensions are 21 ft. by 15 ft., so you can imagine the size of the rooms—but the partitions are sliding paper doors and at night we can open up and get a good breeze. Josephine Walker and Florence (the Chinese girl) sleep on the floor, and I have a spring cot that I brought over from Foochow.

April 14 —— "Little Sister" finally got so mad on general principles that he left and we are all glad to have this place to ourselves. We have learned a few Japanese words and can buy things ourselves, and get on all right.

Please send this letter to the Yakima folks. Mails are very infrequent and I am in a hurry to get this off.

Love to all, Martha

"I have no idea when this life as a 'refugee' will end."

TAIHOKU, FORMOSA   APRIL 22, 1927

Dear Belle,

We certainly must acknowledge that the Japanese are wonderful in their organizing and administrative ability. This island was a den of pirates and savages and full of disease and filth and opium. Now it is a beautiful colony, with great cities and public buildings, and plague and malaria are under control, and a health officer calls every week to see if the place is clean. There are beautiful markets in each ward of this city, clean and sanitary. We buy bread from a baker in the city and it is fairly good bread. Peddlars also bring vegetables to the door. We can go off and leave our door unlocked, and no fear of thieves. In China we had a high wall around our house and a gate woman, and then thieves were constantly getting into our house—even our bedrooms. And what is strange to see—no police on the streets. There is a neat little police station every so far, which looks like a garage, and then there are police, but I have not seen police on duty in the street.

I have no idea when this life as a "refugee" will end, but I hope soon. It will be good to get to a land of chairs again. This crawling around on Japanese floors is too much for me.

Sometimes I get terribly restless, but there is nothing else possible but to make the best of it.

I wonder how you are getting on, and hope that you are not alone. If there is no possibility of return to Foochow for a long time, I might as well cross the Pacific to see the home folks as to sit here. But the great difficulty is to pay so much fare, and if one leaves, it is hard to get back now. Many missionaries will not be sent back and many do not want to return, but I want ten more years out here before I retire.

It is noon and all the whistles are blowing so I must stop and cook a bite. Miss Walker went down town and the Chinese girl is going to a missionary family every day to sew. We don't have much work, but it is enough for me.

When you write address: The American Consul
                          Taihoku
                          Formosa, Japan

Love to all from,   Martha

"Measles is more fatal to Chinese than smallpox."

FOOCHOW, CHINA   MAY 27, 1928

Dear Anna,

Belle's boy Horace [sponsored by Belle] was in the midst of that terrible fighting in Tsinan-fu (Shantung). I had a letter from him to-day saying that he had been in "a remarkable phenomenon." I suspect he was, when the Japanese rained shells into the City. The University disbanded. Americans were evacuated. Consul Price—who was in Foochow when the Nationalists entered and who had such a hard time that he went to the U.S. to resign—was sent to Tsinanfu, arriving just in time for the fighting there. He put the Americans on an emergency train while he himself was under fire. I can just hear him scold even at a distance. He is the one who ordered me to Formosa last year.

A day or two ago Dr. S. and I had a narrow escape from an auto. A wild driver was running back and forth across the road and he was almost on top of us when the ricksha men got us onto a mound of earth on one side as the auto scraped by. It was all done in a second. Sometimes I am weak as a baby when I get home after dodging autos for an hour.

The rain has come down in water spouts part of the time, and the rest of the time the atmosphere has been so humid that a coat of green mold is on everything. Donald is starting to Shanghai to an educational conference tomorrow and has been out here on the verandah brushing off mold from all his clothes.

The measles have been terrible for some weeks. The disease is more fatal to Chinese than smallpox, so Catherine has stayed at home for weeks, and Mabelle Wiley Siek [Hsueh] has hardly been downstairs during that time. So I told Catherine to go to church to-day and I would take care of the baby. She sat on my bed and played while I read. She was 11 months old yesterday and is a lovely child, sweet-tempered and happy. I really enjoy the little one being here.

Martha

"For seven weeks there were seven typhoons and their 'children.'"

350 KULIANG   SEPTEMBER 2, 1929

Dear Anna,

I wonder if your scorching weather lasted through August. For seven weeks we hardly saw the sun shine. There were seven typhoons and their "children"—as the natives call the lesser storms. Fortunately my cottage did not leak or it would have been awful with so many here.

I wrote you about Mabelle almost dying, did I not? She had convulsions and for 24 hours it seemed as though she would die.

. . .

Love to all from,   Martha

FOOCHOW, CHINA   JANUARY 5, 1930

Dear Sister,

I have been waiting for a letter from you to tell of Vina's [Martha's sister-in-law] death. Anna said that she had a telegram telling of her death, but no letter of detail.

Your Christmas parcel was lovely. The present for Miss Hartwell I passed on to Dr. Smith, as Miss Hartwell is too old fashioned for silk bloomers. Ting-mi (Mabelle) was glad of her doll (she calls the doll Isabelle). That was the only one that she got, and her parents were wishing they could get her a foreign doll when yours came, so they all thank you. Their new baby came a year after the other and lived three weeks and died just as the other one. This makes four children dead. Christmas was a sad day here, but Mabelle saved the day. She would climb up on her mother's lap and hug and kiss her when she saw her crying. Three times I have gone through the experience of laying away their babies in the hill-side cemetery. When little Boat died, I was sick and could not do anything for her.

This new year I expect to do more country work and let someone else take the Woman's School. I rather dread the long walks, but if I am in this kind of work steadily I will have a woman go with me and prepare my food and carry my things. The noise is terrible in the villages, and the yelling and swearing makes a person's head ache.

Miss Hartwell has moved to a new house that she has built near here, and has with her Miss Chittenden and Mrs. Carey, an old friend, so Dr. Smith and Donald's family and I are now in this house.

While I am writing now, Donald has come home and is playing his violin and Dr. Smith is playing her typewriter so the house seems more cheerful.

Much love to all your family from,   Martha

"He is holding the lid on until a new government is formed."

FOOCHOW, CHINA   JANUARY 8, 1930

Dear Anna,

I had just got the address written, when a letter came from Mrs. Peet to tell me that she knew of a cat that I could get. We are so over-run with rats that we need the Pied Piper to clear us out.

To-day is a day of stress in the City. Yesterday the Bandit Chief Lu-ting-bang kidnapped six of the Commissioners of departments of the government and carried them off. One of his colleagues in the government invited all of them to a feast, and when they were about through he threw down his wine glass and shattered it on the floor, and instantaneously Lu's soldiers rushed in and seized the feasters, stripped off their fur coats and put gray cotton uniforms on them and took them up the river about six miles away. To-day's paper said that some "trifling molecules" had done this. Pretty good for *molecules!*

Last night we were going to the Culvers' for their regular Tuesday evening prayer meeting, but Donald was greatly opposed to our leaving the house after dark, so we stayed in. Martial law is very strict, as the Commissioner of Police was not seized and he is holding the lid on until a new government is formed. It is said now that the Commissioner of Education and the Vice-Commissioner of Finance were released at the river, and four others sent 90 li farther on. Our friend Mr. Gong, who helped save us from looting two years ago, was at the feast. He dived down among the flower pots and shrubbery and saved himself from being caught.

Now the joke is that this same robber chief, Lu, had given $10,000 to the Fukien Christian University as a fund to build a Memorial to himself. When he makes these old fat officials divide up their loot to get released, he can build another Memorial Hall somewhere else.

The American and Oriental Bank is afraid to open its doors and pay its (creditors) depositors for fear of Lu's soldiers rushing in and clearing out the vaults. The government will not take the responsibility of guarding it.

Dr. Smith lost $6 gold and Donald about $30 by not hustling over to the bank when I told them. I got my last out ($16 Mex.) at noon and at 2 P.M. the doors were closed.

Martha

*"You may see me in the summer of 1932 if
I live to that date."*

MARCH 24, 1930

Dear Anna,

. . .

March 27 —— The bandits are very near Foochow now, just out of North Gate, where we have a chapel. What a terrible condition this country is in. To-day all the City was to turn out and welcome General Lau, who has arrived to put down troublemakers, but such torrents of rain poured down that no one could go on the street.

Donald and Catherine are playing all their cards to get to the U.S. when I go. They want to raise money for Foochow College. My furlough begins January 1932, and they want to go along with me, and from there, east. If Catherine gets on the job she will get it through for her "dear Donald." In that case you may see me in the summer of 1932 if I live to that date.

Love to all from,   Martha

FOOCHOW, CHINA   MAY 27, 1930

Dear Belle,

All the children in my school have had a turn at measles and are just getting out again. We have had to keep Mabelle out of the school so she has escaped. The other day she brought the doll that you sent her to me and told me to "keep Isabelle for my baby." To-day she has got lonesome for Isabelle and has carried her off. She calls her "Isabelle" and another doll she calls after herself—"Mabelle Jr." She does pretty well with English but not as well as "Little Boat."

Love from,   Martha

"There is no Post Office at Sharp Peak and we just hear rumors."

SHARP PEAK   FOOCHOW, CHINA   JULY 8, 1930

Dear Belle,

Such a lot of things are always crowding that I do not write as often as I should. Since I last wrote you we have been through two weeks of fighting around the North and West Gate of Foochow, about two miles distant from where I live. Lu-ting-bang and his 30,000 bandits wanted to loot and burn the City, and General Lau was holding them off.

Mr. and Mrs. Christian decided to come to Sharp Peak and asked me to come along and board with them for a few days. So I packed a basket of things, got a school boy to come with me, and met the Christians on the houseboat.

That night on the houseboat a typhoon struck us, and when the boat tacked one way it was reeking hot, and when it turned, a cold wind blew on us—but the heavy wind and rain did not set in until we got to the American Board Sanitarium.

Next morning I had a good case of inter-coastal neuralgia—that is, the cartilage between the ribs has neuralgia. If you want something excruciating try that. This makes the third time I've had it, twice down here. For these five days I could sit propped up and not move a muscle or I would howl with pain. To-day it has left me so I can get to work.

Poor Horace, your boy, finally had such a severe attack in Peking that he was rushed to the hospital and operated on. He had his appendix and his gall bladder removed. The Superintendant of the hospital wrote me, so he was forced to have the operation which he should have had when a small boy. He will probably have better health now. He has always suffered so terribly with attacks of stomach trouble.

Since I have been here I have heard the fighting has begun again at Foochow, but I do not know for sure, as there is no Post Office at Sharp Peak and we just hear rumors.

Much love to all the Woodhouses from,   Martha

P.S.—Saturday, July 12

Just back to the City from Sharp Peak. Sounds like fighting in the North of the City.

"The '57 varieties of Chaos' is no exaggeration."

FOOCHOW, CHINA   OCTOBER 14, 1930

Dear Jean,

I went down to the country for a tour in September and got an attack of dengue fever down there. I thought I was near the end of my road. I must have had about a 105 degree fever and I was so sick I thought someone would have to bring a coffin for me, but I got home and found that everyone else was raving with the same thing. Dr. Lau came twice to see me and laughed it off by saying the Chinese call it "Peace Fever" as it never proves fatal. The next week she had it good and hard. I was sick ten days with the horrid thing. An old Chinese woman came along and saw that the rash was not broken out so she made me some "tea." I told no foreigners, but took the dope, and soon I was sweating like all possessed and a gay red rash all over me. After that I soon got up, but my bones all ache yet. Dengue is certainly the limit while it lasts. Catherine and Mabelle both had it.

Did you read in the newspapers of the two missionaries who were killed in the North of the province? Miss Harrison I knew pretty well, and Miss Nettleton only slightly. They came from furlough a year ago, so happy to go back to their station, "their own people." The Communist bandits seized them and held them for a ransom—held them three months and then slew them with a sword, just in what manner no one knows exactly.

Miss Harrison was well up in the sixties and the other in the fifties: very lovely English ladies of the best type. For the group of missionaries who came together as a little band over 30 years ago this year has wrought havoc.

Miss Barber died of Typhoid; Miss Otway lost her mind and was sent to England. Miss Andrews had a stroke and is not likely to get well, and these two were killed. Miss Little, a frail old lady, is the one survivor of the group.

All the Shaowu missionaries are in Foochow except one, Dr. Tudd, and the M. E. people are all gathered in except one, I believe. Now we are told to stay at home and be good. I am happy to stay at home and rest my dengue bones.

This fall is very dry and already I have to lock up the wells and dole out water. On account of this I have very little garden started. When I came home from Kuliang, pumpkins were running all over the lawn and we have a grand heap of them. And a vine bean (similar to a lima bean) was doing its best on the garden wall.

Donald had just got out of port when the students began to insubordinate. The next in power will have a merry time with them. I am glad to be out of High School work since China is such a chaotic place. The "57 varieties of Chaos" is no exaggeration. We now have "government by clamor,"—the party that can yell the loudest wins.

What a mess the government is in. To the north of us is a miniature Soviet government. We heard to-day that the English ladies killed were under so strict a guard (for fear some other party would steal them and get the ransom) that they were not left unobserved for one minute during those three terrible months. No wonder one lady lost her mind and one nearly so, before they were slain.

. . .

Lots of love to you and Doris,   from Nana

"Last week Chiang Kai-shek joined the church and was baptized.
He had nothing to gain and everything to lose by doing so."

FOOCHOW, CHINA   OCTOBER 24, 1930

Dear Sister,

The fighting for months around Foochow took all the nerve that any of us had. Mabelle was the only one who was at peace. When she heard the machine gun firing she would say, "Peter Piper picked a peck of pickled peppers," etc. and go on with her play.

The Hsueh family is to go to the U.S. for a year, leaving in February, and that adds to my work, helping them to get their affairs in shape. They will go to New York, so will have no chance to see you as I once wrote you. This will end a chapter in their lives and who knows what the next will be?

For a while, the Chinese government has refused to let any student who was going to a Bible school or studying theology get a passport. But last week Chiang Kai-shek, the President of China, joined the church and was baptized. It must be a real conversion, for he had nothing to gain and everything to lose by doing so. Now the Communists will hate him terribly and try to ruin him. But the young upstarts in the Education Board will have to loosen up a little.

Much love to all of you,   Martha

"By this time my vocal chords had limbered up pretty well."

FOOCHOW, CHINA   NOVEMBER 7, 1930

Dear Anna,

I forget where I left off in my last letter but there is enough to fill another page or two of recent doings.

On Wednesday I got home by 12 o'clock and Dr. Smith said that her thumb had a little black speck on the end and felt stiff. We had dinner and then I made her go to Dr. Lewis to see if it was an infection. He said it was nothing, so she came back with her thumb painful, but was not worried. At 3:30 I went to Wednesday prayer meeting at Wenshan, and had hardly been seated when a note came to Dr. Lewis saying that Dr. Smith had a chill and the infection was going up her arm. I rushed home and packed her suitcase and got an automobile ordered, so all was in readiness for her to go to the hospital if Dr. Lewis said it was necessary. He lanced her thumb and gave her a hypo and we got down to the gate and there stood an old horse-carriage with a horse ready to fall over he was so thin. I was so frantic I could have kicked it all over. By this time the red line had crossed Dr. Smith's elbow.

I yelled at one of the Chinese boys to telephone for an auto—and then Miss Chittenden said that martial law was being enforced and we could not cross the bridge with a taxi. By this time my vocal chords had limbered up pretty well and I shouted to the boy, "Get that taxi here and I'll take the responsibility of getting across the long bridge." In ten minutes Dr. Smith and I had piled into the back seat, with Dr. Lewis and the driver in front, and we were tearing along to the hospital with Dr. Smith beating her well hand like a drum.

We were stopped five times by soldiers but when we got to the bridge the soldiers saw that someone sick was in the taxi and let us go right on.

By that time Dr. Smith had to have her thumb lanced a second time and to have hypodermics to keep her quiet. For two days then, Dr. Campbell came every two hours to see what was doing and to fight back infection. At last she had an anaesthetic and had the thumb bone scraped.

She had a close call, as it was blood poison of a very virulent kind. If we had not got after it at once she would have died.

I got home from the hospital late that night and took dysentery and a high fever of 104 degrees plus. I did not care how sick I was just so I did not die—so that I had no more deeds to look at.

Then last night I was gone for a while and a woman came and left word that "very important business" was waiting and then went off. This morning she came and said that her cousin had been put in prison for a week for pasting posters on the walls and that he had been hired to do so by one of the City pastors. I told her to go and get a squad of women and go to the pastor's and scream and yell and howl and beat the tables and keep it up until the wicked man got her cousin out of prison. He can't read and just went daubing up what he was told to do. I'll think that by this time the pastor is being entertained!

Lots of love to all,   Martha

Dr. Emily Smith and Martha

*"The list is long of the Foochow College graduates who
are now making good in the government."*

FOOCHOW, CHINA   DECEMBER 21, 1930

Dear Wallace,

Admiral Chen, who is now really head of the Chinese navy—though one officer ranks above him—was one of my boys, and he remains a very loyal friend.

Chen Shao-kwan as a student with Martha.

The young chap who is chief bugler on the Admiral's flag ship was an orphan that I took care of for several years—in fact he's Donald's own brother, several years younger. And so the list is long of the Foochow College graduates who are now making good in the government. The officer at the head of this provincial government is one of my former students. One day I went to ask him to give a civil engineer, who had graduated in the U.S., a job.

After a while he said, "I really give this job to you, Miss Wiley. I don't need the man, but you have never asked me anything before so I will take him." The young engineer has been promoted twice by this same official and is now making the most important of these new highways across the province.

It will be 31 years the 19th of January since I left for China. Do you remember that cold, snowy night when you took me to the train and I left by myself for that long journey? There have been many compensations but it has not been an easy life.

For a year I was almost afraid to go to sleep. Now I have adjusted my mind and life to that fact and sleep as peacefully as I used to, and go right on with my work; and when I got to this state of mind most of the commotion in me subsided. I still have jabs of pain but the panic has gone, for which I thank the Lord. I made my will and divided up the few dollars I possess and then I quit all unnecessary worry. What was the use? My life is in God's hands and why should I fear? It seemed about time for me to practice what I had been preaching to these people for so many years—namely, there is peace of mind and heart for a foreign sinner.

Dr. Emily Smith will be leaving for Seattle in February or a little later. When she and the Hsuehs go I will be rattling around in this big house alone until Miss Walker returns, but I will have one of the servants sleep within calling distance.

If my program is carried out I will go to the U.S. in 1932 via the South Sea Islands, touching Madagascar and coast cities of both East and West Africa, and then going to Rio De Janeiro to the World S.S. [Sunday School] Convention, and from there to New Orleans and up to St. Charles. However, the Board may veto this.

Mr. Christian still remembers the bear that he saw at Nachez, and the supper you gave him. The Christians are good friends.

I am always happy to hear that the young generation of Wileys are making good.

On Saturday I sent off about 100 letters and cards, but left my home letters to do more leisurely.

Much love to your good self,   Martha

TIMELINE 1931–1940

1931 — Donald and Catherine have another child (born in Hong Kong) — Marian
— Martha home on furlough

1933 — Martha returns to China
— Foochow College has all appropriations cut by American Board of Missions
— Donald and Catherine have another child (born in Foochow) — Elizabeth
— Another Foochow government "turn-over" — Foochow area bombed

1934 — Admiral Chen considers resigning from navy, is later promoted to fleet admiral

1936 — Donald is in military training camp, and again in '37

1937 — Chinese War of Resistance against Japan until '45
— Martha in U. S. for one year, Hsuehs also in U.S.

1938 — Dugout bomb shelter built on Fairy Bridge property

1939 — WWII begins
— Foochow bombed
— Martha starts rice kitchen for refugees and destitute
— 800 Foochow College students move to Ingtai, (40 miles SW of Foochow) with the Hsueh family
— 600 Primary School students remain in Foochow

4

ROADS TO WAR

"I wish that I could clear out for a few peaceful years."

FOOCHOW, CHINA   MARCH 13, 1931

Dear Anna,

The Hsuehs could not go to the U.S. as I wrote you and they have all been gone to Hong Kong, a week, and I miss Mabelle so much that the house seems empty. I have not heard from them since they left. Catherine expects to stay there until the new baby arrives in June. Poor lady! She is so worried for fear this one will die.

You ask if I am coming home to stay this time. It is like this. I wish that I could clear out for a few peaceful years, but do not see how it can be done just yet. The American Board retires us at 68 years of age. I will be 58 when I get home and by the time I return to China I will be 60—then one more term will be necessary before I can get my pension. If I withdraw before that time I am out my allowance, and I am too old to do anything in the U.S., so it seems better for me to count on one more term.

Besides, there is so much to do here. Of my 40 women only a few are now Christians. If I were not here not a soul would do any of this work. These women will have a chance to learn to read and to know the Lord. Sometimes I think that I cannot go on another day, but when the next day comes I can go on very well. One poor woman is coming to the school who lost four children last month with measles—every child that she had. We brought a lot of children through measles in the school with no loss of life. But hundreds died this winter of measles in Foochow.

Love to all,   Martha

FOOCHOW, CHINA   JULY 8, 1931

Dear Belle,

I will be leaving Foochow on the 14th of July and Shanghai on the 21st. I expect to go by way of Honolulu and Victoria—the place where you and I had such a good visit.

Catherine has a little daughter [Marian] born June 29th. The first four days the baby was perfect, but Donald wrote me that she is beginning to get that yellow color that has carried off their other babies, so they are greatly worried. I do hope this little one will live.

It gives me quite a thrill to be getting off, even though I am greatly disappointed in losing the long trip by the southern route. Across the Pacific will take about 18 days so I ought to reach Seattle the second week in August.

Lots of love until then,   Martha

Donald and Catherine with Mabelle and Marian

"The paragraph about mother is found in Carl Sandburg's History of Lincoln."

Dear Belle,

We have been thinking of writing to you for several days but with four women in the house we manage to keep very busy. Jean has begun on her rug, and the sorting and cutting and dyeing and planning is going on late at night and early in the morning. I have finished the "Sunbonnet Girl" and Anna has set it together. We have made two trips to St. Louis lately and I am now pretty well prepared for "Furrin Parts." Aunt Minnie is making over some dresses for me out of Anna's and those are nearly completed.

If it stays cool tomorrow I will get my picture taken—passport photos. The Board has voted that I may return to China in January and that is what I am planning on now. This trunk that I have here is about bursting and I have not begun to pack the things that I am using. Mollie gave me ten dollars and I have bought a Kodak with the money. You see I am writing on my new typewriter—but very slowly—so slowly in fact that I am doing most of my correspondence by hand, but I practice every day to get used to this make.

. . .

The paragraph about mother is found in Carl Sandburg's History of Lincoln: "Abraham Lincoln, The Prairie Years," page 288.

"A girl skipping along a sidewalk stumbled on a brick and fell backward, just as Lincoln came along and caught her, lifted her up in his arms, put her gently down and asked, "What is your name?" "Mary Tuft." "Well, Mary, when you reach home, tell your mother you have rested in Abraham's bosom."

Love from all of us,   Martha

"A great many of the missionaries are being dropped and I am lucky to be returned."

Dear Belle,

For a month I have been crazy to get out West but it seems that every time I get just about ready something turns up preventing my starting. I told the board that I was ready to leave for Yakima the 24th and got a letter from the office saying that I was to proceed to Boston for a Conference on the Foochow Work with special references to closing the Woman's School.

Anna and I went to the city and found out all that was to be known about eastern rates and I came back expecting to go on my way to-day, but when we reached home there was a telegram on the door knob saying that the conference was postponed until October 16th. So here I am rarin' to go and tied up to that conference! And it seems to be very necessary that I go and plead the case of the Woman's School as that is the main question — to close the school and give the funds to the Boy's and Girl's School.

It must be just glorious now in Yakima. I wanted to get out there so we could go on some of those afternoon walks that we used to take, while it is nice weather. Now, unless another plan appears, I will return from Montclair, N.J., and pick up my things and proceed to Minnesota for a week and then to Yakima.

Dr. Emily thinks that she can get a good place to stay. A great many of the Missionaries are being dropped and I am lucky to be returned, but it is not much satisfaction to return with my school appropriation cut off.

Lots of love to all the Woodhouses,   Martha

"She may send it back to us in bullets."

S.S. President Madison   February 14, 1933

Dear folks,

I sent you a letter from Seattle to let you know that I received your present and at once bought a bed with it. It will be a constant reminder of the Achelpohls.

Mrs. Bressler, Miss Hartwell's niece, and her husband came in a car and took me and my hand baggage to the pier at Smith's cove, and of course Emily too.

At 10:30 the gong sounded and all had to get off the steamer. Just at 11:00 she left the pier and proceeded to Victoria. The first three days I did not pretend to get up. We have had continuous storms, rains, sleet, and snow. The gales split off the canvas like paper. All day yesterday snow fell and the ship's stewards and passengers got out in the wind and snow on the 2nd class deck and had a great snow fight. It was the funniest thing you ever saw — those men rushing around like mad, dodging balls and hiding behind funnels, etc., and basting some unsuspecting person with a snow-ball. I got behind a ventilator where I could peek out and see with no danger to my glasses. Such shouting and laughing.

That is the only bit of fun on this trip — everyone has been so sick. This morning the deck was about six inches deep with snow and the life boats snowed over, and the ropes covered with a thick coat of ice, looking like pictures of the ships in Arctic seas. It is beautiful but cold. This trip has been bitterly cold, and if I had not had my fur coat I could not have ventured on deck at all. I have been sick more days on this voyage than ever before. Cross seas sent up waves that swept clear across the deck. Last night was a twister — seemed like the ship was turning over.

There are 800 tons of coffee on board to be left in Kobe—perhaps for war material for Japan. She may send it back to us in bullets. On the 17th we reach Yokohama.

Love to each and all from,   Nana

" 'Never feah!' "

YOKOHAMA, JAPAN   FEBRUARY 18, 1933

Dear Anna,

Yesterday morning we got to Yokohama in a real blizzard. The wind was terrific and snow, fine flakes that drove into the cracks, was so blinding that the ship had to stop discharging cargo during the afternoon, and as a consequence the unloading has been going on all night, most of it right down over my porthole. We are due to reach Kobe to-day but it seems doubtful. The long line of ships in dock are covered with snow and it is a very wintery scene.

The stewardess has given my lame arm a rub every night, so I got her a few sweet peas from the flower shop and she was pleased. I looked up a drugstore and got a tin of antiphlogistine [a kaolin based anti-inflammatory product] and put a big poultice on my arm last night and hope it will help. By the time I got this done we fairly ran to the ship and got in contact with a registrar.

Later —— We are now out of Yokohama and heading toward the Inland Sea leaving behind a snow covered landscape. Last night I bought the Yokohama Daily and read of Cermak [then mayor of Chicago] being shot and President Elect Roosevelt having escaped injury. "Never feah"! Also that the U.S. Senate has voted to repeal the 18th Amendment [Prohibition]. Garner [who created a gathering spot for lawmakers to drink alcohol] needs a good kick. The Ships Radio news has told us the news briefly day by day.

We have just seen six Japanese destroyers lying here in Yokohama harbor this morning. If the U.S. gets into trouble with Japan she will probably get whipped for a time, as Japan is prepared and the Pacifists in the U.S. don't want her prepared. We Americans, as a government, are too easy.

Lots of love to each one,   Nana

"Kindness only means weakness to a militaristic nation."

AMOY, FUKIEN   MARCH 3, 1933

Dear Belle,

Did I tell you before that in Japan the buses and taxis are now driven by girls, and women are filling into all kind of places to release men for a big war? Most people in the Far East think that Japan will never rest until she proves that she can whip the U.S.A. If she whips China and wins Manchuria, she will have enough natural resources to be independent of the world for raw material. Old U.S.A. had better be prepared. Kindness only means weakness to a militaristic nation.

Be sure to write all the news for I will be waiting for letters.

Love to all from,   Martha

"The next generation of Chinese will be warriors."

FOOCHOW, CHINA   APRIL 3, 1933

Dear Hugh,

To-day is the Feast of Graves—a sort of Chinese Memorial Day when all the population turn out to repair graves and make offerings and have a grand day in the country. My school has gone, and that gives me a free day to write letters and catch up on some other things.

The radio that you lugged to Seattle is now in position and we get Mandarin broadcasts from Nanking, Shanghai dialect; and English from Shanghai; Japanese from Formosa; Cantonese from the South; Spanish and English from Manila. Every evening at 6:30 and 8:30 there is an English news relay from Manila and that is what we look for at the end of each day to hear how affairs are going in the good old U.S.A. and how the battle is going for the day in the North. A day or two ago the Chinese and Japanese got together and fought with knives, reverting to the old time satisfactory methods of warfare. This way of getting the news is quite different from the old days of waiting a month or more to hear from America what had been done in China.

The next generation of Chinese will be warriors if they keep up the propaganda that is on at the present—and how they hate Japan! Some time the future generation of Japanese will suffer for the aggression of the present generation.

With love from,   Martha

"And that is more than I can say of the foreigners—myself included."

FOOCHOW, CHINA   APRIL 7, 1933

Dear Doris,

Having received your good letters so long ago it is a shame that I have neglected you so long, but here goes the news reel. You will want to know first about the Hsueh family, I think. Donald has taken to wearing Chinese clothes and it certainly does change his looks and not for the better. Most of the men who used to wear foreign clothes have taken to the Chinese for both patriotic and economic reasons.

Catherine is just the same dear good person that she has always been, and I do not know how I would get on without her. She is always good and kind and never cross and that is more than I can say of the foreigners—myself included. While I am writing Mabelle is standing beside me pasting up a paper ball. She is a large girl for five years of age and so well trained that it is a pleasure to have her around, but the little one is the cutest now. She is my companion when I have time for her.

April 9 —— I got diverted from my story and will have to break in again. Last night Misses Hartwell, Chittenden, Walker, and myself took an auto and sped to the Y.M.C.A. at the rate of ten miles an hour to a supper and entertainment given in the honor of the famous General Chang and his suite who are touring China for two or three kinds of propaganda.

. . .

I wonder if you would like to order a Peking rug. The agent for the Fetti Rug Co. was here yesterday, and the special rates are $2.50 Mex. a square foot. You can choose the size that you want but 6 x 9 is a pretty good size. If you are interested, now is a good time to buy, as exchange is so favorable. I can send you a lot of photos to choose from. The company sends the photos but they have to be returned.

Lots of love from,   Martha

"The people starve and the rich waste money just the same as in the U.S.A."

EASTER SUNDAY—1933

Dear Belle,

We are all anxious about the way affairs are shaping themselves in the war area. If China and Japan make terms in Japan's favor, and Russia takes the roll that she wishes, we will doubtless see worse troubles in the Orient. However we can only watch and wait and wonder. This province is taxing the people to the limit for the aeroplane fund. Every day the training planes are busy and fly very low just over our house. Little Marian gets out and waves and shouts to them and gets the proper thrill on seeing them.

The radio does not work very well but by listening very carefully we can hear the daily news report from Manila. Yesterday we heard that Mrs. Franklin Roosevelt had imitated the Prince of Wales and fallen off her horse in the park. She will probably have harder knocks before she leaves the White House.

Do you see any signs of the depression letting up? Our funds, allowance, were cut 20% recently. Every mail brings a cut in something. We will have to cut expenses, but I don't see how and do any work.

The college appropriation is cut so much that Donald has nothing to get on with and the government is taxing his grade of teachers 30% every month and that is pretty hard when one's income is so low.

One of my Chinese *friends* has just finished a $20,000 tomb for his wife and bought a concubine to take her place—and yet he *says* that he is a poor man! The people starve and the rich waste money just the same as in the U.S.A. The really decent men like Donald have a hard time to make ends meet.

Give my love to the family,   Martha

"The discipline of life is never lacking."

FOOCHOW, CHINA   APRIL 30, 1933

Dear Anna,

That was a good stunt that the good ship *President Madison* did—namely to turn over in the Seattle harbor. The *S. S. Grant* that I crossed the Pacific on twice, came into harbor on fire, the trip after I enjoyed her comforts for three weeks. So when we take a ship and feel safe we have a sort of fool's confidence.

We try to get the news on the radio every day but often the sound is so faint we have a hard time to hear. Some of the missionaries have expensive radios and they are not any clearer than mine, so there is too weak a current in our electricity or some other major difficulty.

Poor old Donald has been in bed for two weeks. He has been as cross as a bear. He had a week of acute malaria, and then he was determined to get up before he was well, and in two days he came down again, this time with the added affliction of a terrible carbuncle right on the end of his spine. He was afraid of the pain of having it lanced until it reached a place where the doctor just laid hold of him and did the work. He certainly did shriek. To-day he is so exhausted that he lies like a person in a stupor. This stops his campaign for getting money for his school and that frets him. The discipline of life is never lacking.

Mabelle got the dressing down of her young life a day or two ago so she is behaving like a lady. Catherine certainly trains her girls well. The little one [Marian] is very cute now. She is right after me when I am in the house and comes up to "give me something." When she gets my attention she will blow me a kiss.

The sweet peas in the yard are lovely. The portulaca seeds that Belle gave me from her garden make lovely pots of blooming plants now. The little oak trees that I brought from Yakima are growing fine. One has put up leaves a foot long already.

What a lot of repairs had to be done. Things had about fallen down on the heads of the occupants of this compound. White ants were in five places. I had a downstairs place torn out and cement walls and floors put in and if the white ants get that eaten up they will be too exhausted to do any more damage.

The two rooms that I am having fixed up for myself have some good features over the others, one being that they are on the same floor and I will not need to run up and down stairs as much as when my office is below my bedroom. Another is that in winter I will not have a pilgrimage of 40 feet on a windy verandah from my room to the sitting room. But some of the disadvantages are great. These rooms are over the street and all the streets sounds come up, including those of the ricksha stand on the corner. And another is the fact that both sides of the rooms are enclosed with verandahs with brick arches and that darkens the rooms somewhat. I have had a door cut between the rooms making them into one suite, and the office room will be next to the living room. There is a small fireplace in each room, but I have had them fixed so that a stove can be put in if desired.

We had a 20% cut in our salaries (gold) but in spite of that I get more silver dollars for my salary than I ever did before in my life. If silver goes up in value it will work a hardship to all of us in the Orient but may be some use to the business men.

We were wondering to-day if the Japanese are making the threatened drive to Peking. It seems that the old culture of the East is collapsing under the impact of the Western that has been transplanted into Japan, while the Western civilization is falling to pieces under its own where it was developed. If history repeats itself this is quite possible, and may be going on right before our own eyes.

The Superintendent of Customs and two other men are giving a party at a hotel on Tuesday to return my invitation and we will have to put on our best. I am not crazy about a Chinese hotel this time of year, but it ought to be fine if those officials give the party. I have to "be careful" about my food but I get through a meal and eat practically nothing and no one ever notices. I feel quite proud of this ability.

Love to all,   Martha

Dear Anna,

Your good letter came along yesterday and I have read it several times, and every time thought that if you had all this wealth of material that is around me every day to write about, you would make lots more use of it than I do.

Last night at about midnight Catherine woke me up and said that the baby had dysentery and what should she do. I hunted around and found a bottle of castor oil and Catherine gave the child a dose and then her cook and I went to the American Board compound to get the doctor. By the time that we walked there and woke up the gentleman and got into the compound it was early this morning. Dr. Shepherd came down and stayed an hour or so and got the child cleared out and left some medicine, and we were up most the night with her. She was a very sick child and lost a lot of blood and so the family interest has centered on her all day to-day. I was glad that I had rushed for the doctor. The Chinese usually wait until it is too late before they start for a doctor. A missionary family lost a little girl two years old this week from dysentery and it is not to be fooled with.

To-day is Marian's birthday, and I and Mrs. Kiu made a cute little suit out of one of those scraps of print that you gave me and it looks very pretty. The lot of quilt blocks are mostly going into trimming for some of the children's clothes and baby shoes.

Lots of love to all,   Nana

"The depression is already at work here."

350 KULIANG   JULY 16, 1933

Dear Sister,

I stayed on in Foochow until Monday, July 10th, and then got shaken loose and left the City early in the morning, arriving on the mountain top at 10:30. We had sent word up twice to the "house-lord" (care-taker) to have the house opened up and washed. When I arrived it was closed up tight and no one in sight, and when we did find the man and get it open, the smell of mold was pretty bad. A thick coat of it was over the walls and furniture and worst of all, the kitchen and servants' quarters were not ready to use.

This summer the cook is doing all the work that I do not do. He dashed into the kitchen to begin cleaning up and found a very large poisonous snake curled up on the floor. He and the care-taker together killed it, but it made us afraid all day when we moved about for fear of the mate. So I got a village woman to come and cut all the grass around the house quite close to the ground. The care-taker said that last year his sister-in-law was bitten by that kind of snake and died from the poison. Well, the Lord took care of us.

While I was busy on this letter, the cook killed another snake—a little one of the same species as the big one, so I fear that we have a family of them to deal with.

The depression is already at work here. This summer I have just the cook with me and do my own room work and most of my washing—and would be glad if I could do the cooking, too. It certainly is a relief to know that when I put a thing down it is not going to be snapped up and put away by some over zealous coolie, but will remain where I put it.

The Hsueh family has two rooms and I have the room that was once built for Jean Brown, but it has been so rebuilt that she would not recognize the room. I bought myself a new broom and mop—and woe be to anyone who wants the use of them! The windows are not washed yet, but if I just tack some curtains on they will not need washing until next year!

For years I have tried to teach our care-taker but he is still as much of a heathen as ever. His daughter-in-law is ill and so she goes to a medium for advice. She told him that a tree near his house had the nest of a fox-demon in it and that was the trouble. He came back and decided that a very large plum tree in my yard was the home of the demon, so he is paying out more to get the medium to oust the demon. Then a black cat ran into his house and he and the family went on a hunt to scare the cat, which he thinks is a demon out of the village.

In the meantime, the villagers who want the plums come at daybreak to steal the fruit. The last summer that I was here before this, there was a great rustling in the tree at dawn and I slipped on a Japanese kimono and stepped up on the stone ledge around our verandah, and raised my arms to pin back my grey locks, when somebody spied the terrible spectre, and with whoops and yells the crowd surely did disappear. That ghost was worse than the black cat.

There are about 20 feet of slippery path near our gate that our neighbor stoutly refuses to have stone steps cut in. His grandfather's tomb is near, and if those steps were cut in, it would complete a circle that would strangle the dead man. But yesterday I passed the tomb and they had it covered and made into a pig-pen!

Love to all from,   Martha

"He has gone through most of the temptations of public life."

[letter from a former student]   AUGUST 16, 1933

Dear Miss Wiley:

I feel that my salary at present is quite high and I like to do something for your school. My cousin told me about the cutting business and I know how hard you have worked for the poor Chinese women. I promise you that I will give $50.00 more to your school during this coming Christmas. You can write me sometimes about your school and I shall be delighted to hear it.

I still remain your old student,   Uong Siong Bing

Note—The writer was one of my old students and had to have help through Foochow College. He has gone through most of the temptations of public life and has at last remembered the teachings of his school days as a true Christian. A few years ago his wife died and he took a concubine who was a great gambler. She got into debt and asked him for money to pay and when she did not get it she hanged herself in his bedroom on the mosquito net frame. Then her clan set out to ruin him. He came out of this a sadder, wiser and better man. I am getting him to collect money for Donald's work.   M.W.

"My part of the operation was to hold a candle for the doctor."

FOOCHOW, CHINA   AUGUST 17, 1933

Dear Belle,

I am going very carefully as to diet for high blood pressure, and that is better than medicine. And I try to limit my trips up this steep hill to one trip daily and as a result those terrible headaches are less and less frequent. My old cook goes padding around trying to get some appetizing meals for me. He is having a lovely time this summer with just me to work for. He is a one-person servant. When a third person, or *second* I should have said, comes, he goes wheezing around as though the world were on his shoulders.

A woman down in the village that I helped operate on once (my part of the operation was to hold a candle for the doctor) is so grateful that she keeps the house supplied with wild flowers. The beautiful blue hydrangeas are just gone. They make the hill beautiful for a while.

Love to all the Woodhouses,   from Martha

Donald has been in the hospital for an operation for the past three weeks, and is still in the City, as he has to have the dressings changed by the doctor daily.

"We only endanger anyone who is found with a foreigner."

KULIANG, FOOCHOW, CHINA   AUGUST 29, 1933

Dear Marguerite,

This is Tuesday, and on Sunday the consul sent a launch up river to bring down the few Americans that had not come to Foochow. Of course that got us all stirred up, for those that came reported that 30,000 Communist troops were sacking Iong-kau, the farthest south of the stations of our Shaowu station of the American Board.

The next news was that a big village, really in the City, had been sacked still farther south. This morning news came up the hill that the city of Iong-bing, two hundred li from Fooochow, had gone over to the Reds, and if that is so the Red army is only 60 miles from Foochow this P.M. This is the place that the M. E. missionaries left last Sunday.

Catherine and I are waiting for Donald to come up from Foochow and advise us as to the next move. He ought to be here in the morning. Three Chinese ladies and two foreigners took lunch with me this noon and one was sure the Communists were moving on Foochow; one said that it was not a Red army but the old 56th Route army coming to drive the Cantonese out of the province.

Whatever it is, the old Bandit general Lu-Ting-bang has gone over to it with his army. Foochow has not been burned over yet and I hope that it will not have that added to all the other troubles. I would like to get down to the City and pack, if things are as bad as they seem.

Fukien is the Reddest of all China. Some say that it is due to General Chi driving the Reds out of the surrounding provinces. Personally, I think that the Reds that are secretly living in Foochow and could rise up at any time are our greatest danger. In a day or two we will know the worst.

The Consul has sent for gunboats to take off any who might be in danger. It is not much comfort to be carried off and leave the Chinese friends to take the brunt of it, but we only endanger anyone who is found with a foreigner.

The Reds kill off the foreigners, the Imperialists, the capitalists, the intelligentsia and those over 40 years of age. The young people are put through their "reconstruction program"—that is, made over into Communists.

In all this confusion I have to stop and remind myself that the Lord is still in Heaven and still has the power to restrain this horde.

The 19th Route army—the division that distinguished itself in Shanghai—has headquarters in Foochow City, but the troops have practically all been drawn southward, and those left are largely raw recruits. We can hear the reports of the big guns in the City every little while, and we suppose that the gunners are limbering up those old pieces.

I would certainly hate to have a lot of those soldiers get into our house. They just defile a place so that, it cannot be used again by foreigners. Well, we will just have to sit tight until the Consul gives us directions how to proceed. We have gone through these scares so many times that one ought to get used to them, but each time seems to have some new features that give us the same thrills.

We were saying a day or two ago that this has been the most peaceful summer in years, with no typhoons or other disasters, but we forgot to touch wood and so this happened! If I have to move I will go to Hong Kong. Japan will not be a very cordial host now; the feeling against America is so tense. Many people think that the white race will not have many more years to work in Eastern Asia, so we will have to get the native church strong enough to take care of itself if that day ever comes.

When these Communists reach a place they order all the deeds of property to be brought in and all are burned and the Soviet leaders begin to administer affairs to suit their own interests. Sometimes I wonder if it is possible for Russia to spread her propaganda over the world in the course of time. Well, we will wait and see if we live long enough.

August 30 —— News has reached us that the Red army has been stopped on its march southward, and the British, French, Japanese and American gunboats are in port. So we will be quiet another day and go on with our work.

Foochow College got all its appropriations cut by the American Board, so I have had a busy time since I reached Foochow, helping Donald with his publicity campaign to raise money to keep the College from being closed. We have had sufficient results to keep the wheels going for another year or longer, and so that will give him time to plan for the future. Also the Woman's Bible School is in about the same fix, but the budget is small and more easily handled. If Franklin D. is going to bring good times he had better get busy.

I sent you from Japan, via St. Charles, two small Japanese pictures. Your art training will show you that a good artist made them. Last week I mailed you a Chinese doll to put in your collection, and hope that it will not get its face mashed, as I did not have a suitable box here on the mountain to pack it in.

I have some pots planted with vegetable seed, in preparation for planting, or setting out, when I go to the City in about ten days. If times are hard, we will at least have a good garden.

A thief stole some of Donald's clothes off the line in our yard about a week ago, so some of our things may be gone when I get back to the City. It is a job to "pass the days" as the Chinese say.

Mabelle (Ting-mi) has outlined almost enough of those animal blocks for a quilt this summer; pretty good for a six year old. I will get the sewing class to make quilts this fall—nothing like passing on a good thing.

Later —— Donald arrived and said that the Communists had been diverted from Foochow. It is a seaport and the navy would interfere with their operations, as well as foreign gunboats. But he came up to plan with his family as to what should be done in case he sent a code telegram if things should take a turn for the worse. I am going down to the City to make a few plans "in case," as we keep saying, but the scare is over as far as Foochow is concerned.

Martha Wiley

"The Consuls request that no one remain longer."

FOOCHOW, CHINA   SEPTEMBER 11, 1933

Dear Doris,

An American mail came at 6 P.M. yesterday and I read until 12 o'clock, then woke up at 3 o'clock and could not sleep, so at 5 o'clock lighted the lamp and began a letter to you.

Catherine and the children went down just a week ago this morning. Donald got scared when the Communists got so near, and thought that we might be cut off from communication with the City, so he came to the foot of the mountain in a "gas-cart" (automobile) and Catherine and the children met him there—but I decided to stay longer and have had four days of storms out of seven.

I am fond of the children and they are wonderfully good obedient girls, but it was rather a relief to have a quiet house for a few days. Before I am up, Marian's little feet come pattering into my room and she calls out in English, "Good morning, Gu-Gu," and if she is put to bed without telling Gu-Gu goodnight she fusses until she is taken up and brought into my room.

If the storm abates, I plan to go down on the 13th and then the hubbub begins. All schools, except mine, have had to postpone the opening because of military conditions. I always begin late, so did not have to change the date.

We certainly did have a narrow squeak from having the Communists take Foochow. If they had done so you would have had this letter mailed from Hong Kong.

The Southern troops came up through the central part of South China, and the Communists either had to come to Foochow with the army behind them and the navy in front, or retreat N.W., and they chose the latter. The communist force is variously estimated from 30 to 100 thousand—most probably the latter as they force raw recruits into the army. Just now the 19th Route army is digging trenches and putting up entanglements at Water Gate, about three or four blocks from my home. Nobody knows whom they expect to fight, as the Communists retreated, unless they fear that a secret force of Communists will rise up in the City and begin to burn and loot.

Refugees in great numbers are surging about in Foochow and suburbs. Our compounds are filled with the Christian refugees from up-river stations. I dread to make the plunge into this condition on Wednesday, but after the first day or two we get used to it somewhat.

The soldier guard here on the mountain will be withdrawn on the 15th, so we will have to go down by that time, as the Consuls request that no one remain longer.

Lots of love to you and the family,   Nana

"The refugees that are pouring into the City
would make anybody weep to see."

FOOCHOW, CHINA   OCTOBER 5, 1933

Dear Sister,

I wrote you that Donald sent for us to go down the mountain September 4th and Catherine and the children went at that time. It was so warm that I thought that I might as well be killed by Communists or bandits as to run into that heat, so I stayed on at Kuliang until September 12th and then came down into the heat and turmoil.

The large Communist army got to Iong-Bing, just up the river from Foochow, and everyone thought that it was a matter of hours until the army would reach Foochow and that secret Communists would fire on the City. Donald wanted Catherine and the children with him in case they had to flee. The Communist army always kills the moneyed people first and the educators next. As Donald is the best known principal in the City they would soon be after him if they got into the City. Catherine said that she and the children could hide but there was no way to hide Donald. They planned to escape to Sharp Peak fishing village if they needed to flee.

The refugees that are pouring into the City would make anybody weep to see. We had a house full but they got away early and are pretty well fixed now. Just to-day Pastor Chen of our up-country station arrived with a party of refugees that are the worst ever. They were nearly starved and had been hiding in the hills and travelling by stealth until they could get out of the Communist territory.

He said that on the last day's march they saw at least 40 dead babies by the roadside. One stretch of travel covered 25 days of hiding and starving. Mrs. Chen gave out and could walk no farther, and two Chinese men of the Anglican Mission got a board and put her on that and carried her for days. That was better than walking, but clinging to a board up hill and down dale would be mighty hard work too. Pastor Chen is a prominent man in Iong-Kau and he would have been one of the first to lose his head if he had been caught.

Hundreds of these poor persecuted people are lying on the ground with no beds, no change of clothes. The Shaowu missionaries are working hard on the job. Josephine has a squad in the basement making and dyeing clothes, and is buying up beds from the pawn shops where they can be bought cheap. She is working hard to help out. I have not got into the relief work, as the Shaowu missionaries speak that dialect and are free from other work, so they can manage that.

In spite of all this we seem to go on day by day about as usual. My school is full of nice women and we are getting on all right so far. My nurse left for hospital work (with my consent) and I thought of another nurse, but did not know where to find her. One day she came along glad to get a job, so we were all happy. She is such a nice capable person and carries responsibility without being urged, that I am glad to have made a change. She was a poor abused little widow when I first took her into the school. She graduated here and was a Bible woman for three years in a country place until run out by bandits, and then went to Union Hospital and had three and a half years of training, but as she couldn't pass in English she could not get a diploma. The lack of diploma as well as the old friendship made her willing to take my small wages—$16 Mex. a month—about $5 gold.

Poor Catherine has another hospital experience before her in December, and she does not want to go to the Mission Hospital where she has lost so many babies, but she does not know where to go or how to plan.

. . .

Martha

"Admiral Chen is now the 'Minister of the Navy.'"

FOOCHOW, CHINA   OCTOBER 24, 1933

Dear Anna,

Muk-huak, the cook, is going to take a week off for his 14 year old son's wedding. I feel like kicking him, but will have to give him a present of two dollars instead. No one could make him postpone the date for a few years, as his wife wanted a good servant in the fields.

Mabelle and Marian come to my room every evening and play hide and seek for a while before going to bed. Can you find some beads, fine and medium size, of all colors and shapes, in the ten-cent stores? Mabelle is just crazy for some. One day she swiped another girl's handful and brought them home. Catherine had a long session with her, and when Mabelle found out that other people call that stealing she about cried herself into a fever. Finally Catherine found a few for her and she has strung and restrung them hundreds of times. Yesterday Marian got into that little box and scattered her beads, and Mabelle cried all afternoon that her precious beads had been partly lost. If you can get some, a large variety, do send them on.

October 28 —— Yesterday some friend called "Hannah," who might be "Eve" for all I remember, sent me a pair of beaded slippers from Singapore. Mabelle got hold of those slippers and begged for the *beads* on them. This bead business is getting serious! Do come to the rescue!

This week I had a nice friendly letter from Admiral Chen. He is now the "Minister of the Navy," the very top of the Chinese navy. He has just completed five gunboats and has two more under construction, from his private fortune, besides what the government is building. He is an awfully nice man. Catherine says, "What a pity that he does not have a wife"! His gunboats are his lady-love!

Martha

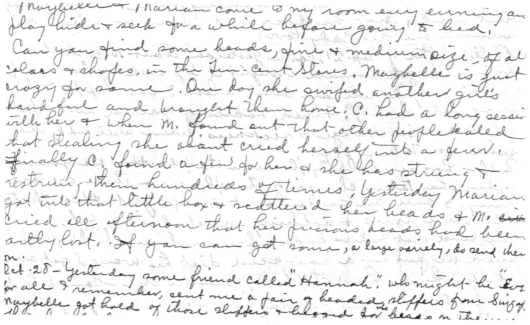

Example of a handwritten letter of Martha's.
(We were always glad when her typewriter was in good order!— Pat and Kathy)

"The government in Foochow had
one of its frequent 'turn-overs.'"

FOOCHOW, CHINA   JANUARY 1, 1934

Dear Home Friends,

This is the very first letter of the New Year and, in fact the first letter for a number of days. Perhaps you have chanced to read that the government in Foochow had one of its frequent "turn-overs," and we have been in a state of turmoil ever since, and we were told that letters were censored and what was the use to write letters that may never reach you!

For several days it has been rumored that "hi-gis," aeroplanes, would bomb Foochow City, but we thought that it would be like other times—be only rumor, so went about our usual Christmas celebrations regardless of it all.

On the Saturday before Christmas, I went to a Christmas celebration at Au-Seu, a village on the plain, and was late in returning. On reaching home I found that the servants and students in the school were very much excited, as Japanese planes had appeared and dropped a few bombs here and there in the City and suburbs. All sensible people would have taken the hint and prepared for safety the next day, but all of us were not sensible. Sunday afternoon, eight planes came back ready to do more than on Saturday. I had gone to Christmas service at Sang-bo in the suburbs and got home very late. Miss Walker and I were just finishing a late lunch when we heard some planes near the roof of our house and had just remarked that they sounded strangely like the French planes that we had heard when—crash!—some thing had happened!

I ran the length of the verandah to find the children, as their mother is in the hospital with a baby two weeks old [Elizabeth]. It happened that Donald had gotten home from the hospital and was taking the children to the lower storey, so I went back to get the servants out of the upstairs and found the school nurse and the house maid on the living room davenport clinging to each other. After chasing them downstairs, we discovered that the Woman's School students were crouching under the camphor trees in the yard. It seemed a little safer to get under the brick arches of our house, so Miss Walker and I called them over to our house. With two exceptions they were very quiet and stood together and prayed that God would take care of them. The two hysterical ones clung to me as though I could keep off the bombs. Mabelle climbed up me like a squirrel up a tree and hung onto my neck. Our cook said that our house shook with the concussion of a near explosion, but I do not know, for there were too many shaking knees about to be conscious of the house.

Our house is nearly in the center of an area surrounded by a wireless station, an official yamen, a military camp, and some temples filled with soldiers—and so we were likely to have a bomb fall on us if there would be some random throwing. It certainly did seem a bit fearsome with eight planes in action right over our heads. The roaring of the planes and the firing from the forts made an unusual noise for those of us who had not been used to world wars and hundreds of planes in action.

By evening we got out and gathered some news. One bomb fell in a two storey house and killed two adults. The shock broke down the walls of the house next door and shattered the glass in the Senior High dormitory of Foochow College and in the assembly hall. A bomb came through the roof of Lau Memorial Church and struck the gallery floor but did not explode, yet shattered hundreds of panes of glass. Fifteen minutes before, there had been a crowd of children there for a Christmas service. No one was injured in this church.

Near our little chapel at Siong-Huong, which is near the aviation field, a number of bombs fell and 11 in one house were killed. I do not know how many soldiers were killed in the explosions in the yamens and forts. The air was fairly good, as the planes came down very low. The Bible women at the Siong-Huong chapel moved out early next day, as the aviation field is too near. There were explosions on both sides of the chapel.

The usual wild rush from the City took place Sunday night. All night the street past our house was filled with refugees carrying what they could. Ricksha men and automobile companies reaped a fortune from other people's misfortune.

Daily bombing rush from the city

Monday morning I got up at 3:30 and took the cook and went the rounds of all the gates and bolted and propped them with heavy timbers, except the large front gate. Then got our school cook up and she had breakfast ready by 6 o'clock—also the servants and Shaowu refugees in the house next to us. The latter felt badly that I did not give them time to go around and sing the carols they had practiced, as this was Christmas morning—but there was not peace in our corner of the earth. By 8 o'clock everyone was at the gate ready to depart, if not already on the way to a place of safety.

Donald had taken the children out of the City that evening so he could be free to go to the hospital early in the morning and plan for Catherine, and when Mabelle saw that I was not going she certainly protested. "Gu-Gu, I can get a quilt for you—or you can sleep under part of mine."

Christmas morning at 8 o'clock I stood at the front gate looking for a ricksha, and the coolies asked such a price that I was wondering what to do when Sik-bo-so, a little woman from one of the Kuliang villages, came running to the door where I stood. She said that she and her little twin girls had not slept all night worrying about whether I could escape from the City or not. She had put on straw sandals and thin clothes and started at dawn and run down the mountain to see if she could be of help to me. She was a great help, for she took the roll of bedding and bag that I had and carried them to where I was going and that left me free to go on my way.

At the first sound of danger both the gate woman and the gardener ran away, so we had to get a man who thought that he was willing to watch the house for a week for a large bonus. When this was settled Miss Walker and I went on foot across the City to North Gate to see how Catherine and the baby had escaped, or rather how they were getting on, after the bombing of the day before. We found Donald there ahead of us and getting a sedan chair to take Catherine out of the City to some relatives. She hugged her little sick baby up to her and cried when she saw us. We had a prayer together, and then Miss Walker and I went out to West Gate and on to Mrs. Newell's at Union High. Sik-bo-so had got ahead of us, and left our baggage and came back to meet us—six or seven miles.

As this was Christmas day, the foreign faculty was having a Christmas dinner at Mrs. Billing's home. They kindly took us in and we were having a good helping of chicken when the bombing planes came back and were more generous of their bombs than the day before, but as we were well out of the City where most of the soldiers were supposed to be, we felt no personal concern. But one small bomb fell about 100 feet from the Newell house. Miss Walker and I stayed all night, and in the morning I took a walk up to the top of a nearby hill and sat down to read when suddenly I looked up, and groups of soldiers were coming up the hill with their personal arms and machine guns and hiding in the tombs and holes in the hill side, so it seemed time for me to withdraw in their favor.

Then Miss Walker and I came back to the City compound to see what was likely to happen next, and found most everyone at their work and expecting to run under the hospital building when the planes appeared. A warning gun was sounded and one plane appeared, but no bombs came down in the City—only on the village.

Then we were asked to get out of the City until it was evident that no more bombs were to be dropped, and we went over to the M. E. Compound and stayed three nights, and also during the time the planes were likely to come, and the rest of the time went about our work. The planes had to come from General Chiang's headquarters in Kiang-si and could arrive not earlier than noon, and if the mornings were cloudy they would be later, and as they were in enemy territory they could not land and had to get back to their starting place. On the days when there was low visibility we had no fears of their coming. We have just had a week of this and it has been a great nuisance.

The General wants to clean out this nest and was having the planes aim at the forts and yamen and other places where the soldiers of the 19th Route Army were stationed. It was remarkable what a small number of civilians were killed considering the number of bombs that were dropped, but the great suffering is on the part of the people who have been so frightened that they have left their homes and paid such exorbitant prices to get moved out of the City. And again this is not to be compared to the number of refugees from the Red area of this province, who are in 26 places on the island where there are old temples. The next thing that may happen is to have a clash between the Nationalists and the 19th Route Army. Bags of sand for barricades are very much in evidence throughout the City and in one place I saw a barbed wire entanglement.

If this present "pink" government wins out and becomes completely Red, there are indications that a bad time is coming for the Christian church along with all other religions. This Mission may suffer as the Shaowu Mission has and as the Russian Christians have been persecuted. However, we will wait and see, for it does not seem possible that the Nanking government will let one province secede and set up for itself. Eugene Chen of 1927 fame is furnishing the "hot air" for this new regime. It is reported that he went south by air three days ago and immediately the weather turned cold!

This province has been bled white by the Cantonese, and now this new group is trying all the ways possible to get more out of the poor people. And the unusual thing about it is the population is not in sympathy with this new movement—not even the fiery student class. Everyone acts ashamed of the whole thing except those who are concerned in setting it up. You will remember that the 19th Route Army was the one that fought so bravely at Shanghai and became the idol of the people. It is a pity that they are mixed up in this, and have largely turned Red.

Our Women's School students have scattered and I do not think that I will try to get them together again until the spring term as we had only two weeks more before they would have gone anyway. We can give the examinations before taking up the spring work.

All the schools in the City have disbanded temporarily. The newest government ordered all of Dr. Sun Yat-sen's pictures taken down and the worship of the same discontinued. But Dr. Sun would be infinitely better than Lenin—if it comes to a choice between them.

Strange to say we can go about in safety and carry on our evangelical work and meet only friendliness. This is an anomalous condition, surely.

January 2 —— Planes dropped a few bombs on a village north of the City to-day and now the village people will be moving to the City, probably.

Love to all from,   Martha

"This place agrees with your definition of love—
'One fool thing after another.' "

FOOCHOW, CHINA   JANUARY 3, 1934

Dear Anna,

There has been so much excitement that I had no time to write and thank you for all of the lovely Christmas things. The dress is lovely, and the white leather pocket book and stockings.

Mabelle loves to sew and your gift of scissors and thimble pleased her greatly, and the tooth brushes will be in use when Mabelle gets her teeth again—the first ones are lacking now.

Catherine was in the hospital and could do nothing for Christmas, and on the 23rd,

24th, and 25th there was bombing of the City, so we all scattered and did not get together until December 30th. On the Sunday after Christmas I set up the tree and let the children decorate it. When they got home they did not let me out of their sight for a day or two. They are crazy about the little sister (Elizabeth).

Yesterday Josephine and Miss Burr and I walked over to the North Gate Hospital to see Catherine (who moved back to the hospital when the baby got worse) and she and the baby look a lot better. The baby is three weeks old to-day and the jaundice is fading a little and it seems as though she will pull through. We have been holding our breath almost, so anxious about her. This place agrees with your definition of love – "One fool thing after another."

Yesterday the planes came again and seemed to know where to spot the soldiers. When I get up in the morning I dress for decamping at a moment's notice – pin my valuables on me, have my hand bag ready and William's suit case packed – then I go about my usual routine. One thing we feared was that in the mix up the children might be stolen. When they left the house we had two trusty coolies watch them all the way, as the ricksha men and servants cannot be trusted.

Love to all from, Martha

"The soldiers are seizing coolies to carry ammunition."

FOOCHOW, CHINA JANUARY 10, 1934

Dear Anna,

It is still dark and I am sitting up in bed writing. I dreamed that some one was getting in and when I opened the door a charred skeleton walked in! That was such a bad dream I thought I'd better wake up and do something pleasant. The Seventh Day Adventist missionaries asked me to supper last evening, and maybe the pie made me dream. They live about two blocks away.

Now we are living in daily dread of fighting in Foochow between the 19th Route Army and the Nationalist troops of General Chiang Kai-shek! However, they may compromise as Chinese usually do – or retreat. This is Wednesday and since Sunday the sound of big guns could be heard if one stood high on a building or on a hilltop, so the fun is going on fairly close. The streets are very quiet.

The soldiers are seizing coolies to carry ammunition and so all the coolies that can hide have done so. Yesterday morning my cook saw the ricksha men going out of Water Gate lickety-split, hunting a place to hide. He is mighty glad to stick in my upstairs kitchen and eat from our garden truck.

The garden comes in mighty handy when it is not safe to go out to buy things. I am so hopeful of better times that I planted more seeds yesterday.

Donald and the children went to South Side Monday and I have not seen him since.

Catherine is still at North Gate Hospital with the little baby. It seems as though this baby will pull through. She is four weeks old to-day and the jaundice is fading a little. It has been a great strain to all of us, especially to Catherine. When she leaves the hospital she will go straight to South Side and I hope will have little baby to take with her.

Yesterday when the Seventh Day Adventist missionary called, my stove blew up the lid and the two of us nearly bumped the ceiling—we did not know whether a bomb or a bullet had struck us—and we looked at each other and burst out laughing. This upset has "pepped" me up so that I feel better than I have for a year past.

On the 19th of January it will be 34 years since I left Yakima for China. I never forget that snowy night when I boarded the old Northern Pacific train and started off, as innocent as a lamb about the great wide world.

January 13 —— Yesterday I had a great working spree—got up early and got the cook and gateman and gardener and Eu-nguk all going strong when—bang! two guns went off—cannon and machine guns began. I thought that the Nationalists and the 19th were fighting in the City and so put on my hat and coat and started for Water Gate with Eu-nguk. When I got there I remembered that my passport and cheque book were in my desk so I went back home to get them. By this time hundreds of people were pouring out of Water Gate and they were shouting that five planes were overhead. I did not know whether to go to Water Gate and to South Side or to Peace Street. So I backed up against the wall and prayed and soon found my feet going well on the way to Peace Street and my head following. When I got to Mrs. Christian's the planes were pretty well through with their morning work, so I sat down by her fire and she washed clothes. After lunch the cannon went off again and we took to the place under the McClure house and everyone else gathered there too, but as the planes were high and some flew away, we went out on the hillside to watch them—over 20 bombs could be heard falling and probably more that were not heard. The Nationalists were bombing the soldiers on the river bank several miles away. The machine guns always scare me because if you can hear them that means the fight is close.

Mr. Shepherd of the Shaowu Mission is going to Central China to undertake the rehabilitation of the devastated area reclaimed from the Communists by Chiang Kai-shek's army. He will be in a danger zone, surely.

The drawing book you sent will go to one of the Shepherd children. There are three girls and a boy in the family. They would go to the gate and watch for the postman to see if something had come from America for their Christmas. But nothing came for them—so Mr. Christian and I are making up a fake parcel for them, since they are leaving right away to go to Central China. It is certainly hard on the kiddies to get nothing from "home." The two larger girls got the dresses that you sent, the red and the blue.

My servants have not dared stick their heads out this week. Now the present government is seizing all kinds of people to impress into carrying lead for the soldiers who are fighting. If they cannot carry they may give $15 and go free. No coolie can give that, but cooks and others can, so more revenue gets into the Army. It is said that the Nationalists have determined to finish up the job by January 20th. The quicker the better, I say.

To-day is so cold and foggy that perhaps no planes will come. At least I am counting on a quiet day of writing. In ten minutes I can get from this house to the open country as we live so near the City gate.

Here's hoping that you all have a peaceful 1934.

With love to all the A's,   Nana

"Soldiers are sacrificed to the foolishness of these half dozen propagandists."

[partial letter]   JANUARY 14 [1934]

. . .

Wonders never cease! The brave 19th Army has taken to their heels, and Friday night all night long poured out of the City garrisons by thousands. Yesterday I walked to North Gate to see Catherine and the remnants were hobbling out in squads—the sick and distressed soldiers, many of them little boys. The real veterans are evidently at the front fighting.

The children came home yesterday evening and they surely have pestered me this morning. Catherine will come home tomorrow if nothing breaks loose again! Rumor says that the Navy (Chiang Kai shek's Party) will come in tomorrow, and that the apparently retreating 19th will turn on the Marines, but it seems ridiculous to think so.

I had confidence enough in a peaceful day to wash my hair this forenoon and have unpacked my emergency bag. I think that there will not be any fighting in the City, but may be more up river a little way. Something ought to be done about those "hot air" parties that started this fracas. They came in by air and left yesterday in three planes. They will go elsewhere to stir up another fracas. The population is impoverished and many lives lost, and the soldiers sacrificed to the foolishness of these half dozen propagandists. Schools simply flew to pieces when this began.

Martha

FEBRUARY 8, 1934

Dear Anna,

. . .

Chiang Kai shek is enlarging the Aerodome and making ready for more planes to have headquarters here and soldiers are pouring in, and all looks like a war is in preparation against Canton. If he starts that he has a big job ahead as the Cantonese are the best fighters.

All our mission work is cut to the limit. My school is cut from $1,000 Mex. to $595 — not enough for the teachers — and the Bible women are cut fully half and the Committee this P.M. is trying to cut more.

Much love to William and you and Jean,   Nana

*"People live and die, but accounts have to
be rendered in both worlds."*

FOOCHOW, CHINA   FEBRUARY 10, 1934

Dear Belle,

Your boy Horace passed on into eternal life on February 6th. I went down to Pagoda Anchorage for a few days of change from the continual confusion of the City on February 3rd and stayed over Sunday. On Monday his adopted mother came to the house to let me know, and I was away.

This morning someone told Miss Walker that he was dead and also the family address, so I went there at once and found that Horace was dead, in his coffin, and that he was carried out to a little shack of a rest house on the hills outside of North Gate. The sister led us out there and we saw where the mortal part of the dear boy was at rest. He had three operations for gall stones in Peking and could not be cured, as the "sand" continued to form in the liver and could not be drained off or collect as stones. He suffered terribly most of the time and it is God's mercy that he was released from such suffering, for there was no cure.

With his fine training and gentle spirit he would have done something worth while in the world if his physical strength had been equal to taking up the burdens of life. I cannot but be glad that his suffering has ended. Norman [Belle's deceased husband] was always interested in him and I hope that they have found each other in that land where "the inhabitant will not say I am sick."

I am so sorry not to have seen him again and to have found out what was on his mind that he wanted to tell me. Every time I leave for a few days there is always something unfortunate that happens.

Of course you would want to know about him so I have written fully. To-day is such a lovely day that it is a pity to be inside, but I must get back to accounts. People live and die, but accounts have to be rendered in both worlds.

Martha

"I am still Irish enough to revive when a real fight is on."

FOOCHOW, CHINA   MARCH 10, 1934

Dear Anna,

There is a young lieutenant in the Navy who occupies a seat in our living room a generous part of his time, trying to get free English, and now a new youth has appeared, a business man. That latter brought his wife to place her in the Woman's School. She was so pretty and charming that I liked her at once and did not enquire very fully as to her education but found out later that she was his concubine. There is a rule not to take in that class, but I did not want to send away this girl who had no choice in the matter—so just told her to keep quiet about her home affairs and she could stay on.

Now I have 52 women besides the children and the teachers, and a good part of them are "guests"—non paying. The Board gave me $585 Mex. for the whole year—about $150 gold to run the school or close it. Three people on the Executive Committee wanted to close it. The treasurer for lack of funds, one Modernist woman missionary for theological reasons, and one young pastor who is a "smart alec." The Chinese women got together in an all day prayer meeting, 60 women, and prayed the school into a new year of existence, and now more women and better have entered than for a long time.

Some special gifts have come already—the last mail $30 gold—the mail before $425—and some local gifts. Very few of these women are Christians and they are as raw as possible. One is being cured of itch, others of trachoma [a contagious bacterial infection of the eye]. But my little nurse is wonderful. She said that she came back to me as a "prodigal to her old home" and there is nothing that she will not do to help me.

To-day is Saturday and in the afternoon I do not have to be on duty so am writing in my favorite position—on my back. Old high blood pressure bothers me at times.

On my birthday Donald and Catherine and Mr. and Mrs. Christian had two tables—20 guests for a Chinese feast at the Christians'. I told them to absolutely cut out anything this year, as we are all too poor, but Chinese-like they could not let pass a year making a decade, especially the 60th year.

My garden has improved a lot since I wrote you. I now have cabbage, lettuce, parsnips, onion, kale, carrots, radishes, turnips, kohlrabi, beets, celery and tomatoes—and beans and asparagus coming on. I have almost enough for the Woman's School. Over in the school yard we have several kinds of Chinese vegetables and Swiss chard and New Zealand spinach. I just planted the corn this week. Frost killed our papayas. There was so little frost it could hardly be noticed but they simply fell right to the ground. This garden is my life-saver. I work in it for rest.

The City is full of soldiers, but "Nationals," so we are once again under the central government. There seems to be reason to think that affairs may remain quiet for a time.

Hundreds of soldiers march past our house every day marching to hymn tunes—"Glory, Glory, Hallelujah," the "Year of Jubilee," etc. Last week a state funeral was given to the late Admiral Yang and as the cortege passed our house the band was playing "Nearer My God to Thee". He was an exceptionally ardent Buddhist and all the monastery priests were waiting to receive his coffin at the end of the cement road and carry it to the monastery up in the mountains. He had no son, nor wife, in the procession but an auto of concubines. The coffin was in a truck, and the truck was covered with a canopy that was most elaborate, and there were thousands of marines and soldiers marching, and with hundreds of beautiful silk banners. When my admiral, Chen Shao-Kwan, has a state funeral I hope that it will be Christian. But he will not be able to manage that.

This 1934 year I am going to stop working on Foochow College and get my own work back into shape. Donald is well again, Catherine and the baby are all right; the Board has put Donald and the dean on the payroll again. When I arrived a year ago, Donald and the school were on the ragged edge. Donald was mad and sick and the Board was cutting off all finances.

I wrote letters and documents for Donald and did a good many other things to get Foochow College on its feet, which only the Lord and I know, and which Donald has a slight appreciation of. The Treasurer had advocated the closing of the college and the Board was glad to get rid of that expense.

Last week the treasurer said in a business meeting that, "the Board had committed itself to closing Foochow College but Donald's letters had completely changed the situation." That made me feel we had gained this hard fought battle *in fact*, not just guess work—and that I got to Foochow again just in the nick of time. Now the same Treasurer advocated closing the Woman's School—wrote the Board to do so. The Board sent out the appropriation in a lump sum to the Executive Committee. This committee is largely these same greedy old pastors. They never cut their salaries but cut the Woman's School from $1,000 a year to $585.

My expenses are about $150 a month or $1,800 a year Mex. After that all day prayer meeting even the garden seemed to grow better and money is coming in and we will not close up until things are far worse than they are now. If this Bible school were closed it would be a blow to the women's work of the whole mission. I am still Irish enough to revive when a real fight is on.

Nana

FOOCHOW, CHINA   MARCH 18, 1934

Dear Sister,

The newspaper tells more of last night's fire that swept over the island in the river and completely burned down all the houses. The tide was out and no boats could get to shore and no one could wade through the deep mud. Some tried and failed, so the island was swept clean. Two men on a new launch that was under construction got into a quarrel and got off the launch to settle the trouble and left a small boy on the boat with a candle as a light, and he went to sleep and the candle fell into some oil—and to-day hundreds are without a home!

Love to all from,   Nana

"My ears ring just like an acetylene lamp sizzling,
every conscious moment."

FOOCHOW, CHINA   MAY 31, 1934

Dear Anna,

I'm glad to know that you do not have high blood pressure. You can tell that yourself. My ears ring just like an acetylene lamp sizzling, all the time, day and night, every conscious moment. It makes me terribly discouraged sometimes, but I decided that I wasn't going to say anything about it, not keep harping about. People soon get tired of other folk's ills.

. . .

It is hard to buy curios now. The Japanese have bought everything up.

Lots of love to all from,   Martha

FOOCHOW, CHINA   JUNE 8, 1934

Dear Sister Belle,

To-day we heard that the Communists got into the city south of Foochow, and killed and tortured the Christians and carried some of the women off in the mountains. That is their usual procedure—to carry off the women. Now the Nationalists will have to chase after them. Some of the Communist party is shut up here in the soldiers' barracks. They are a vicious lot. The reason that an army cannot get them is that when they are pursued they all scatter. Some go back to their shops and fields, and others take to the mountains, and others to fishing boats, and they are at once a part of the population, which an army cannot collect. I do hope that we can get through the summer without such scares as we had last summer, and at the end rushed down the mountain ready to take a steamer.

Yours with love to all,   Martha

"I am writing to the accompaniment of machine gun fire.
Tomorrow we will get the facts—from the milkman."

[unknown recipient]   FOOCHOW, CHINA   AUGUST 7, 1934

To-day I am writing to the accompaniment of machine gun fire and larger field gun firing. For several days there have been disturbing rumors and the sound of some firing in the distance, but to-day it is much more distinct. Ten bombing planes are operating at present, near enough for us to hear their explosions and also the firing from the planes. Just now a cannonade was very near.

Donald came up this morning and reported that all was quiet, and before evening this heavy fighting so near! One never knows what a day will bring forth. A gang of Communists several thousand strong, starved out of the N.E. part of the province, started to Foochow and on Sunday was only fifteen miles from the City, but there must have been a dash for Foochow or we would not hear the firing so near. Airplanes were scouting about this morning very near our house here on the mountain and evidently found something.

Personally I do not have the least idea that we will be disturbed. We have gone through these times so often that the thrill is all gone. Tomorrow morning we will get the facts—from the *milk-man* who comes up from the City! It does seem that Chiang Kai-shek could clean up the Communist element in the province without so much delay.

It is now dark and the firing continues. Airplanes have just gone over our Kuliang houses so near that it seemed they would surely scrape the roofs. The latest is that a lot of discharged soldiers were trying to get into the City. Unless it is too hot we shall sleep as peaceful as usual. More firing! If the troops can aim at all, there will be many casualties on that ridge just beyond here.

This forenoon Mrs. Christian and her household and I gave a morning "coffee" for 20 friends. The ladies brought their knitting and there was no lack of conversation with so much trouble everywhere.

Good-night,   Martha Wiley

FOOCHOW, CHINA   DECEMBER 6, 1934

Dear Anna,

You are probably on your way to St. Charles this week and will have given everybody a good stirring up in Yakima, as well as a good time. I was certainly glad to get your long letters and read them over and over again.

The lacquer firm has sent the boxes of lacquer. If it is too late to sell without a lot of trouble, just stack it away until next year. If it can be sold it will be a great help to the work here, but if not, do not bother very much about it.

The list that I am sending is just a guide in fixing prices, but the firm gave me a very big reduction—they are hard up, too. If things can be sold for approximately these prices in gold we will not lose anything. If some things are not in demand, let them go cheaper.

Happy Christmas to all the A's and B's—

from,   Nana

"If a thing cannot be changed by good will, then there is nothing left but to endure the trouble or go in for a row."

FOOCHOW, CHINA   JANUARY 18, 1935

Dear Sister,

Just a month ago, Mrs. Beard was pitched out of a ricksha and struck her face on a pile of stones by the road side. This resulted in having the bones of her nose fractured just between her eyes. Mrs. Christian did the entertaining of the prayer meeting group for her that month.

This week Mrs. Christian was pitched out on a busy street. Her right arm was dislocated and the top of the bone that goes into the socket was crushed. Mrs. Beard's nose had got down to normal and she entertained for Mrs. Christian this month.

What a gang has been in to see me this day! When I see a person heading toward my door I know that a problem has arrived. I had a rumpus with a neighbor. He put a sink hole near the well and spoiled one of our wells, then he rowed around and said that our drainage went into his sink hole.

We have some of the meanest neighbors that could be imagined. One is sort of a detective and he is "some pumpkins." One is determined to spit down into our yard onto the women's washing. When I am in the yard he gets his head in but otherwise he puts his head out of the window and calls names and spits. A person is absolutely helpless in such a case. If a thing cannot be changed by good will, then there is nothing left but to endure the trouble or go in for a row. We cannot round up the cow and put her in a pen as you did when you were bothered.

January 19 —— If you were here I would go with you for a long bus ride this cold, sunny day. One can go most of the length of the province now by bus. The progress in road making is one of the surprises to all travelers now.

Much love to all the home folks,   Martha

***"It seems that my Admiral Chen Shao-kwan got mad
and resigned from the Navy."***

FOOCHOW, CHINA   FEBRUARY 10, 1935

Dear Sister Anna,

It seems that my Admiral Chen Shao Kwan got mad and resigned from the Navy. It seems that he gave an order that Captains and all others of lower rank were to have some special training in navigation to bring them up to date. Two Captains did not wish to study and stirred up a row and Chen resigned as Admiral and Minister to the Navy.

I wrote him to "get back to his job!" Cheeky, wasn't it? But as I was his benefactor when he was a little fellow I felt that I had a right to speak my mind. But he did not go back until he got those Captains out of the Navy and on land in some civil job. It is rumored that he will come to Fukien and clean up the province. I was surprised that he planned to return to his native province.

Got stopped here, as a woman with a nine-year-old girl came to see me and the youngster kept picking *things* off her hair and kept me wondering if one of them would fly over to my newly washed hair. The child looked about my room and whispered to her mother, "So beautiful!" Hard on her heels came a group of women from a distant village. One woman had lost a son and a daughter in the same week of a fever and her husband died soon after, so this woman took the heavy silver hairpins from her hair, pawned them for two dollars, and bought raw opium with which to commit suicide. Someone saw her and seized the opium. And now her father-in-law wants to sell her. She is 31 years old and refuses to be re-married. So HERE she comes! I am glad to take her in and help her find comfort in the GOSPEL and in women who really care for her. The best part of our work is to bind up the broken hearts.

I wish that you might see the big lantern parade going by under my window just now. Huge! Gorgeous! Marvelous!

Much love to each, Good-night,   Martha

"I must keep on until it seems the square thing to withdraw."

FOOCHOW, CHINA FEBRUARY 23, 1935

Dearest Doris,

I introduced the woman who tried to kill herself with opium to a bath tub and soap and then to a good hair wash and started her to washing her clothes. Next day I gave her a grubbing hoe and told her to get busy digging up the garden. She went about it as though she were making embroidery. I suggested that she "pep up" a bit and she answered that, "since her children had died she devoted herself to weeping". She has been here a week and she looks a different woman. She is able to smile feebly, help cook the rice, give a smashing blow with a grubbing hoe, and read a few sentences in the Gospel primer.

I wrote you a lot about the Foochow College Primary School building that Donald and Catherine worked so hard to collect money for. Now, the contract has been let and the trench for the foundation is just about finished, at a cost of $7,500 Mex. About $2,000 has to be gathered up yet, but they needed the building so much that they had to begin, for the students were dropping off because of the old building. The raising of money dollar by dollar has been a great strain on all of us.

Yesterday was our Anti-Cobweb Society and it was held at the English Mission Compound. This is a monthly affair and deals with some live topic and is usually well worth attending. Yesterday the speakers took up the "Three Principles" of Dr. Sun, and the New Life Principles of Chiang Kai shek. These addresses were made by English speaking Chinese. One address was made by a missionary. Every one goes early and has time for tea and a social hour.

. . .

Sometimes I think that I must give up this work and then when I see the need of the women I take fresh courage and go on again. But each year is harder than the previous one and I've just passed my 61st milestone! Missionaries are fewer, more work demanded, and no money to do it with—but the Lord still lives—therefore I must keep on until it appears to be the square thing to withdraw.

With much love to you and Belle,   Martha

"What to do without creating a panic was the question."

FOOCHOW, CHINA MAY 22, 1935

Dear Mrs. Slipp:

One of the worst experiences of a life of trying experiences came to pass this month. One of our students had a queer eruption and I sent her to a foreign hospital and to a foreign doctor thinking that she had some form of venereal disease but the doctor said there was nothing the matter with the girl. I waited a little to see if the matter cleared up, but as it did not I sent her to a Chinese doctor and he made a microscopic exam and the disease proved to be leprosy.

What to do without creating a panic was the question. I had to send up to the mountain chapel to get the Bible woman who had brought the girl. When she came she was utterly broken up at this disaster, for the sake of the girl, and also for the blame that would come down on her head from parents of the other students.

She and I packed up the girl's things and got her started homeward with the Bible woman and one of the servants, and I did the disinfecting. The school did not get an inkling of what was the matter until my gossiping gate woman voiced her suspicions, but by that time the danger of a panic in the school was averted. While the Bible woman was taking the girl home, I went to the leper village and saw what could be done for her there. The school nurse was terribly frightened as she had had so much contact with her, but she went with me to the village and we arranged to have a place repaired for her and thoroughly cleaned. I sent the furniture that she had used in the school, and her registration fee and rent and various charges for other things, and then the Bible woman and the parents of the girl took her there to stay and have the Chaulmoogra injections once a week at the Anglican hospital.

Give my regards to your family and much love to your good self,   Martha

"He planned to marry her at once and sell her
into a Buddhist nunnery."

FOOCHOW, CHINA   MAY 23, 1935

Dear Anna,

Yesterday I went to a wedding of one our Woman's School girls. The bride is a girl that I took in five years ago and wrote you the story of her troubles. She was a field girl who had to swim the canal in the mornings to get to her field work. The sister of the man she was engaged to went with her. One day the tide took the other girl under and drowned her, and then the man said that this girl had a demon pursuing her, and he planned to marry her at once and then sell her into a Buddhist nunnery.

The bridegroom is one of our mission boys, now an army doctor, and they met several times before the engagement was really made, and both seem well satisfied.

Her friends came in here to get the bride's bouquet. They picked just what they wanted, and when we saw the creation we wondered. It had Easter lilies and sunflowers and phlox and red roses and asparagus tops and heavenly bamboo all strung together.

Lots of love to all from,   Martha

"It has been surprising how well the mandate has been enforced."

FOOCHOW, CHINA   NOVEMBER 4, 1935

Dear Home Folks,

The Saturday following this past week we had to get ready for a wedding. Donald's young brother who is in the Navy turned up and announced he had a month's leave of absence and had come home to be married. He was engaged to this girl four or more years ago, and he has sent money right along to keep her in the Woman's School. Now she has had four and half years of study and has become a Christian and was baptized and joined the church, and is a very good little housekeeper.

On Saturday at 5 o'clock the ceremony took place in our living room with palms and many lovely flowers and potted plants for decorations. The bride was just as pretty and sweet as a bride should be, with a long veil that kept two or three persons busy to keep in order. The groom wore a black "tux" and was dolled up to look fine. Well, I just stood there during the ceremony and reviewed the past.

The boy had no other home but mine for the years of his life beginning at three and lasting till he went in the Navy. I nursed him through typhoid, had his tonsils removed and adenoids, tried to educate him, tried to bring him up a Christian, had to take him with me through the summers and give him special food, and had no small task in the problem of discipline. When Donald graduated from Yenching he tried to take him in charge, then when Donald went to America this boy went to the Navy and enlisted.

He was soon a very good bugler and was bugler on Admiral Chen's flag ship during the stirring times on the Yangtse, then took signaling and was promoted to the radio service, and is now in the Admiralty in Nanking in the radio office of Admiral Chen, and sends out and receives the Admiral's telegrams.

November 5 —— Yesterday I saw a Chinese woman smoking on the street – the first instance for more than a year. Chiang Kai shek vetoed that almost two years ago and it has been surprising how well the mandate has been enforced. It would be a good thing for the women of the U.S.A. to have a few Chiang Kai sheks in power.

The end of the day and the end of the paper seem to coincide so I will have to close this sheet and get my sleepy self to bed.

Sincerely yours,   Martha Wiley

"I asked him to arrange an 'audience' with
Madame Chiang Kai shek."

NANKING HOTEL   NANKING, CHINA   FEBRUARY 17, 1936

Dear Anna,

I mailed a letter to you telling of my travels up to the point of arriving at Kirakiang, several hundred li up the Yenztse. When our boat got there it had to wait until other boats got away from the dock. Mr. Wong and his wife and their personal rickshas were waiting for us. Mr. Wong came out in the river on the Hsia Petroleum Company's launch and met us there, but the customs would not let us off until we docked.

Away we went, far out into the suburbs to the Wong estate with two large foreign houses, a big pond with boats, a soy factory and large gardens. His office in the APA is down on the dock. Evidently he owns most of the suburb real estate.

It was Saturday P.M. when we arrived, and as soon as discreet we began our propaganda for Foochow College. He was just interested in me as his old teacher but not especially in his old school. The Hsuehs and I unfolded the needs of Foochow College that evening.

That Sunday we had a great dinner and all P.M. I continued my screed on Foochow College. Monday morning Mr. Wong decided to take us to Kuling, a summer resort in the mountains. Off we all started at 8 A.M. by auto to the foot of the hills. There Mr. Wong had a cottage, but he took us to Journey's End Hotel, a little place tucked in the fold of the hills, and the manager is an Englishman who made a million and a half in the APA and then lost it all in speculation in stocks in Shanghai. His wife and daughter went to England and he and his son are in this wilderness. He looks dirty and discouraged. Every vase in the room was full of dead flowers. The pots of dead plants stood in the rooms, and icicles adorned the eaves. It was a weird place. Mr. Wong was just introducing us to his distinguished English friend—then on we went up the hills for four hours.

At noon Mr. Wong had two tables of guests (20) in his downstairs drawing room, where there is a stove. About half were M. E. missionaries, and in the middle of the twenty courses Mr. Wong got up and made a speech about his old teacher, and if you had heard it you would know what a nice person "Uoi-Su-Gu" is! I'll venture to say none of us has ever attended such a swell feast. His adopted daughter, 19 years old, planned the menu. Frog livers, of frogs shipped from Manchuria; great bowls of duck tongues; shark fins; and bird-nests. Our glasses were kept filled with grape juice—no wine. I had to make a speech at the end of this entertainment.

Mr. Wong came from his office early and I had a chance for a confidential talk, which was my effort for Foochow College—still no promise. We packed up that evening and planned to take the boat the next morning. Mr. Wong said that he would see to our tickets, as he had to go to his office anyway, which was near. We were all reduced to utter humiliation at our failure. We were ready for tears. Mr. Wong put us on the steamer that I had arrived on, but every cabin was full, so we all went ashore and clambered on to another, a China Merchants steamer, and found that Mr. Wong had paid the fare for all of us to Nanking. But still we were crushed. About half an hour before the boat sailed I said, "Senghu, just what do you want me to say when the Shanghai students ask about your interest in Foochow College?"

He replied that he would be responsible for $10,000 endowment in honor of his mother, and as soon as I got to Foochow he would begin by remitting $500!!! I just began to stutter. After all the nervous strain, I'm afraid I shed a few tears.

We got to Nanking, and in the morning Mr. Ding took us to the Metropole Hotel to lunch—the grand hotel of the capital city. Mr. Ding is one of my old students. He really is, in rank, governor of two provinces, but is called Control Commissioner. I sat at his right and Admiral Chen on my left. C. J. Wang and other celebrities were at the table not far from us. It was most interesting to be with these old "boys" who were now such fine men and in responsible places.

After this dinner Commissioner Ding sent us home to where Dr. and Mrs. Hinman were staying. At 6 P.M. we had a dinner engagement with Mr. Chang, principal of Madame Chiang Kai shek's school for orphan children of soldiers. It seemed queer to me that children of common soldiers should be brought up in such luxury. Probably propaganda to let soldiers think that if they die in battle their children will be better off than if the father had lived.

This Mr. Chang is one of my old students and has nothing like the ability and culture of Donald, but he gets $330 per month and all furnished—other teachers accordingly. This is Madame's pet. Catherine was invited to Madame Feng's to luncheon and the rest were invited to the Admiralty for luncheon with Admiral Chen. What fine taste in all his apartments. After the way those upstarts in Shanghai treated us this brought back my self-respect.

Sunday morning Admiral Chen brought his nephew, who is adopted by him, to call on me. This is a very inadequate hotel to receive a distinguished guest, but I managed a cake and tea in a private sitting room, to receive the two greatest men in China. I asked him to "grant the audience" to Catherine and Donald at 3 P.M. today to tell him about Foochow College, also to arrange an "audience" for Donald and me with Madame Chiang Kai shek for the same purpose.

February 19 —— Catherine pulled a contribution out of Madame Feng, and had an interview with Madame Chiang Kai shek. Today she and I will get a letter and our publicity material to Madame Chiang. Donald will see the Vice-Commissioner of Communications. Tomorrow—if it is not storming we will go to Wuhu. It is 9 o'clock and the Hsuehs have not stirred yet. They are tired out. I get up pretty early and get a bath before the amah appears or she makes me pay a fee—I can turn the water on cheaper than that. No towels or sheets in this hotel, but lots of spittoons.

We have all suffered for our precious school. I do not know what more we could have done to create interest among the Alumni and old students.

Love,   Martha

"I pay a watchman to patrol our street
from 11 P.M. until daylight."

FOOCHOW, CHINA   MAY 8, 1936

Dear Sister Belle,

Just now we are all agog about thieves. Practically all the houses of foreigners have been entered in the last three months and their goods stolen. The thieves burn a hole around the lock and remove it and get in that way. Our premises, the school, had three or four such visitations last term, but this term, none yet. The thieves especially want men's clothing. Most all the American Board compound have lost their overcoats.

My puppy is going to be no good as a watch dog so I am trying to give him away. He is just a "play-dog." The Hsuehs' dog is better than mine, and another Chinese dog in the school is learning to bark at strangers, but this pedigree spaniel is just no good.

I might mention that, besides the dogs, I pay a watchman to patrol our street from 11 P.M. until daylight. My share is $2 a month and a street full of neighbors make up the rest.

We are all so grateful that the hot weather is delaying its arrival. This year there is an intercalary fourth moon, and the Chinese say, that holds up the weather for a month. That is, we have two Mays to make the calendar come out right at the end of the year. I hope that Earl and Myron and their families are getting along all right and that for them the Depression is over—or at least the worst of it. Will the Woodhouse boys vote for F.D.R. this next election? From the papers he is losing votes pretty fast—but how can he be defeated with so many voters on the payroll? His pictures look like a big smart aleck to me. I'm sorry I cannot vote against him. I'll trust you to do that. And Eleanor! Did you read what Alice said about them? When she thought of Frank and Eleanor in the White House she felt like grinding her teeth to powder and blowing them out of her nose!

Write when your garden interests give you time.

Much love to all the family,   Martha

"She became melancholy and tried to kill herself by taking Lysol."

KULIANG FOOCHOW, CHINA   AUGUST 20, 1936

Dear Belle,

Perhaps Anna wrote you that I had an accident—fell down on some of these steep steps and got up with a compound fracture of my right wrist. So I have done but little writing up to this week. Now I am trying to catch up with my correspondence by writing with my left hand, and it is terribly slow.

I still have a cast from my elbow to my knuckles and it is so heavy that my arm is tired out all the time. Catherine has combed my hair all summer, but the rest of my personal needs I could look after myself. The cast will be taken off this week and then I will be free of this weight, even though I will not have much use of my hand for a while longer. It is very inconvenient not to be able to sew or sign my name.

Yesterday all the foreign children were at play on the club lawn, and the three Hsueh children were among the group, when a crazy woman led a water buffalo onto the lawn. The cow swooped at a man with her long horns and sent him sprawling and then she tried to tramp on him. He dodged under her and she started for the next and struck little Billy Bishop, the son of the new missionaries who work for Miss Hartwell. She missed him with her horns, but began to tramp him and skinned his back badly before she could be beaten off. The three Hsuehs came running up the hill, yelling but unhurt.

Mrs. Kiu, one of my teachers, has an adopted sister who was taking nurse's training in Shanghai, and she became melancholy and tried to kill herself by taking Lysol, so the hospital sent her back to Foochow, and I am having a time to keep Mrs. Kiu from bringing her into the Woman's School. I had two years of nerve strain from having one teacher's husband parked in the Woman's School, and every so often he would go violent and want to kill someone. This girl wants to kill herself and the canal is right at the front door, altogether too convenient, so I have notified Mrs. Kiu that she cannot come to the school, but since I am on the mountain and not at the front gate, I understand that the girl has been brought to the compound. I will have to read the riot act.

After the civil war began in South China, General and Madame Chiang Kai-shek did not come to Foochow. The City spent $50,000 to fix up a place grand enough for them to live in, and everybody had to have their compound walls whitewashed at their personal expense to welcome the illustrious ones, so the bill for whitewashing will come down on my head when I go down the mountain.

Senator Bingham's son has come to the mission with his young wife. The young wife is the daughter of Foochow missionaries. They are awfully nice youngsters. It is strange that young man should land in a mission field, as he has so much money. His mother was a Tiffany of New York, famous for the jewelry store. He is a very quiet, kindly chap.

Much love to all the family,   Martha

*"We never tire of watching the thousands of little crabs
running around down there like little Fords."*

[letter from Leona Burr]
SHARP PEAK   AUGUST 27, 1936

Dear Miss Wiley:

I was about to write you as we end up our restful, happy life in your house, when your note of the 24th came.

We are leaving here Tuesday, September 1st, by launch with the Christians and Miss Plumb and will get to the city in the P.M. If you and Mrs. Hsueh and the little girls come down here the next day, we could leave everything clean and ready for you to step into. We would leave the dishes out and in every respect you could see how we have arranged the things as you wished to. I think it would be a fine way for you to end the summer if you do this. The water is holding out very well—plenty, in fact. We are leaving the two little lamps that we bought and the washboard and some other things. The chimneys to your big lamps broke or cracked first and then slowly fell apart as we sat by them. We used them very little and the chimneys seemed very thin. We shall not put the braces at the doors but tell the woman that you will be coming so it will be easy for you to open up the house. I think you can get word to me whether or not you are certainly coming. Otherwise we would shut things up as securely as we found them.

All summer as I came and went up the hill to the house, I picked up cones, branches and scraps of twigs and put them in the fireplace, where on the last Sunday night, I was going to have a fire and a real ceremony of parting with the most restful summer of my life. The days have been so hot that I am doubtful that we can endure a fire even to burn up my answered letters so if you find a colorful lot of material for a quick fire when you get here, you will know that that was one plan, too impractical to be carried out. You may find it just right to do before you leave.

We have liked the beach below this house best of all. It is wide and so gradual that it seems perfect. No matter if it is called "Dead Man's Beach," it is a wrong term, for the floor of the beach is as hard as marble and we never tired of watching the thousands of little crabs running around down there like little Fords. We made a path down there that takes just ten minutes from the house. We go down to the regular place for company's sake sometimes.

It has been like a game watching who actually got to come after planning to rent a room up here with us. One student was packed to come when his mother got Typhoid fever. Another could not come for financial reasons. The sick boy could not come at all because his fever has fluctuated all summer and he could not leave the hospital. So I have received $15 from Dr. and Miss Wang (Union Hospital) who spent three weeks here. One student spent two weeks and paid $5, which makes $20 in all, which lacks considerable of being $50. Miss Loland wrote that she certainly would come and then did not write again nor show up. So I am adding $10 to make it up somewhat, paying $60 as I said I could if necessary for it has been so good to be here. I am writing a check for this amount, having paid my $50 to you in June.

I have worn, almost every morning, the pajama suit you gave me. The trousers were too long, and I am not modern enough to wear trousers in the day time so I turned them bottom side up and made a skirt, and with the jacket, it has made a perfectly comfortable morning rig. I seem to remember much that you have given me all these years so I am very glad to pay some extra rent for your grand house. I hope that if you do rent it next year that you can get the full amount. Mrs. Diamond asked me what the rent was and I said $200. She was greatly impressed with the bigness and fine water supply, etc.

If I see you in Foochow, I can tell you some funny things too, but for now, this closes with a hope that you do come and enjoy the house while it is clean and while the weather is fine.

As ever,   Leona Burr

"The coolies fell down and rolled me out of the chair."

FOOCHOW, CHINA   SEPTEMBER 10, 1936

Dear Anna,

Last Sunday I took a terrible pain that I could not conquer, and after three days and nights I took a sedan chair and started down the mountain to the hospital. On the way the coolies fell down and rolled me out of the chair—and with my broken wrist in a cast! I felt abused. I had three days in the hospital with all kinds of tests to prove that I had appendicitis, but ALL signs failed and I came back to my room in the City with a little bottle of dilute hydrochloric acid, in exchange for my cheque for all that monkey work in the clinic.

Did I tell you that when Admiral Chen heard that I had broken my wrist he sent me a long telegram regretting the accident and that, too, when he was on his way to Kwangsi to help General Chiang. He is a thoughtful, kind-hearted lad and I love him just as I do Donald.

Love from,   Martha

"I found that bandits were cutting down our trees, quite large ones."

FOOCHOW, CHINA   NOVEMBER 26, 1936

Dear Doris,

I wanted to go to the Peak for a change. Last Friday I told the cook that we would leave the house the next morning at 6 o'clock to catch the boat. We got down the river to a place called Guang-tau by 10 o'clock and then had a hard time to get a sampan to take us the four miles to Sharp Peak. The wind and tide were against us and it took four hours to get across. If the wind is good, one hour is plenty of time. We got up to the castle by 3 o'clock and all had to pitch in and open up the house and sun the mattresses and then get the dishes out from the attic where they are locked, and fill the lamps, etc.

I found that bandits were cutting down the trees, quite large ones, and so I had to tramp around the hill to see how many stumps there were freshly cut, and then had to blow up at the care taker and arrange a meeting with the head of the village to see if this could be stopped.

Everybody in Sharp Peak was busy cutting sweet potatoes and putting them out to dry for winter use instead of rice. The hills were a busy scene all Sunday. So we had a change, but it consisted of three days that were most tiresome.

Lots of love from,   Nana

"He convinced his captors that they must all work together if China is to be saved."

[letter from George Hinman]   DECEMBER 27, 1936

A CHRISTMAS MESSAGE FROM CHINA

My Dear Friend:

Such a wonderful Christmas we have just experienced! At the end of the two most anxious weeks of suspense, at last came the dramatic relief on the afternoon of Christmas, when the radio told us that General Chiang had been released and had flown back to his headquarters in Loyang, Honan province, from the city of Sian, in Shensi province, where he had been held by the rebel troops of General Chiang Hsueh Liang, son of the old governor in Manchuria.

Of course everyone was anxious and troubled about the fate of the one whom it was hoped might be the deliverer of China, and the thought of this situation and what it might mean for the country colored all the thoughts and the prayers of the Christmas celebrations. It had been thirteen days since General Chiang had been surrounded by rebel troops and seized, after a large part of his personal body guard had been killed. There had been a great wave of excitement in Foochow when a false rumor of his release came.

Every day we looked anxiously for news. The Central Government was pushing a punitive expedition to surround and overcome the rebels, and at the same time Madame Chiang and her brother T.V. Soong were using every effort to secure the personal release of General Chiang before his life should be still further imperiled.

When all could see the strong loyalty and unity of the Chinese people swiftly developing under the strain of the great emergency, then it became for the rebels simply a question of securing the best terms they could for releasing their captive and obtaining their own safety. Apparently, at the end, General Chiang's release was without conditions, he having convinced his captors that they must all work together if China is to be saved. It was a personal spiritual victory for General Chiang, won by his patience, his courage and his loyalty to the established government of China.

Day after day we waited in suspense, but when the news late Christmas afternoon came over the radio in Foochow College, where the students were listening eagerly for some encouragement, there was a quick rush to the street, and parades were started in which all the schools were soon participating.

The celebrations of the day after Christmas, beginning with the great assembly of all the students, ended with a monster lantern and torch light procession, in which perhaps eighteen thousand students, soldiers, police and firemen took part, while probably a hundred and fifty thousand people lined the streets. There was an incessant roar of firecrackers and the illumination at the South Gate was a dazzling globe of brilliance. Saturday night and Sunday morning the papers reported everything in full, making a special feature of the address by an American expressing the good will of the western nations.

Cordially yours,   George Warren Hinman

"A few drops of hydrochloric acid in a glass of water at meals,
and no more pain in my stomach."

FOOCHOW, CHINA   DECEMBER 28, 1936

Dear Anna,

I want you to consult a doctor about the use of dilute hydrochloric acid. Since I was told to take it I have found out that most old people have to take it—that part of the stomach secretions fail as we get old and it has to be supplied. Mr. Christian went to the hospital in Hong Kong thinking that he had cancer of the stomach; he had such pain after every meal. He was there three months and came home well—with a little bottle of hydrochloric acid! I had a week of those tests and have been taking the hydrochloric acid, a few drops in a glass of water at meals, and no more pain in my stomach. It stops all the fermentation that creates "heartburn" and acute acidity. It will be no harm to investigate and may just be what you and William need.

. . .

Admiral Chen always writes or sends a card but he considers his $500 a year to Foochow College as a gift to me. He still thinks that I am in Foochow College.

Love from,   Nana

"Risking even life itself for the peace and progress of China."

[letter from Catherine]   DECEMBER 29, 1936

Madame Chiang Kai-shek,
Nanking.

Dear Madame:

My associates on the faculty and all the students of Foochow College wish me to tell you of their great joy at the release of our great and beloved leader, and to assure you that all shared with you in the anxiety of those long dark days of waiting, and in the prayers that were offered by all Christians in China for his deliverance.

. . .

Assuring you of the utmost loyalty of the teachers and students of Foochow College, and trusting that many of them may follow the example of Generalissimo Chiang in risking even life itself for the peace and progress of China.

I am,

Faithfully yours,   Catherine Lin Hsueh

"Here I am at Sharp Peak in the 'Gingling' house."

FOOCHOW, CHINA   FEBRUARY 10, 1937

Dear Anna,

Here I am at Sharp Peak in the "Gingling" house. You will see that at last I have found a name for the Kinnear place. "Ging" means Kinnear and "Ling" means forest or woods. Dr. Hinman paced the circumference of the hill as far as he could and figured out five acres, but he reckoned as a flat surface, while the real surface is that of a truncated cone, so I suspect that the number of acres is some more than he estimated. I think that Gingling has a pretty good sound, don't you?

Now, about how we got here. After school closed I got things together, and every old thing that was in the way at the city house I loaded on a launch to bring down here. There was a third of a ton of coal, a big stove that was not being used, 24 baskets of charcoal, a good lot of stove pipe, a big drum that has a place in the middle to heat water, one spring bed, a big tin box for locking things in, water jugs, bedding, provisions for a month, and goodness knows what else that belonged to me.

The personnel were; the cook who was so angry because he had to come that he was not especially helpful. He always carries a coolie load with him if he goes to stay over night; Eu-nguk and her baskets of personal things; two of the big girls of the Woman's School that I am tiding over this vacation, with their rice and vegetables for a month's stay; Donald and Catherine and two children for a little visit and to see the house, with their bedding and food; two masons with their luggage and eats and Catherine's cousin who was sponging a way home for the China New Year, besides the boat crew. And I almost forgot Mr. Faurot, the new teacher.

Martha's summer home given to her by the Kinnears

The weather had been fine for several days, and we thought that it was going to be just the time for us to be off, but that morning when we left the house at 6 A.M. it began to blow a head wind, and most of the way it was terribly rough and our launch was loaded too heavily, and with the high waves and the contrary tide several of the people on the boat were seasick—among the number were Catherine and the children. It kept me busy passing in a crock for the seasick folks and emptying it again. Donald was saying over and over again "de-nguok" which is Chinese for "hell"! Though I could not see just why *he* was any worse off than the others.

When we got to Sharp Peak landing, the waves were so high that the launch could not anchor and just kept turning around and around. We yelled our throats sore to wake up the pirates ashore to come over and take us off in their small boats and finally got some of them to come over. All the seasick ones hopped into the very first rocking canoe and were off to shore, and the rest of us followed as we could along with the cargo.

In the meantime the rain had begun to come down in dead earnest. I sent the cook on ahead with the keys to open the house and get a fire started. He was so rattled, that he could not get the door of the woodshed opened when he did get to the top of the hill. When Mr. Faurot and I arrived, he was standing by the door of the woodshed, regardless of the rain, holding the package of keys out to me. Well, we soon got the door open and had a grand fire of dry wood and later some of the coal that we had brought down. My shoes were soaked through and also my heavy coat, but there was no chance to change until the loads came, and everyone had some hot soup and were drying out their clothes. Donald took a hand and soon had everyone fairly well dried out, but all the time he was saying "chieng-chieng-uang-uang"—ten million bets on it that he would never come down that river in a launch again.

By supper time the house was so cosy, and the supper so good, and the children so happy that no one was concerned over the noise of the waves beating against the cliff behind the house. A good night's sleep was a fine cure for all the discomforts of the day.

The next morning the sun came out and it was a glorious day. The entire group went down to the seaside, and the children gathered moss and shells and came back for lunch so enthusiastic about the lovely place. Even Donald said that he wished that he could stay for a week—and that he was coming again in the spring. Mr. Faurot brought the camera that Mollie gave me ten dollars toward getting, and took some snaps, copies of which I will send you if they turn out well.

Love from,   Nana

"The 'Pool of Blood Temple' was open for business."

FAIRY BRIDGE   FOOCHOW, CHINA   JULY 1, 1937

Dear Home Friends:

Thursday, June 24th —— The school nurse and I planned to make calls, but at 5 A.M. a drizzling rain did not seem encouraging, and at six there was a downpour.

Friday, June 25th —— On our way to the address of a student on our list is the Holy Roller Church. The nurse had never been inside so we stepped in. A preacher just from Borneo looked the traditional part. He showed us a room lined with pictures of thousands of Holy Roller church members throughout the Orient, and said that in his province alone they had more than 100 large congregations. So flourishes an implausible doctrine, and so burns a strange fire!

Across from the church we entered a very narrow alley, looking for a widow and her daughter, and we wound back and forth for so many blocks that I quite lost my sense of direction, but at last we found them sewing busily to earn a living during vacation. The daughter brought us out into the main street by an even more winding route, and as we came into the wide street we faced a sign: "Haik Die Mieu." The "Pool of Blood Temple" was open for business. The nurse was curious to see this phase of Buddhist idolatry so we went in.

"But where is the 'pool of blood?' May we see it?" A man drew back a curtain made of dirty sacks and we peered into a room so dark that it took a minute or more to be able to see that the walls were lined with idols and that in the middle of the room was a stone trough about eight feet long by four feet wide and perhaps four feet high, and around the foot of it a stone ledge. It was level full of water that looked black and sticky—and it is under *this* that the souls of women who die in childbirth are supposed to be held until ransomed by the prayers of relatives, and by offerings cast into the water, and by beating the head on the ledge until the blood flows. Sacred motherhood, for the supreme sacrifice, so punished!

On Canal Street we made several calls, stopping for a few minutes at the home of a lovely girl who was married a few months ago to a man who beats her cruelly—no "extreme mental cruelty" this, but just old-fashioned beating with no Reno in the distance.

June 26 —— Heavy rains again. The Bible Women came in for the last monthly meeting of the first half year, but had to hurry home at once as the floods began to rise so fast that they feared being caught separated from their families. As we stood on the hill we looked down on the Foochow Plain transformed into a lake. The farms that a week ago had waving rice fields are now utterly desolate. Fishermen were dragging nets over the soldiers' drill ground, and sampans were plying back and forth over what are normally busy market streets.

As our house is in the old native city the heat will soon drive us to the hills where we study, teach, write, and prepare for the autumn work.

Your fellow-worker in His service,   Martha Wiley

Drill ground—old city wall in foreground

"Admiral Chen is having interviews with diplomats and audiences with the rulers of Europe."

FOOCHOW, CHINA   JULY 30, 1937

Dear Sister,

Donald has just come out of the military training camp. Last summer he was in a local camp and this summer he had to go to Kiu-kiang in Central China and has had a terribly stiff lot of training. He has lost all his fat and looks thin and tired and old. He had just one day with his family and then went down to the City for the entrance examinations of the College for the fall term. Lots of the men who were in the camp fainted and were carried off the drill ground, but Donald did not get to that point.

One trip was a 30 mile trip up and down the mountains in the boiling sun with only four little biscuits to eat, and in the middle of the trip they had to stand at attention for two hours in the sun, without hats, on very sloping ground. When a man fell out from sunstroke or exhaustion the Red Cross soldiers were there to carry him off. Donald says that in spite of everything he feels better than when he went away.

Admiral Chen is still in Europe, and we see in the papers where he is having interviews with diplomats and audiences with the rulers of Europe. H. H. Kung is doubtless doing what he can in the U.S. for the financial support of China during this crisis. No matter what subject we begin to talk about, we always get back to the present war conditions.

Much love to all the Wileys and Woodhouses from,   Martha

"In case I ever write anything in code it will be postscript."

FOOCHOW, CHINA   AUGUST 1, 1937

Dear Jean,

Just now Catherine is going down the hill to Foochow, to consult with Donald as to what to do if the daily expected invasion of Foochow takes place. The children are standing on the crest of the hill watching her depart and the smallest is crying for her mother. *Jittery* is the word for all of us.

It is almost unbelievable that another "Ethiopia" could take place soon but it seems to be coming. I am going to get off all the letters that I can this week, for no telling when the Japanese will be in Foochow and the first thing that they take over is the Post Office, and then censor all the mail.

I wonder what you hear in the U.S. Do send me the clippings from the dailies, as I want to see what is going on in the minds of Americans in regard to the Orient. Today is very cloudy and a thick fog hangs over the mountains and comes into our rooms and dampens everything, but it is nothing to the cloud over the people. Every time Catherine speaks of the conditions of China and the army she begins to weep. Even the children go about quiet and subdued.

We hear by radio that Frank wanted to bring all the U.S. soldiers out of Tientsin [the first city occupied by invading Japanese troops]. Would he defend his own capital if the Japanese should sometime decide to hold night manoeuvres in the suburbs? I wonder. What a slaughter of civilians it was in Tientsin because they could not be given refuge in the other foreign concessions. The Italians refused to give them refuge.

It is said that an ultimatum has been given to Foochow, and it is not unlikely that bombing will begin if it is not agreed to soon. In that case, just what the foreigners will do is a question that time will settle, as the Americans are not approved of by Japan.

The wonderful library in Nang-kai University in Tientsin was burned, along with all its books—the best library in China, it is said. This morning an airplane circled over us, maybe a Japanese scouting plane and maybe just a Chinese passenger plane—but no matter which, it keeps the population on the alert.

In case I ever write anything in code it will be postscript. In the first word read every other letter, beginning at the first—in the second every other letter beginning at the last—in the third every other letter beginning at the second letter of the word—in the fourth every other letter beginning at the end of the word—then begin the same routine all over. In Manchuria it is impossible to get any letters out without censoring and that may soon be so in Foochow, if it turns into a major war. Very likely this is nonsense, but no telling!

August 2 —— We are all in a perspiration about our bank accounts. If Japan takes over Fukien the currency will deflate to nothing. Tell William to wait until November 1st or later to send me the $300.

Martha Wiley

"The truth about China's attitude and activities will be her strongest defense."

[letter from Catherine]

FOOCHOW, AUGUST 10, 1937

My dear friend:

You will want to hear directly from China about the terrible conditions here since the Japanese have started their long-planned drive to take over North China, and make it a second Manchukuo. You have doubtless heard a great deal through the papers; but will want assurance from us here about actual conditions and the plans of the Chinese to meet the Japanese invasion.

There is no question that the Japanese army has determined on securing control of all North China, the five provinces of Hopei and Charhar, and Shantung, Shansi and Shensi (perhaps Honan). The outbreak at the Marco Polo Bridge was not a simple accident. It fitted into a plan, which had been made long before by the Japanese army. They were only waiting for an opportunity. At first the Chinese armies had little success at holding their own; but the Japanese had abundant reserves, which they had all ready to throw into North China. They did not wait for any negotiations, but went right ahead sending troops and ammunition and air planes over. They insisted on having all the troops they could muster quartered on Chinese soil before they would talk terms.

The Chinese insisted that troops of both sides should be withdrawn before negotiations could be carried out on a fair basis, but the Japanese would not hear of withdrawing their troops. They kept moving in new reinforcements. When the Chinese troops objected to the continuous flow of Japanese troops and ammunition, the Japanese thought they were justified in starting "punitive measures," which were absolutely nothing less than aggression to carry out their real purpose to occupy the whole of North China.

It is significant that one of their first acts of aggression was to bomb and set fire to the great Nankai University. Japanese seriously object to the Chinese schools and colleges, where they know the teachers and students are ready to give themselves for their country. You may expect that wherever the Japanese go they will try to control or else destroy the schools. America has a tremendous investment in the schools and hospitals and benevolent institutions of North China. Japan is among other things, very jealous of the influence of America in North China, established and supported by American money.

Here in Foochow we are not in immediate danger, though if the war becomes general it is all together likely that Foochow will be one of the next points the Japanese will attempt to seize. We are directly across from Formosa, and for several years large numbers of Formosans under Japanese protection have come across to Amoy and Foochow to engage in all sorts of illicit business. They have established many pawn shops, which receive stolen goods, and are run in close partnership with gambling dens, opium shops and houses of prostitution. All are under Japanese protection, and the local police dare not interfere.

Chinese and foreigners here have had many serious losses from theft, but there is no recourse. The goods go to, in all probability, one of their pawn shops, but only occasionally can they be recovered, even by paying the shop considerable sums to redeem them. In many parts of Foochow there are Formosan shops, displaying the sign "Foreign Hong (business place)," where opium is sold openly. The police dare not interfere. Before the trouble began even the Japanese consul in Foochow complained of the trouble these Formosan adventurers caused him. But under war conditions they may be extremely useful to the Japanese, just as the renegade Koreans are in North China, now serving as plain clothes spies.

The risk of early occupation of Foochow by the Japanese is shown by preparation of the Fukien government officials to move their offices to a large city up the Min River about a hundred and fifty miles from here. It is probable that the Cantonese armies will strongly garrison Foochow, as it was part of the agreement with the Cantonese government when they were unified with the national administration, that they should take the responsibility for guarding southern Fukien. The Cantonese armies are specially well drilled and efficient, and should give a good account of themselves if the Japanese attempt to come in. Already our local Japanese consul has asked permission to quarter three thousand Japanese troops in the local barracks, and has issued a circular to the foreign community assuring them that they have no territorial ambitions in China.

My husband was called to Kuling this summer with thirty-six hundred military officers, government officials, middle school teachers and principals, for two weeks of intensive military training. They were addressed by General Chiang-Kai-shek, and given special detailed instructions as to the general policy of the government. Each one was asked to sign for a particular service. My husband signed for publicity work, and will try to give out information locally to our foreign friends about actual conditions.

We feel sure of the sympathetic attitude of you all in this crisis of China's life, where all its marvelous progress of the last few years is threatened by the ruthless aggression of the Japanese militarists; but it will be so easy to be deceived about the facts of the conflict. I am sure that the truth about China's attitude and activities will be her strongest defense; so we plan to give ourselves definitely to this work of telling our friends about the shameless premeditated attempt to occupy and control China.

Catherine Lin Siek [Hsueh]

[Note: Siek is Foochow dialect; Hsueh is Mandarin dialect.]

*"Of course the Japanese attitude toward missions in
Formosa, Korea, and Manchuria, is world news."*

FOOCHOW, CHINA   AUGUST 10, 1937

Dear Miss Williams,

You probably get more accurate news in the U.S. than we do right here. The people believe that when Japan goes into the war in earnest she will take all the main ports and that will include Foochow, and then the customs will be Japanese controlled. The narcotic importation could not be worse than it is now with all the smuggling that goes on. But if the Chinese banks have to stop payment, all the paper money will be so deflated that everyone, missionaries and all, will have a hard time to continue. Of course the Japanese attitude toward missions in Formosa, Korea, and Manchuria, is world news.

The small boy that I have had on the mountain is ready to carry the war on single handed! The Hsueh children are also on the defensive. Last week the cook bought a few bananas, and the oldest Hsueh girl informed the family that she would eat no bananas until Japan treated China fairly, and the second child looked very wistful at the banana offered to her, but would not touch it. These bananas come from Formosa.

The beginning of school is a problem, but as my school is comparatively small I shall open at the stated time, unless there is some very definite war condition to prevent. Also women are steadier than the youths in the schools. Donald has a tremendous responsibility these days with 800 plus of inflammable youngsters to keep steady. The introduction of military drill in the schools was deplored greatly, but there is one bit of help from it, and that is that the army officers who train the students put some fear of disobedience into them, and they are better controlled than they were three or four years ago.

With very much love to you both, and hoping that you have a comfortable summer, as ever,

Affectionately,   Martha Wiley

"Donald has bomb-proof cellars enough for the students."

FOOCHOW, CHINA   SEPTEMBER 3, 1937

Dear Sister,

Dr. Rawlinson, who was killed in the accidental bombing, was a member of the American Board and editor of the *Chinese Recorder*, the oldest missionary journal in China. When I was in Shanghai the last time, I was entertained in his home. Mrs. Rawlinson and daughter Jean were in the car with the doctor, and when they were on their way saw everyone looking up, and Dr. Rawlinson got out to look. He did not come back and Mrs. Rawlinson got out of the car to see where he was—and he was dead, killed instantly by a fragment of shell piercing his heart. She saw many people all lying on the ground and turned to them to help her lift her husband into the car, but no one responded—all were dead and 25 cars had been struck and all were blazing up. She and Jean, the 16 year old daughter, lifted the body into the car and took it to the undertakers. That was just before the great evacuation took place. The other horrible things that you have read are rather minimized than exaggerated. Stragglers from the Shanghai area are getting through over land, walking most of the way. But the Chinese are fighting hard against the heavy handicap of poor equipment. At Nankau Pass they charged with battle axes, and regiment after regiment fell before the Japanese artillery.

The consul does not wish the American missionaries to leave the port (in case we are asked to evacuate) though we do not seem to be in any danger other than an occasional bomb dropped to destroy the Chinese morale. Donald is opening school today, and with about half the usual number. He has bomb-proof cellars enough for the students, and also the new hospital in our compound is five storeys high with concrete floors on each storey, and the basement is the best bomb-proof place in the province. Our Woman's Compound is too far away to reach after the signal is given, so I will not open school until after the 27th, and not then if there appears to be danger, for I cannot assume responsibility for the lives of the women who would come because they had no other place to stay. So in that case, I might as well stay here on the mountain for two more weeks.

Lots of love to all from,   Martha

[Note: Martha is in U.S. for one year]

---

*"Coal here is $44 a ton, and I do not see myself
buying very many spoonfuls."*

FOOCHOW, CHINA   NOVEMBER 20, 1938

Dear Sisters,

There have been no further upheavals since the great one the Tuesday after I arrived. [More information about return trip, in 12-25-38 letter.] Everything seems as peaceful as at any previous time. The students of the Woman's School are gradually coming back, so I plan to open school on the 24th if no further flurry occurs. Those who are already in the school are making clothing for the refugees, and we will have 30 or 40 more garments by Wednesday. There are a lot of camps here of people from Amoy and other places that have been bombed. Our turn may come, but it looks as though Japan has her hands full now without adding one more place that would be of no particular use to her—so we may escape.

You probably know the general news much better than I do, as all that I get is the meager account in the Chinese language daily, and the much delayed papers from Shanghai.

I am moved over to the large compound on the hillside, but as soon as school begins

I will be running back and forth most of the time and it is not going to be very satisfactory. The other missionaries thought that I had better move over and I agreed with them when the scare was on, but since then I thought that I had better have used my head a bit and stayed where I was. This house is going to be a fright to keep warm. Already I am sitting around in the big black coat that you gave me, Anna. Coal here is $44 a ton, and I do not see myself buying very many spoonfuls. Yesterday Seng-Seng and I went around and looked over the trees at Fairy Bridge and found a few mulberry trees and one camphor tree that I told him to cut down for firewood, but it will be very wet unless some dry wood can be bought.

By the way, Miss Deahl has at last bought a house boat and is going to get it fixed up and live in it. Miss Little, with whom she is now living and who has carried on the work among Boat People, thinks that it is very foolish to want to live on the river, but that may be the safest place if any more bombing takes place. We are most afraid of the fires if the City is ever invaded, for the "scorched earth" policy is terrible, and a boat would not be as likely to burn as a house on the land.

Martha

✦

"Our house at Fairy Bridge was much injured by the bombing last summer."

THANKSGIVING DAY NOVEMBER 24, 1938

Dear Donald and Catherine,

. . .

Our house at Fairy Bridge was much injured by the bombing last summer. On your side, large areas of the plaster on the outside of the house have fallen off. I do not want to have this repaired until I think such troubles are over. On my side, the kitchen looks as though it would fall down. There are great cracks in the main walls as wide as an inch, or in some places more than that. We will have to have some iron supports put in so that we will not be in danger. While the school is running we will be over there most of the time, but will keep the house in the main compound so that we will have a place of refuge if a sudden emergency arises.

Martha

*"As those eight legs carried me up the mountain it occurred
to me that my 'car' was an eight cylinder."*

FOOCHOW, CHINA   DECEMBER 11, 1938

Dear Sister Belle,

The rain has been coming down for a day and night, and it is to be hoped that there will
be water enough in our many wells to keep the compound supplied. This evening I made
a fire in the grate—the second time this season, for we have had a wonderfully mild fall.
On Tuesday last I went up the Mountain to Kuliang to see about some repairs, and it was
a glorious day and along the way the butterflies were out and flying about. The road had
been torn up in several places and the bridges blown out, so that I could not go very far
by ricksha and had to go in a chair, which seemed slow after riding at 50 miles an hour for
a year. As those eight legs carried me up the mountain it occurred to me that my car was
an eight cylinder.

On the 9th, five bombing planes passed over the City and circled about for a while. The
sirens blew, and we stood in one of the school rooms under the shelter of a big tree so as to
be in an inconspicuous place while the callers were passing over us. They came very near
and I felt very creepy for a minute. The students were all very quiet and self-controlled. At
3:00 another squad came again and did the same thing. Then people began to move. We
had settled down to think that the Jones family [Martha's term for the Japanese] had forgotten us—but not so. I wonder if you heard about this on the radio.

I have rice and wood and olives and salt in store, so that if we have to run to the big
compound there will be food for all for two weeks. I hate to stay so far from the school but
it seems best for me to hold onto this house for a place of refuge—and if I moved back to
Fairy Bridge I would have no control of this house.

Affectionately,   Martha

*"I've never gone clear through the inside, as it is a very
gruesome place in spite of the electric light."*

CHRISTMAS MORNING, 1938

Dear Anna,

. . .

The amount of potted plants that the woman gardener got started last year is appalling,
something like 300. I shall have to dump out most of them, for we do not have water to
keep them up. Among other things this week I have had a well dug much deeper, which
nearly gives me nervous prostration, for digging in the fluid clay is very dangerous. We

dump all the unwanted pots of flowers on the dugout [bomb shelter]. Already it looks on the outside as a very green and colorful little hill. I've never gone clear through the inside, as it is a very gruesome place in spite of the electric light.

Affectionately,   Martha Wiley

Dugout bomb shelter

**"The China Sea was a wild lake of chocolate foam;
but disturbed nature was less alarming than
the violence of man's making."**

FOOCHOW, CHINA   DECEMBER 25, 1938

Dear American Friends:

Yes, I reached Foochow after a very tempestuous voyage, just exactly one month from the date of sailing [see 11-20-38 letter]. Storms assailed our good ship all the way from Victoria to Yokohama, and there a belated typhoon met us; but as we took the inland sea passage we had a quiet night, while the more venturesome passenger steamers that took the open sea route were "frightfully buffeted." The China Sea was a wild lake of chocolate foam as the typhoon lashed its surface for two days.

The *Empress* docked at Hongkew the day and night that the terrorists were giving Shanghai its worst experience of the kind, but only the morning papers made us acquainted with their activities. Such terrible wreckage along the river as we approached Shanghai—miles and square miles of desolation! After one sight of that wanton destruction it would be impossible to be "pro"—one simply would be an outspoken "anti."

The Formosa Channel was in one of its angry moods and very choppy; but disturbed nature was less alarming than the violence of man's making. At the mouth of Bias Bay a great airplane carrier lay sprawling, with war-birds hopping off it to carry on their deadly work ashore, for that was the fateful day in South China. Loaded transports were entering the Bay and the empty ones going north. With sad hearts and much foreboding we entered Hong Kong.

Hong Kong was crowded with both foreign and Chinese refugees. I was grateful to have a cot in the drawing room of the boarding house. Water was scarce and turned on only at special hours. Vegetables were not being brought in. Refugees from the mainland were crowding the places where shelter from a projecting roof gave them a temporary home. Sometimes a whole family would be gathered around an oil tin of thin rice that was simmering over a tiny fire, and often there was not even that comfort. The fall of Canton took place during these days in Hong Kong, and there was such dismay and tragedy in the faces of the people that it was unforgettable.

Our little party boarded the first steamer that left for the north via Foochow, and for the first time since leaving Seattle the sea was quiet. The steamer was loaded with refugees. These poor people had been scattered all over the recently invaded area, and now were going back to their former houses to endure still more hardships. We touched at an unfrequented port and they were put ashore, except a few going on to Foochow.

A Chinese nurse just returning from America banteringly asked the captain to give her a job on his ship. The captain wheeled about and exclaimed, "Are you a nurse? I'll give you a job this minute!" Half an hour later a little Chinese babe registered his disapproval of coming into this troubled world as a refugee.

After four days and nights we sighted the hills of Fukien lying back of Foochow. Our steamer anchored for the night at the mouth of the River Min. Chinese launches dared not come out into the region of gunboats, so we continued on our way 45 miles up the river to a British launch. The sun shone gloriously on the familiar hill, and the wayside rest houses gleamed under the banyans; friends, foreign and Chinese, were waiting on the Foochow pier—oh, it was good, this getting back again!

And what about the homeland? Were there no thoughts left for it? Yes, indeed. Apples $12 a box in Hong Kong, and none at any price in Foochow! And the cottage cheese, the nice yellow butter, running water, English language dailies, and just everything good! Who could help having some special thoughts about America the Beautiful?

Two days of getting settled and learning from frequent callers that now, there was nothing to be alarmed about—then rumors came thick and fast for a day, culminating in a rush from the City of an estimated 100,000. My school left in the darkness between 3 A.M. and daylight. Relatives took the students away to country places. They were planning to avoid going through the horrors of an invasion, if there should be such.

Quiet was soon restored and our school again assembled and a time of peace seemed to be possible, when the airplanes came roaring over us twice in one day. Not one student was hysterical. They stood here and there and some said together Psalm 56:3, but the children and servants had made a short circuit to the dugout.

Refugees have been coming into the Foochow region, and we as a school and the women of the churches have been doing our utmost toward getting winter clothes for them. The women of the school cut out the garments, and the outside women come for them and help with the sewing, which is voluntary. The garments are made of hand-woven "patriotic cloth" (which is the name for gingham) with a generous wadding of cotton. One bolt cuts out six garments, but as there must be lining, it makes just three complete garments. The gingham, cotton, and thread reaches just $1.50 per garment, in local currency, which reduced to U.S. currency is *30 cents* for material.

We could have made many more if the material had been more plentiful. Remember please, that 30 cents U.S. currency at present buys the material for a wadded garment, 15 cents for a single garment. The sewing is contributed. The winter winds are wet and unbelievably cold. The mails are now reaching us unmolested. The Hong Kong and Shanghai Bank in Foochow is functioning.

Refugees are still in need and will be. Yesterday a woman wandered into my house. Her husband had been killed in Amoy by a bomb. She and her baby were sick and starved looking. Usually the refugees stay in the camps so I asked her how she happened to come. She replied that she saw the foreign house and knew that foreigners are kind. I hope that I may live up to that reputation.

There is mass education, mass production and other things en masse, and now I am learning the feeling of mass misery, mass suffering. It bears down on one like the heavy clouds, and yet we in Foochow have just touched the fringe of it all. The people keep up their morale marvelously. They go about their accustomed duties patiently and cheerfully.

In the year that I have been away, many things have been done that surprised me on returning. Among these is the building of a new home for the aged, and another for the incurables, and a fine up-to-date little hospital for unwanted infants. If the war had not been thrust upon an unwilling people, they were all set for wonderful achievement in all humanitarian projects. What a pity they could not have been left to work out their ideas in their own way!

In spite of war conditions, the Mission business goes on inexorably. The Woman's Organization, the Bible Women, the Woman's Bible School, the committees, the visiting in homes, the long, long walks with callers, the repairs on buildings, the gardening, the sewing for refugees—and many miscellaneous demands—help to fill the days—and what priceless days they are! There are contacts everywhere with every class of people who need just what we came to give.

This letter will be a belated Christmas greeting, and it carries to you all my gratitude for the many kindnesses received while on furlough in America, and the memory of gracious friends will make the days in war-torn China seem less difficult.

Most cordially yours,   Martha Wiley

"But one gets so the alarm is not alarming."

FOOCHOW, CHINA   JANUARY 13, 1939

Dear Donald and Catherine,

Every day or two the sirens sound the alarm to get out of sight, or if at night to blacken out, but one gets so the alarm is not alarming. We go right on with our teaching and class work. Most of the planes are very high, passing on to the interior for their deadly work. Foochow seems so quiet with so many people moved out and the schools most all gone. The dugout is getting to be a very colorful hill with grass and vines all over the top, and the pots of plants that I have dumped on it.

Did I tell you that I sleep at the American Board compound? The Mission thought that I had better do so—and I agreed so that I could hold this house for my use, in case the school had to leave Fairy Bridge compound, and we might have this as a refuge. I have rice and olives and salt stored away in case there is a rush to this place—which does not seem likely until a new campaign begins in the spring.

Our work for the refugees continues. We tried to make 100 garments a week for them, but I could not get money enough to buy the cloth for so many as a steady thing. The women of the churches are glad to do the sewing if I get the material, as many of them are without warm clothes themselves. I'm glad that I worked like a slave to get most of those Chinese curios sold, so I had a little money ahead to show that we Christian women are not so heartless that we did nothing practical to show our interest in the suffering. Yesterday I went to the camp to see how things were going and was glad to see some of the garments that we had made in action—quite literally so. But most of our sewing has gone to the refugees in Amoy.

Martha

"It is wonderful how friendly the Chinese are to us in spite of the scrap iron that goes to Japan."

FOOCHOW, CHINA   MARCH 22, 1939

Dear Home Friends,

Perhaps you heard over the radio that Foochow had a visitation from her neighbor yesterday. All morning a heavy rain was falling and in the afternoon a slight rain and mist prevailed so we felt secure from aerial trouble for one day at least, but just at 2 o'clock the siren blew and we quietly waited for a squad to pass over as they had been doing—but not so.

We stood out in the yard of Fairy Bridge home and saw four of the planes following one after the other over the barracks about a half mile or less from us. Suddenly they turned four abreast and began to pepper the barracks where the new recruits are stationed for drill. And on they came right over our house — they seemed not a hundred feet from our roof — with a deafening roar. They were too near to make us comfortable.

Round and round they went, back and forth over our Fairy Bridge Compound and that region, for exactly one hour. They were hunting something and dropped a few souvenir bombs but continued hunting. Finally they departed and the release siren blew. In an hour they returned and began circling us, this time dropping three bombs on the Military Academy about a third of a mile from our house. I went over there later and saw the three big holes in the grounds, each about as big as a good sized room. Fortunately no one was killed. Farther over at pier 6, one bomb was dropped and a pig killed and a man wounded. The real killing was done in the barracks where the poor youngsters were quartered, but the outside world will not know how many.

A good many in the compound took to the dugout, but most of us prefer the open sky, and the noise does not seem so terrible if the planes can be seen. They let loose the bombs about a block from us, but the speed and the height made them drop farther on. I must say they were fair marksmen. The women in my school were very quiet, though the new ones cried softly. A visitor who happened to be in school came full tilt toward me and there she clung until all was quiet. Most of the women sat with bowed heads and prayed. One teacher said, "I am a very timid person and only the grace of God enables me to sit here quietly" — and so said I.

Some of the bombs fell near the home of a man-teacher in my school. He stayed and finished up his day's work and went off to his home. On my way home I met the hospital accountant going towards his home near the barracks, and he was in a quandary as to whether to move his family away or not. It is wonderful how friendly the Chinese are to us American Missionaries in spite of the scrap-iron that goes to Japan. As I went to look at the shell holes, every one along the way spoke kindly and a soldier led the way for us. I wondered if those holes had been dug there by American iron, and if the dead boys in the barracks lay dead because of the greed of a so-called Christian land. It does not make us feel so proud of ourselves when we know the wickedness of our own land.

Martha Wiley

*"The Manchu Quarter in 1912 was child's play
compared with the situation here now."*

FOOCHOW, CHINA   JUNE 11, 1939

Dear Miss Pepoon,

The people seem to have enough trouble with the Japanese without anything more, but the flood comes nevertheless. Probably half of the population of Foochow has moved out somewhere, but that leaves about 300,000 of the poorest with all their business gone, and with the incessant bombing and business being carried on at night—what little there is left—the situation, from the standpoint of food scarcity, is to say the least appalling.

When you helped us with the destitute in the Manchu Quarter in 1912 there were many who were suffering, but that was child's play compared with the situation here now, and with the sure knowledge that the conditions are to get worse and worse. I started a "rice-kitchen" in the Woman's School for the poor of my immediate district and am giving out 50 meals a day, besides those who get help at home, and Bishop Hind has provided for two "rice-kitchens" in the City with 100 meals a day in each. As the destitute come I take them in for meals, and it is probable that my place will be crowded before long.

Yesterday evening after the last siren, I went to Fairy Bridge to look over those who had collected and took in several more, mostly women and small children. One little seven-months-old child just lay still and whimpered he was so hungry and weak. Those who need a bath and sulphur ointment [for scabies] get that extra. It is very inconvenient to live over here in the Peace St. Compound and have my work at Fairy Bridge, but it would be difficult to have the sirens going all day and be living over at Fairy Bridge where the compound is surrounded with barracks and government buildings, all of which are the targets of the bombers, for the aim might not be accurate sometime.

Since February there have been 36 (now over 40) bombings of Foochow, and this does not count the dozens and dozens of signals when the planes passed over to do their wicked work somewhere else, and the many bombings of the places near—so near that we could hear the explosions and see the fires. It is certainly a busy time for those of us who are left in the City, and a very trying time for those who had to move out to the country places and endure all kinds of hardships. And this is not as hard as the real refugees are enduring, where home and possessions are destroyed and nothing left for food. We are better off yet than most of China, but just wonder what will be the outcome of affairs here before the war ends.

This morning I woke up before 4 o'clock with the conviction that I ought to send someone over to Fairy Bridge to have one person take the responsibility of sweeping out the dugout every day to see that there are no snakes in it before the people rush in for shelter several times a day. These heavy rains bring out the snakes. I have had one of the destitute boys in the hospital for four weeks with a hand bitten by a cobra. He says that the cobra just scratched him as he kicked it off or he would have died. As it was, he narrowly escaped an amputation of his hand. Now the question is to get him a job.

And he is just one of hundreds and thousands out of work and starving unless helped. The government has done wonders, but as this is not an invaded area it cannot give this area much attention. The government home for old folks was bombed—also all government buildings, all the government school buildings, a large per cent of the business block, and here and there areas of homes. Some days there are only demolition bombs, but mostly incendiary bombs are dropped.

There is no telling when this letter will reach you for there has been no mail in for almost a month now—that is, no foreign mail. The Post Master said that he was going to send our first class mail down the coast and have it picked up at a small port where the Japanese are not bothering yet. This will have to be carried on men's backs for a long distance, so I surmise that not much of it will go at a time. I keep on writing just the same when I have time, as it is bad to get too much behind.

Much love to you, dear friend, from Martha

" 'To be living is sublime'—or is it only sordid?"

FOOCHOW, CHINA   JULY 1, 1939

Dear ones at home,

Today is July 1st and we Foochow folks are still sitting tight. Yesterday was to have been the limit of the patience of the "Joneses" but something went haywire and the City is still in the hands of the Chinese. There was to have been a flight of birds over us at midnight of the 28th—but they went somewhere else. The next day was the end of the "patience" of the Jones family—so we were informed and that all foreigners that were not looking for trouble were warned to get out. All are at their usual places.

We have rumors as to what the haywire was (the siren again, twice this morning) but it would be better told than written—the Joneses are sensitive! On the 28th, incendiary bombs burned the main building of the Union High, which is several miles from the West Gate of the City. This building stands out all by itself way out there in the country. It had an enormous U.S. flag on it—unmistakable. The first bombed missed and killed two little children playing in the yard; the next missed; the third made a direct hit. Soon the whole building was in flames. Two workmen in the basement crawled out unhurt. We watched the fire from the roof of the hospital. The students have been gone for months, so there seems to have been no motive other than wanton destruction of American School property.

This is the fourth day we have lived in this tense atmosphere, expecting an invasion each day. In the meantime we have got the refugee work all lined up, and when the scramble begins we can direct them to their places of safety. The planes are in the distance, their sound getting plainer. When they get too near, I duck under the house or the hospital. The noise is so terrifying! Seven planes visited us yesterday and then passed on over to do their wicked work farther up country. It is now almost 9 A.M. and the second visit is near. We have been anxious about Foochow College since Union High had such a disastrous visit.

The gruel-kitchens are the most popular institutions in the City at present. There is another terrible flood on today and the Water Gate region will be washed over again. Two weeks ago there was a similar flood, but this one today is two feet higher on the level. Our front gate is waist deep, and when the tide comes in and backs up the water it will be considerably higher. (All clear has sounded.) Our Fairy Bridge Compound is beginning to be covered in places. I hope that the front gate will be passable so that the "guests" can come for their meals. It looks odd to see sampans with the matting covers lined up near the hospital at Peace St. front gate.

> "We are living, we are dwelling,
> In a grand and awful time—
> In an age on ages telling,
> To be living is sublime"—**or is it only sordid?**

[Excerpt of hymn with Martha's addition in bold]

I thought that there would be no one to call on me today, but floods cannot keep the population from seeping in—have just wangled three in through the back gate to the hospital, one a woman with both wrists broken, just as mine was.

Glory be! It begins to look as though we are not going to have an invasion—at least not for the present. The rumours are all in favor of none at all. Heavy rains and fog may keep the Joneses away. When this flood recedes I dread the tidal wave of humanity that will start this way. If they can only be headed toward Fairy Bridge they can be managed, but not at Peace Street.

Martha

"Perhaps something had to be done to check my mad career."

FOOCHOW, CHINA   JULY 15, 1939

Dear Anna,

Such a procession as passes in review here day after day! The worst case today was a mother with her boy whose foot was gangrened and the toes mostly gone because she had fled from Amoy and was a stranger and had no money to take her boy to a doctor. In their flight he had hurt his foot. The little chap is now in the hospital.

In the morning nine of Mrs. Jones's birds came over and made straight for our part of the City. I ducked for the hospital, and as they came nearer and nearer I thought that the lowest floor would suit me best! On the stairway my ankle turned and I fell only one step down, but that was enough. By August 7th the cast can be taken off—not too bad!

I fractured two bones in my left ankle and as there was no electricity to run the elevator I was carried up to the fourth floor and, at night when the electricity came on and my foot was x-rayed, it showed two bones slightly fractured, one on each side of my ankle—which is mysterious. For three days I lay flat with my foot packed in ice. Then the cast was put on and I stayed three days more, and then a pair of crutches made and I was carried home—to the top storey of this big house on the hill. Since then there have been sirens galore, but no actual dropping of eggs on this city—but many on the interior of the province. I never get used to the noise. Perhaps something had to be done to check my mad career—the pressure was becoming so great.

The soup kitchen now has 160 guests a day. Up to the end of this week I have been paying for the rice, but then the International Red Cross will give me the rice, and I will have more for the sick and afflicted ones.

Last night after the household was asleep and rain coming down typhoon style, the postman brought a letter from Josephine saying that she was coming down the river soon and expecting to spend August with me at Kuliang. I hope that she will not run risks on the river. Every day or two a river launch is bombed. While I was in the hospital a wounded man was brought in and operated on, but died next day morning, and I could hear his little widow weeping. He was running a launch that was machine-gunned. The next day the same thing happened.

The rumour today is that on the 17th there will be a bad day for the coast cities, especially Hinghua, just south of here, so more of the suffering population are trying to move out of the City. One thousand ricksha men have just been commandeered to go into the interior to carry loads.

Love to Belle and others,   Martha

"The steamer does not declare her destination, the passengers
taking the risk of getting off where the steamer
will land them."

FOOCHOW, CHINA   SEPTEMBER 26, 1939

Beloved Hinmans,

At 2:30 A.M. September 20th there was a knocking at the door and when the door was opened there stood Donald. Were we glad to see him! For days many people had been praying that he might arrive in safety. It is not easy to pass Mrs. Jones's door now, but he came through to Shanghai all right but with a few anxious moments at the ports. On the steamer Donald had to be satisfied with deck passage and put his cot up in the only place available near the engine. So the two nights on the steamer he had very little sleep. The steamer does not declare her destination, the passengers taking the risk of getting off where the steamer will land them.

Martha

[Note: The Hsueh family traveled to U.S. in 1938.]

*"The students classes were held in the farm houses
and country sheds."*

[letter from Donald]   FOOCHOW COLLEGE   INGTAI, FUKIEN, CHINA   NOVEMBER 25, 1939

Dear Friends in America,

In view of Foochow College being threatened to be occupied by the Japanese, my wife and I with difficulty and with much prayer decided that I should come back first and alone and leave my wife and three little girls in Oberlin for a while longer. It was hard to separate from my family as our family motto has been, "Hsuehs always stay together."

Marian—7½, Elizabeth—5, Mabelle—11½

Ordinarily it takes only two days and two nights by steamer from Shanghai to Foochow, a distance of 200 miles. When I came back two months ago, it took seven days. Foochow had been blockaded by the Japanese for months. The dirty, small freight steamer carrying the British flag could not land at Foochow. The steamer stopped at Santau in our province to the north of Foochow, and then I had to travel on land for four days.

The next day after my arrival, the Japanese planes came to bomb again. When the siren alarm sounded, I was on the Southside and was caught in the street not knowing where to run and hide myself. As different places with dugouts were not known to me, I followed the crowd. Half an hour later the 3rd jetty near the Big Bridge on Southside was bombed and about 30 people were killed. The jetty was only a quarter of a mile from where I first started to run. On this day, another place at Upper Bridge was bombed and several people killed. In fact, for the two or three days I stayed in the City, the siren blew six or seven times from 6:30 A.M. to 5 P.M.—each time being one or two hours long. You simply couldn't do a thing except try to hide yourself in some place.

When I went around to see our Foochow College buildings, I found nobody except one office clerk who was asked to stay there and watch all buildings. Later in the evening, I found that 300 refugees came to our school to eat rice. Our Assembly Hall has been turned into "The dining room for refugees." In fact, the whole college campus has been earmarked as one of the five refugee camps in Foochow. The College clerk told me that the Church Relief Committee in Foochow has decided to put 1,000 refugees in our school if actual occupation by Japanese takes place.

Before I went down to Ingtai, a faculty representative and a representative of the student body came up to welcome me. I went down with them. Ingtai is just about 50 miles southwest of Foochow and is the temporary site of our work.

Think of our students in Ingtai—getting up at 5 o'clock and after breakfast scattering themselves over country places from 6:30 A.M. to 4:30 P.M. every day. At night all come back to the larger country houses to sleep.

One missionary, after having seen our widely scattered area, made a joke saying, "Your College Campus now is larger than Yale University or the University of California." In fact, some students had to walk three miles every morning and covered the same distance coming back during the evening. Their classes were held in the farm houses and country sheds. It is most difficult to walk during rainy days, for the country roads are very bad. Mosquito, gnats and filthy paths and bad odors, etc., would be enough to make anybody sick. I marveled at the sacrificial spirit of both teachers and students especially our American Board missionaries who follow our students and live with them.

Please send your good letters often. My family is still in America and letters from there seem very good to me.

Sincerely yours,   Donald Hsueh

East Gate Park — Foochow

Ten Thousand Year Bridge — Foochow

TIMELINE 1941–1946

1941 —Foochow College moves to Shaowu (220 miles NW of Foochow)
—Japan invades Foochow

1942 —Martha teaches at Foochow College again because of teacher shortage

1943 —Foochow College is divided between Ingtai and Shaowu for one year

1944 —Martha retires from mission service but remains in China
—Foochow is occupied by Japan (4 months)
—Refugees in Ingtai—students sleeping in abandoned Buddhist temple

1945 —Return to Foochow

1946 —Fire destroys campus building of Foochow College, library, and all books burned

1946 —'49—KMT—CCP Civil War

5

WAR AND UPHEAVAL

"Then the gate is opened and floods of destitute come in."

FOOCHOW, CHINA   FEBRUARY 15, 1940

Dear Sister Belle,

Every morning I have to get up at 5 o'clock — and you know how I like to sleep. Have roll call at 6:30 at Fairy Bridge and breakfast for 120 children — 40 go to Foochow College Primary; 80 stay in Fairy Bridge and have two hours of "books." Then the gate is opened and floods of destitute come in. The nurse looks after their sicknesses. At 12 o'clock dinner is served to 80 more — then washing tables and house cleaning. At 4 P.M. the next squad come in for supper. I teach them from 4-5 P.M. On Tuesdays we give out cash aid to the old and sick that cannot come to Fairy Bridge.

Please let the rest of the relatives know I am still hale and hearty and soon 66 years old — how come?

Love to each of your family from,   Martha

"It is a risk of life to get into any port now."

Dear Anna,

After we got a cablegram from Shanghai about the arrival on the 29th of Catherine and the children, we heard through the shipping company (I think) that the party might start on the 30th to Foochow. If so, they are all in a terrible typhoon. We hope that the captain was too wise to start out in such weather, especially as it is a risk of life to get into any port now.

The cook and I have got all the hinges and metal fixtures oiled and ready for leaving. I hate to close up the house when the walls are so damp.

There has been a regular scourge of thieving at Kuliang. People have had the meat stolen from their kitchens between the buying and getting it ready to cook. Window glass has been taken out of many houses, and in some the doors are hacked down. Potatoes are dug at night and taken from the fields. Nothing is safe from the thieves. I will take the best dishes down the mountain, and the rest will run the risk. I'd hate to have the tubs and kitchen things stolen, but they are too bulky to move. I often wonder—if the work of packing to come here, and the same to get settled, and then closing up, and the housekeeping during the time here, with the difficulty of buying food, and the number of people who come up the hill to find me—if it is worth the effort. Yet each year I come.

I want to get down the hill and meet Catherine and the children when they come. They must have had a very rough voyage if Bertha Allen broke her leg on the way.

Lots of love to all,   Nana

"Children should not see what we see every day."

SEPTEMBER 21, 1940

Dear Anna,

Cholera is getting bad here—one shocking case in our compound yesterday. If the Hsuehs were going to stay at Fairy Bridge, I would have to move the "destitutes" elsewhere, or rather my place of work for them. Children should not see what we see every day. But in a few days, when they get rested, they will move up to Ingtai. Josephine will be going to Shaowu, and my crowded house will be a quiet place then.

We are on a search for rice again today, so I will close my letter and get the men started. Donald thinks that he will have a hundred bags (160 lbs. each) in a day or two, so he will risk beginning school. The strain on him is terrible. He certainly needed Catherine's help.

Lots of love,   Nana

"Sharp Peak has been planted to poppies."

FOOCHOW, CHINA   OCTOBER 12, 1940

Dear friends in Old Home,

The island (Sharp Peak) that Mrs. Jones has acquired (where my summer cottage is) has been planted to poppies. It is bad enough to have them live in our property, but it makes one boil to have them use the island for such a purpose. Retribution must come some day, but that is a poor consolation for the debauched lives right now.

Much love to you both, from yours gratefully,   Martha

AMERICAN CONSULATE
Foochow, China

OCTOBER 28, 1940

TO ALL AMERICANS IN THE FOOCHOW CONSULAR DISTRICT:

This consulate has been instructed by the Department of the State urgently to suggest to Americans in this consular district, and particularly to American women, children, and men not detained by essential and urgent considerations, that they take advantage of the steamship transportation to the United States now while facilities are still available. It is impossible to guarantee that transportation facilities from the Far East will remain available indefinitely.

It is accordingly requested that all such Americans communicate with this office.

(No one plans to go from here.) M. Wiley

Edward E. Rice   American Consul

"It may be the same if F.D.R. goes in for a third term."

NOVEMBER 4, 1940

Dear Sister Belle,

Your letter was so newsy that I carried it around and read it over and over. Today you will be thinking of how the elections will come out. With this distance between America and us it does seem that Willkie ought to be the choice of the people. You have only a choice between two democrats—and between New Deal and anti-New Deal. Perhaps next week will find the U.S. plunged into war. You remember how everybody shouted the slogan for Wilson: "He kept us out of the war," when he had already planned to enter the war the day after the election? It may be the same if F.D.R. goes in on a third term.

Our Annual Meeting will begin next week and I am hoping that Catherine and Elizabeth will come and stay with me, even if Donald cannot get away. Donald is having such a time to get food for his 1,400 that he may not get here. I just paid for 200 mattocks that he has had made and wanted sent up immediately to Ingtai, so that the boys could get to work making a garden.

Write again soon, one of your newsy letters. It is good to know that there is one land of plenty on the face of the earth.

Love to all the W's from,   Martha

"Many students are still sleeping on the floor until beds can be made."

[letter from Catherine]   FOOCHOW COLLEGE   INGTAI, FUKIEN, CHINA   NOVEMBER 15, 1940

Dear Friends,

By this time perhaps you have received my last letter telling about our safe arrival in Foochow. Now we are at Ingtai, an interior place where Foochow College is, about thirty five miles from Foochow City. The trip from Foochow to Ingtai was harder than the one from America to Shanghai.

After staying in our home in the city for two weeks, we began to re-pack our things for Ingtai. On September 8th we left Foochow at midnight on a sampan towed by a small launch. The next morning, early, we came to a rapid where we had to change to a "rat boat" which is smaller than a sampan.

Ingtai River is very narrow and has more than twenty rapids on the way between Ingtai and Foochow. When the boat came to a rapid, the four boatmen jumped into the water, one man at each end of the boat to push it up, and the other two men to pull on a long bamboo rope tied to the mast. It required a skillful man to handle the long oar at the end of the boat. One of the boats in which we had put some baggage crashed against the rocks in the rapids and was wrecked, and all the games our American friends gave to our children were lost and some of our clothes spoiled. Fortunately we had put most of our baggage in the boat in which we were.

After two nights on the way, we arrived at our destination. The children were very happy to get on shore. We went to live in a Chinese house, which is not as good as most of the barns in America. We cleaned it and repaired it and made some stools out of old boards and made some partitions of some pieces of cloth, and the children picked some wild flowers for the first decoration. Now, since we are used to it, we realize that it is better than thousands of other people's homes.

The children go to school while I keep house and teach five hours a week and help Donald with his school work so as to make contacts with the students. This year we have about 1,400 students in Foochow College, 800 in the High School at Ingtai and 600 in the Primary in the city. The 800 students up here have a very hard time for they have no proper place to live. Many are still sleeping on the floor until beds can be made.

There is no place to buy nourishing food. Sometimes we see some carried on the streets but the price is terribly high. The students are hungry most of the time, because all they have to eat is old rice and a little bit of vegetable to make it palatable. My children always come from school hungry, and after searching the cupboard, exclaim that our cupboard is emptier than Old Mother Hubbard's.

Even though the students have a very hard time, they have never complained. They are very ambitious to prepare themselves for future usefulness.

Not only the students have been patient during the transition from the city campus to this barren hillside, but also the teachers have borne all the discomforts bravely. Not one teacher or his family has been free from malaria. Rice has been so scarce and so expensive that the teachers have suffered great hardship. Still they remain faithful to the school. Sometimes it breaks my heart to see these educated men suffering for enough food. Because the price of food is so high, and salaries in mission schools are so low, these loyal teachers have partly starved, and their families never really have enough food.

We ought to do better by these educated, trained workers. If not, at the close of this war these people will be exhausted. How I long for just a share of the good things of America to pour into my suffering country! You can imagine how hard my husband has tried in every way to better the conditions of his teachers and their families. His responsibility is truly heavy. Will you remember him in your prayers and in your planning for the new year, that his health and courage may continue? There are marvelous opportunities in our work right now and we want to meet them bravely in a Christian spirit.

How glad we are that friends provided so much quinine! Every day the school nurses give it out to many patients. It is like part of our food now. Every week we have to take some in order to prevent our getting malaria.

Since my husband came back from America in 1939, he has been struggling to make the hillside more comfortable for the students. Because of limited finances, our development is very slow. We have a proverb in China: "Even a skillful woman cannot cook a meal without rice." No matter how good the plans are, we cannot carry them out without financial help. Now we are still in need of funds to build sanitary bathrooms for 800 boys. When the school fled to Ingtai, the health conditions were unspeakable. During this year my husband has made all the improvements that we had money for and has engaged a trained nurse and a graduate doctor, for there is no other medical help nearer than Foochow City. In spite of this, we are finding it impossible to fight against skin diseases, which the students get from lack of bathing facilities.

A contractor has estimated that $250 U.S. will be sufficient to build enough bathrooms to keep the boys in health and cleanliness. May God open some way for us!

Affectionately yours,   Catherine Lin Hsueh

"I took in a little girl of 12 whose mother was selling her off
as a slave girl because they were starving."

FOOCHOW, CHINA   MARCH 29, 1941

Dear Sister Belle,

This morning I took in a little girl of 12 whose mother was selling her off as a slave girl because they were starving. She is as pretty as a picture and has been in school for three years. Today is rainy and the children cannot work in the garden. I found this girl off in the corner learning the Ten Commandments—to catch up with the others.

. . .

Write as often as you can, for I am so glad to get letters from home.

Lots of love from,   Martha

FOOCHOW, CHINA   APRIL 16, 1941

Dear Miss Hartwell,

This month makes two full years of running this rice kitchen with never a break. It seems to be a miracle, as I look back on it now, that this could have been done with no resources but gifts and a small grant from the Red Cross. Besides those who have had meals, there is a regular number who come in for cash aid on Monday, and another group on Tuesday, and many who come at any time.

My school nurse still runs the clinic and the main discomforts are itch, malaria and beriberi. Many die every day of real starvation and others of mal-nutrition diseases. Some evenings I think I cannot go on another day—but when the next day comes I get up and go on with renewed purpose.

Affectionately,   Martha

"We have to move our school to Shaowu."

[letter from Donald]   FOOCHOW COLLEGE   INGTAI   APRIL 26, 1941

Dearest Gu Gu,

We are still alive and well and o.k. Sorry to cause so much trouble and worry. We have decided to go to Shaowu, as we have to move our school to Shaowu. There are still over 300 youngsters left. Mr. Ting Chao Wu wrote, advising me to move to Shaowu where there was lots of rice. Our government urged me to move too. Now it is the time. We have to begin everything again. At least I am not discouraged.

There are several things we'd like you to do. Please move our rugs and one trunk that Catherine brought from America, the newest one, and two bicycles, and my own clothes in the Dieu and the drawers at Fairy Bridge house, also electric fan in the Dieu.

Please go with Sing Dong to my room, (not bed room) in Cowan Hall to take money out from the drawers of the high filing case. I think I have left $180 in one bundle and $60 in another drawer and some other money. Please take the money for yourself. Sing Dong has all my keys.

If possible, remove all my own books from Lincoln Hall to your place. Sing Dong and other coolies can help.

Love,   Donald

*"Our vegetable garden has kept a good number from having beriberi.
Keep putting in a packet of vegetable seeds."*

FOOCHOW, CHINA   JUNE 21, 1941

Dear 1103-ers,

The food supply has been cut off from the outside, and it is reported that five times five score in Foochow alone succumb to canis lupus at their door, daily. Our vegetable garden has kept a good number from having beriberi. [A disease caused by a deficiency of the B vitamin Thiamine, often fatal if untreated.] When you write, keep putting in a packet of vegetable seeds—Swiss chard first—then cabbage, turnips, collards, lettuce, and kale. The Swiss chard, lettuce and other leafy vegetables, and Kentucky wonder beans, we do need. I have tried to get seeds from this year's plants in order to keep up the supply in case mail does not get through, but yesterday when we looked over our collected seeds most of the pods were empty. The rains and the mildew are too much for these imported vegetables.

You would be amazed at the people of the higher class who are in dire necessity and come for help. Most of the money that has been used in Foochow has come through those of their family in positions out of the province. Since the Post Office and the banks have not functioned, the source of supply has stopped.

Martha

*"I used to think bombing was the worst thing ever, but now
I think to live among starving people is much worse."*

FOOCHOW, CHINA   JULY 9, 1941

Dear Miss Williams,

We have no idea whether letters reach you from Foochow or not—since we are not receiving mail. I have sent three letters telling you that your two letters from St. Paul had reached me with the cheques and the quinine, for all of which I send my grateful thanks—for the cheques came in time to be exchanged before the banks stopped taking in gold, either U.S. or sterling. Today the radio announced that exchange in Shanghai was 20 to 1, but that does us little good until business begins.

Can you imagine a city, that until the incident [Japanese invasion] had a half million population, with practically no postal service! All government banks have departed for the interior, leaving those of the population with money in just the same condition as those with no money. We were spared all this turmoil for almost four years while other parts of China had to carry the burden of suffering, but now we are in the hands of the sadists.

So far I personally have had sufficient for my needs—and the other foreigners also—but that is small comfort when we work with those who are starving for the foods that would keep them from beriberi. What a long tale it would be to tell of the things that we have seen in these last two months. But there has been one relief—no bombing. I used to think that was the worst thing ever, but now I think to live among starving people is much worse.

Always with grateful love to you and Miss Katherine,   Martha Wiley

*"All Red Cross funds are now cut off at the
worst time since the war began."*

FOOCHOW, CHINA   JULY 10, 1941

Dear Sister Belle,

If this letter ever reaches you, you will see that we are jogging along just as usual—only more so. I sent you a letter through the Foochow P.O. last week, but doubt if it ever leaves the P.O.

It surely does get wearisome, living in such an atmosphere of depression and starvation and fear and suffering and general wickedness. All Red Cross funds are now cut off at the worst time since the war began.

I am sending this letter out by a man who is going to the north of the province. Hope that it reaches you, to assure you that I am all right and wish I had one of your good raspberry pies.

Love to all the Wileys and Woodhouses,   Martha

CABLE ADDRESS "FERNSTALK" MISSIONS CODE
AMERICAN BOARD MISSION
FOOCHOW, CHINA

MARTHA WILEY   AUGUST 7, 1941   FAIRY BRIDGE

Dear Emily S. Hartwell and Miss Richardson,

Your letters written me on February 2nd came August 2nd!—a very leisurely voyage across the Pacific. You know perhaps that all credits are frozen and Mrs. Jones is clamping down hard on all farms and enterprises. We are feeling the iron heel already. I am glad that both of you are out of this. We are practically in i-t-t (internment) camp as far as independent movements are concerned.

The perspiration is dripping off me at 9 P.M. All afternoon I was at the government offices begging rice without success for the starving children and old people. Grants of aid are made to Buddhist monasteries and nunneries—but none for my poor folks. This is a time when we must appeal to God "with strong crying and tears." How the "father of lies" must be enjoying himself during these terrible days.

All told there are just 13 in this compound. If I can get out of port I will go to Shaowu, but there are restrictions now about getting through the lines—by Mrs. Jones and also by "our folks." What a mess—and what is it all about? There are a thousand details that I should love to write but it is prudent not to do so.

Today I had a letter from Catherine and she said that Josephine was far from well, and that Dr. Scott had lost 40 lbs. and Dr. Leger 25. (If they were peaches the loss would be $1.70 a pound.) If I go up there I will gain—I am just that contrary. Edna Deahl is just about the same—not much work on the river possible. Even if we cannot resume work in our day, the past three years have been the most fruitful of any in my life time, spiritually.

With much love to you both,   Martha Wiley

*"I have used largely of my personal funds to
keep the women's work in tact."*

FOOCHOW, CHINA   AUGUST 18, 1941

To the treasurer of the Foochow Mission:

Dear Sir,

The sum of $1,800 U.S. sent through the American Board Office, Boston, was sent at my request. Formerly this fund was held in the Old National Trust and Union Bank of Spokane, Washington, and was drawn on by me as need required. It was a personal gift to me and remains so at present time with only one limitation, and that was that it should be used for the purpose of Bible teaching under my direction or that of some one whom I should designate.

Knowing that in a few years my retirement would be necessary, I have used largely of my personal funds and other gifts to keep the women's work of the Foochow area in tact, and I have kept this Ida A. Woodward fund for this period of special difficulty in carrying on women's work.

Very truly,   Martha Wiley

*"There is only one lavatory on the launch and at least 300 women
and children — the rest you can imagine."*

SHAOWU, FUKIEN, CHINA   OCTOBER 3, 1941

My two dear friends in Old Home,

Just before leaving Foochow, I wrote you possibly I might come to Shaowu — and now I am here, as I supposed, for a vacation. There had been many hold-ups by bandits on the river and also bus lines, since the people are starving, so I had some qualms about venturing. But nothing happened to me.

I left Foochow on the "Queen Mary" — as foreigners name the little launch on which we "set." It can hold 200 — but 600 crowded on. I had reserved one of the two shelves on which we are supposed to sleep. An impossible man got the under shelf. I finally paid for both shelves and had the man moved. The uproar had hardly stopped at midnight when the "steward" put his head into my window and said to shut the window as we were nearing the place where bandits always begin to shoot. The windows were two small iron doors.

Just at that minute a foreigner put his head into my "window" and said that his sampan captain refused to go on with him and his family and that there was not a square foot of deck space and would I take them in. Of course I did and father, mother, baby son, grandma and amah all piled in with their luggage, and sat in a row on the lower berth (or shelf) and their luggage was stacked up on the two feet of space in front of the shelves. I stayed up on my shelf until 6 o'clock P.M. the day after leaving Foochow. There is only one lavatory on the launch and there were at least 300 women and children storming the place. The rest you can imagine.

All that day we were chugging up rapids—in some places being pulled by men in addition. Not a shot went across our "Queen Mary," even when stuck in a rapid. My cook and his boy and a man who was with me lay on the floor of the passage way inside my cabin, and were so tired they let people step over them. My lunch basket was underneath the missionary's family baggage. The cook got a bowl of rice for me during the day. About 5 P.M. we caught up with another launch as loaded as ours, and another missionary family called to us. The bandits had shot across their deck and seven persons were killed and a number wounded.

When we got to the dock at Nanping, six other launches were docking—among them, two loaded with General Li and his soldiers. The general had left Foochow a week before I left, and had got to the bandit nest, and had gone into another cabin to visit when a bullet passed over his bed. He was furious and turned about, telegraphed to Nanking for soldiers to come down there and clear out the bandits, so his launch arrived the same evening as mine.

When we reached Nanking, the man who was with me hopped off and ran to the hotel to get a room for me. Every one was occupied by a military party, so I went to a native inn. Their rooms were all occupied except two that load carriers used and they smelled to heaven, but at least there was a roof over us. Lots of people were setting on their baggage roll in front of buildings, and the rain was pouring down. My cook cleared out the contents of the room, put newspapers on the bed and over that a large sheet of oil paper, and hung my mosquito net, and somehow the hours went by. The military party started from the hotel at day break, and a neat little room was washed and I moved over. My cook "borrowed" a friend's kitchen and cooked for me.

The man—the cook—and his son, spent 48 hours buying bus tickets to Shaowu, so great is the traffic. They took turns standing in line so as not to lose their turn. In the meantime I had the opportunity of making the acquaintance of General Li. The manager of the hotel is an old Foochow College student and he took me to call. The General had called on me one morning at daybreak—but I was not up, so he set 7 o'clock for me to call. We had a long talk and he promised to do his best to alleviate the suffering of the starving Foochow people. Nanking is full of Foochow people, and I picked one of my refugee girls and took her with me to a school in Shaowu.

While at the hotel, Mr. Talbot—a Foochow missionary, arrived from Shaowu, and said that when he was a few miles from Nanking a telegraph pole was thrown across the road to stop the bus, and the bandits came on and searched everyone and threw the contents of their suitcases on the floor of the bus, and as people fought for their goods there was an awful time. He was relieved of $200.

Next morning I was to go over this road, leaving at 5 o'clock. I was ready to leave the hotel at 2 A.M., and the two men and a boy each took a parcel and we got to the door of the bus station. It was very dark, but a lot of people were ahead of us. The man took my suitcase on his shoulder and edged up to the door. When the bolt was drawn people poured in like a flood—only one bus and so many wanting to leave. The men got into the bus and got one seat.

Finally from a distance I saw a crowd of people waving, and at last we were in Shaowu. All the Hsueh family and Foochow College teachers and Shaowun people who had been refugees in Foochow—Foochow people who are now refugees in Shaowu—turned out to greet this old lady—and that was not a small thing to do, for the bus station is across the Min River far from the City, and walking is the only way to go.

Love from,   Martha Wiley

SHAOWU, FUKIEN   OCTOBER 10, 1941

Dear Sister Belle,

Hardly had I gotten here when General Li—the present governor, now in Foochow—sent me a telegram asking me to return to Foochow at once and begin a Relief campaign in co-operation with his staff. But I could not undertake it so soon. A few months away would do me some good, and the governor could get someone else to help him.

I had to go to South Gate and watch the moving out of a family from the shack that I'm moving into, and get a couple of men started to white washing the walls, and some more to start scrubbing, and a carpenter to stop up the chinks and change a partition. I hope that the rats will not eat us alive.

Josephine got to Shanghai on October 8th and sent a telegram from there. She left for Ku-Kong on September 20th on the last thru bus. Reached there in time for a bombing of that city by 62 planes. Some planes dropped bombs so close that dirt thrown up showered her. She had to fly from there to Hong Kong. The steamer was delayed a week so she got it. These days it is not good to travel unless one has urgent business.

Love,   Martha

[partial letter to Belle from the Hsuehs]

Dear Auntie Belle:--

How are you? I think of you very often. I wish that you could see the lantern parade. I like Yakima apples and I like you. Good bye love to you.

Elizabeth Hsueh

Dear Auntie Belle:--

We all think of you, especially today because it is your Birthday. We are all very happy to have Miss Wiley with us. She is well and we are glad that she could be here to have a change after her three years hard work. With much love to you from all the Hsuehs, and please remember me to your family and a hug to the baby Isabella.

Catherine Hsueh

Dear Aunty Belle:--

Today we have a happy day because today in China is something like July fourth and I make a big lantern and we put a candle in it so light that I can see every step I go. My daddy sends love to you too. I am going to end now so goodbye.

from Marian

Many Returns of your Birth-day. This is not hard to remember, for it is our National Holiday, the double ten (the tenth of the tenth month). We never forget our happy time in your house in the summer of 1938. May God bless you, always.

With love to you from Donald

"I am told that our Kuliang houses have been looted and gutted."

SHAOWU, FUKIEN   JUNE 4, 1942

Dear Sister and others,

When will the U.S. begin to get in some effective licks at the Joneses? To us out here everything moves awfully slow. The Joneses have everything their way so far. The U.S. was just like China—too optimistic in the beginning to be adequately prepared. Mr. Faurot has been getting home mail. Try air mail. Once or twice a week we can get a scrap or two of news from a defective radio and a small sheet of Chinese characters—called a newspaper. But though we are so hard up for foreign news, we did get word over a London broadcast that Foochow was taken, which was hardly accurate, as Foochow City was not invaded, but just Sharp Peak and the neighboring towns. I am told that our Kuliang houses have been looted and gutted. Sharp Peak home not reported yet. Fairy Bridge still cared for by Duai So. My furniture, and other belongings in all places, widely scattered. But I will gladly let them have all the things if I just do not have to move again or hear the bombers too often.

The tomato plants, that I trusted to supply me with fruit, just reached the blooming stage and then sicken and die. Even the University experts cannot find the cause. The soil is very sour, but when that is remedied the plants wither up just the same.

Poor old Donald! He had just got those terrible old buildings cleaned up and the Delco Lights established when a new disaster came. He will have to turn his boys out for the cadets that are coming. Tragic! Tragic! How the Chinese who are in places of responsibility stand this I do not know. Their endurance is beyond understanding.

If William has another $300 of mine lying around idle he may send it to Mr. Belcher [ABCFM treasurer], as before. Mr. Belcher has ways of getting funds to us. Besides my expenses I give to the hungry ones. I have to be grandmother to all the boys of Foochow College, and the Foochow people who are sick and distressed come to me. Around $126 U.S. got through in April. That is all, besides what William sent to Boston that has come through in months, besides my salary.

This week we are holding the term exams. How interesting to be teaching in Foochow College under much the same circumstances as 42 years ago when the Boxer uprising was stirring the world—and us especially! But the Boxer antics were play compared to what is on the carpet now. The very latest news just in is that Foochow is being prepared to resist. So no food is being shipped in. Poor people!

Martha

"More and more soldiers pouring in on wheelbarrows,
stretchers, and on foot, crowding all homes
and taking their furniture."

SHAOWU, FUKIEN, CHINA   JULY 25, 1942

Dear family,

It is said that the 86th regiment is coming here so we fear that the bombing will begin in earnest along with the machine gunning. I am starting a dug-out in the yard for those who want to go in. I never once went into the one Donald and I made in Foochow—preferring the open air.

It will soon be a year since your last letter—and what may have happened in a year. Are you women in war-work as during the last war? How useless the whole mad war is, and the condition at the end will be even worse, with the financial and moral breakdown that always follows war.

Life goes on here—in a mixture of fears and spells of quiet. The towns in the districts bordering Shaowu have all been terribly bombed and machine-gunned and many burned. Shaowu has had and still has many alarms. The former crowd of wounded soldiers has moved on, and a new lot of several thousand have moved in, and every nook and corner oozes soldiers. Every alley and doorway is unspeakably filthy, and the one principal street is clean only on the row of stones in the very middle of the street. The soldiers snatch whatever they want. Donald got up early and went a long way to buy a piece of meat for his family. Just as he had paid for it, a soldier snatched it out of his hands and ran. And the poor fellows are pitiful, too—sick, filthy, hungry, neglected, paid nothing, and ragged.

The extremely hot weather has been late in coming, but now it is 90 degrees in my bedroom, which is low and shut in by walls—but how glad I am not to move out. If one could get to Foochow it would be cooler and safer just at present, but the way there is dangerous and the risks too great during travel—so here we stay. Throngs of soldiers now pouring into this town will increase the food problem.

Foochow College will open the first week of September—unless!—and I will do full time teaching. Donald has a wretched time. Shortage of funds and teachers, panics from fear of Japanese invasion, difficulty in getting food, and a thousand other things. He looks old and weary. Five years of war is a long time. Will it be a "Seven-Years-War" or a "Hundred-Years-War"?

Refugees report that the Japanese are becoming more and more cruel and malicious. They looted the German missionaries' homes just the same as the American.

July 28 —— More and more soldiers pouring in on wheelbarrows, stretchers, and on foot, crowding all homes, the Hsuehs included, and taking their furniture.

Martha

***"The sick and wounded were carried in here and
often dumped on the street to die."***

SHAOWU, FUKIEN, CHINA   FEBRUARY 15, 1943

Dear Mrs. Blandon,

The cholera and malignant malaria raged in this town, especially as the sick and wounded were carried in here and often dumped on the street to die. For a time, several would die on the street in front of my house each night and cry out until death claimed them. Most of them were cholera cases, and we had nothing to give them. When our students were ill, the nurse had to boil herbs for a tea to check the cholera. Only one student died of cholera and one of cerebral malaria. At last the summer was ended, and the cold weather came and checked the worst ravages of these two diseases. Then the matter of clothing for the suffering was always before us. In Foochow we could buy clothing at the beginning of the war, but now just coarse cotton calico is $27 a foot. I brought to Shaowu every scrap of anything that I had that could be made into clothing—even the porch curtains—and most all has been used. My house maid loves to make clothes regardless of who wears them. One quilt (patchwork) was made into trousers—and did they look funny? They made everyone who saw them laugh.

Martha

"Interesting to see what false prophets most wise men are."

MARCH 11, 1943

Dear Anna and the others,

We get a typed sheet of radio news from one of the missionaries who has a radio, when he has the time to take down the news. The same comes a day or two later in a Chinese language news sheet. I have just read through a Readers Digest of 1939! Interesting to see what false prophets most wise men are—and also because of nothing new to read. In the summer I was reduced to reading Jane Austen's insipid stories. Only a few magazines came in 1941, none at all in 1942-43. At least we are relieved from reading stacks of painful detail.

. . .

Martha

"There is no glass in the school rooms and when the wind blows it fairly howls."

SHAOWU, FUKIEN, CHINA   APRIL 14, 1943

Dear Sister and other Relatives,

Already we are into the springtime, and here the hills are red with azaleas and every bit of uncultivated land in the valley is yellow with buttercups, and in another week the wild roses will be out and covering some of the broken walls that are so unsightly.

Anna is always worrying about my food. I have just finished my dinner which consisted of a potato (Donald brought me a basket of them from Foochow) and a tiny piece of bacon (also from Foochow) and a bowl of cauliflower (raised in our front yard) and a biscuit (with maltose syrup), and a pomolo, native grown and hard to buy and harder to eat! So that is ample for one old lady to have for lunch. For supper I will have soft-boiled rice and some kind of vegetable.

This week Donald bought a lot of tea oil for the school, and he kindly told me that I might have a tin of it—a kerosene can ¾ full, at $600—which is much cheaper than if I had bought it at retail (if I could have got it at all). Then the cook found that a wounded soldier had 20 pounds of sugar to sell and I bought ten pounds for $200. My charcoal had run out and I bought enough for a month for $110. The syrup had run out so the cook got some made at a shop—three baking powder tins for $25. This tea oil is supposed to be good for both cooking and lighting—but my insides do not agree. Lard is not on the market and very seldom is any meat. This does not worry me at all, but I would like more fruit, and soon the loquats will be out and will make us all happy. I have had AMPLE FOR ALL MY NEEDS and no one need worry about me. The cost is appalling at times. Rice in Foochow is now $700 a load (100 lbs) — normal price is $7. So you see that most of the staple foods have gone up in price 100 times while salaries have increased two or three times, which is very hard on salaried or white-collar workers.

Eu-nguk sews and mends and the cook does buying and odd jobs. At last Catherine's fierce servant left her and Catherine decided to try doing her own work. It was rather hard for her to get out and boil rice and have it ready at 5:30 every morning so that Donald and the girls could get to school before 7 A.M. She calls on my people when she has something urgent that she needs to do. We have spells of letter writing when she must do less housework. She is not adapted to heavy work, but she felt that she should try it as the family expenses are becoming so high. They had to move, and the only house that they could get, rented for $200 a month, so they sub-let one half of it. As a result my "palace" is piled high with their trunks, since they think this a safer place than their own.

Mabelle had to give up her music for this term, as in June she must take the government Uniform examinations, at the end of her Junior Middle School. The examinations are very stiff for the youngsters. Mabelle was the only girl in a class of 70 boys last term, and she got second rank. She fell behind in Chinese literature because of their long stay in the U.S. Marian is doing very well with her violin, and gave a recital all by herself on Sunday afternoon. Elizabeth practices on the piano and is doing well. I keep on teaching English all the week days and Bible all day Sunday, so am happy and flatter myself that I am useful.

For the past two weeks, it has been so cold that I had a fire night and morning. The temperature was down in the 30's most of the time. The school rooms have mud floors, and when the weather is damp they are rather sticky. There is no glass in the rooms, and when the wind blows it fairly howls. Pioneering must agree with me for I did not have a cold, and no malaria, and did not miss a day of school all of 1942, and now hope that I may have such a good record in 1943. Of course the Joneses have broken up school for many days. When the siren blows, the boys land outside and with a whoop of joy start for the nearby hills. The crestfallen teacher goes home and waits for the "all clear" before going back. We are right in line with an objective that the Jonsies are after, so have to be pestered with them very often—but no matter as long as they leave nothing with us.

I would love to see your grandchildren and your flowers and walk about the peaceful roads with you and see no wounded soldiers. I suspect that you will soon feel the distress of war when many of the young men fail to return, but let us hope that no enemy ever sets foot on the homeland, and the scourge of invasion never takes place.

Affectionately,   Martha

"Sirens still break into our class work, but nothing worse."

SHAOWU   APRIL 28, 1943

Dear Miss Williams and Miss Katherine,

Today is so quiet in Shaowu that it cannot seem credible that there is so much turmoil. Wild flowers in abundance decorate the landscape. The surrounding mountains are an indigo blue. Springtime in Shaowu is really lovely.

Donald and Catherine are going through a great mental strain to decide whether to stay on for a term or go back to Ingtai in the summer. In Ingtai rice is $700 a load (150 lbs.), buildings even worse than in Shaowu, and the constant menace of being near the coast in case the Joneses make a second visit, as is threatened often. Alas, if we give up the present quarters they cannot be had if we go away from Ingtai again—and moving is a nightmare.

But the number of pupils is dwindling. Sickness is a constant fact. This term one student died of meningitis and a second now has it, but is recovering. Injections cost $450 each, and worse, every drop of serum is used up and no more is to be had. The older teachers are often sick, and at present the dean has a large carbuncle between his shoulders, and has been dangerously ill for days. Injections by the army doctor cost the usual $450 each.

Prices still soar. A spool of thread costs $24 and cotton cloth $37 a foot. A thief came into my house and stole my fountain pen, now worth over $1,000! Donald and Catherine caught him and got back the pen. Sirens still break into our class work, but nothing worse. Neither the Hsuehs nor myself could have gone through the past year on our income (salaries), but beloved friends have enabled us to help others from their gifts. God bless you all.

Abiding love,   Martha Wiley

"I would like to have a home in Foochow for the few
remaining years of my sojourn on earth."

SHAOWU   JUNE 3, 1943

Dear Mr. McClure,

There is one matter I would like to talk over with you and know what your reaction is, and that is hard to get from a letter. However I will write the gist of the matter. For a long time I have been thinking seriously that I would like to have a home in Foochow for the few remaining years of my sojourn on earth. According to the Board rule, when one retires from active work she is supposed to get off the American Board property.

As you probably know, the major part of the Fairy Bridge property was bought by money raised by Miss Hartwell and me. In fact, Miss Hartwell was to raise one third and I one third, and the B.M.I. a third, for the original purchase. Then we kept adding small pieces on our own responsibility and including them in the compound. The last piece along the canal was paid for from my personal funds—when U.S. and L.C. [local currency] were almost equal (land and wall $1,600), and one piece was $280 U.S. that I paid for, as I remember. Besides this, I have been personally responsible for most of the upkeep all these years—and that has not been a small amount as the white ant season came on each year.

Of course there might be a howl that old missionaries would be troublesome—and no one is a competent judge of herself and the feelings of others in regard to her peculiarities. At any rate, the first step is to have a home that would in no way conflict with the comforts of the missionaries and their "work." This would be possible at Fairy Bridge with the Hsueh family on one side and Chinese workers on the other, each with his own allotted place.

Now I could manage the finances of this while Miss Williams is still alive—but it would be harder after she is gone. She is now nearer 90 than 80 and time is precious. If I returned to the U.S., I would be just one more old missionary derelict hanging around somewhere, and not especially welcome anywhere. I have no delusions about old people being so charming that people do not weary of them. The best way is to have a home of one's own somewhere and then retire to that. If I follow the age limit of most of my people, I will have eight more years to endure myself—and not, I hope, make anyone else endure me. Up to this date I flatter myself that I have been useful, but times are changing.

Now please write me frankly if you think that this is feasible or the right thing to work toward. If you do, I will plan to go to Foochow this summer and talk it all out with you and/or your property committee. If you think this is not possible, and an unwise procedure, just say it out "right from the shoulder." I value your opinion.

Good-bye,   Martha Wiley

SHAOWU, FUKIEN, CHINA   JULY 5, 1943

Dear Sister Belle,

My cook has gone to Foochow for the summer. Eu-nguk and I are glad that he has gone for a while, as it gives us a good chance to scour the kitchen and all the utensils. The buying and dishwashing has been my job so far, but when the weather is settled I will increase my activities.

All of June and the first week in July has been one continuous downpour. The river Min has burst all his banks—and such floods! The current changes with the high water, so makes travel by boat to and from Foochow exceedingly dangerous. Three days after

Donald started down river a boat captain arrived, and said that a Foochow College boat had been wrecked and several Foochow College people drowned. If Donald had not sent a telegram about some school business from a town farther down the river just at that time, there would have been some lusty wailing in the Hsueh household. Even yet we do not know what started the rumor.

The Mission Treasurer said that his office would pay the travel to Foochow for all the missionaries in Shaowu, if they would go to Foochow for the summer. My home in Foochow is closed and all the things packed and scattered here and there. The Kuliang cottage has not been occupied in three years, so it will be about eaten up by termites. It would take a month to get settled and then it would be time to return. And coming up river is not a pleasure trip. Only three missionaries decided to go. Besides, in the summer is when Catherine and I get off our main correspondence of the year. One might as well swelter here as in Foochow—but in Foochow there is better food. My cook will do a good many errands for me and can two dozen cans of peaches. Do you remember my former dislike of canned peaches? Now, with such a scarcity, fruit of any kind seems most desirable.

These few days I have kept to the wide street of town, for walls are falling here and there with no notice. Continued rain and floods have softened the lower part of the walls, and all at once they come down broadside with the sound of a cannon. Some lives have been lost during the week. Three enormous walls at Foochow College have gone down, but no one in the school injured. I called a mason to look over the walls of my house and yard, and he said that they were all O.K. and dry as a bone. That night a big section of the garden wall fell down! So I do not think much of expert opinion about walls.

This P.M. I plan to go to a mission meeting at the University. We have to walk everywhere—just go wading through the mud and water. These two years my only way of getting anywhere has been on my two feet. It keeps a person young to have to walk several miles a day. Yesterday I was weighed and my weight was 135 pounds—not thin for me. I still have one pair of rubbers that do not leak, and that is more than most people have.

After five years of no new clothes and sharing with others occasionally, I find myself with plenty of clothing; such as it is, except stockings. My stockings look as though they all had varicose veins, except two pairs that I keep for emergency. All summer we either wear socks or go without anything but sandals. The boys in Foochow College come to class barefoot and with their short scout trunks, and look too much unclothed. Now that school is closed for the summer, there has been not a single siren. Before that, days at a time, we were interrupted and the boys had to take to the long grass of the hills. Perhaps the rain has something to do with our quiet.

Love to each and all, Martha Wiley

"A big cobra is tormenting me more than the Japanese."

SHAOWU, FUKIEN   AUGUST 9, 1943

Dear Miss Williams,

Plague has been terrible in Foochow this past spring and is still bad. It is reported that one hundred persons a day die of it in Foochow now. Dr. Liu tells me that inoculations are not certain to develop immunity. Often people who have taken inoculations become reckless, not knowing of the uncertainty of being immune. Donald has been in the midst of that for six weeks at least. Both bubonic and pneumonic types have prevailed.

One of our teachers who made a quick trip to Foochow, came back with a skinned spot on the back of his head, where a piece of shrapnel took him when he was in a bus on the way home, not far from Shaowu. Sirens have been pests for a good while this summer, but no planes here. A big cobra is tormenting me more than the Japanese. Twice this week he has crawled to the kitchen door, and one day I looked out of the screen door of our sitting room and he was very leisurely passing before the doorstep. The war whoop that I gave started up his pace, and he got into the grass of the yard, and there he may be yet. If my cook were here he could soon kill it, but women and children are not equal to attacking a cobra for they turn and fight. We all go about as though we had delirium tremens. At dark we shut up all the outside doors, and whenever we move about take a light.

Affectionately,   Martha

"When she was small she had to run so hard to keep up with the older brothers that she had no time to grow."

SHAOWU, FUKIEN, CHINA   AUGUST 31, 1943

Dear James and Belle and John,

This will soon be the birthday season for all of you, so I will write you a joint letter. Jim will now be in the eighties and John not far behind—and Belle trying her best to catch up with them! Mother used to say that the reason Belle never grew larger was that when she was small she used to run so hard to keep up with the older brothers that she had no time to grow.

I wonder how the war is affecting you farmers. At the end of World War I all prices but farmer's produce were high. But if high prices mean INFLATION, almost anything is better than that.

Your letter, Belle, dated May 13th, reached me exactly three months later. The last month of that time was covering the distance from Chunking to Shaowu. TRANSPORTATION

IS NOW at it's lowest. It requires ten days to get mail from Foochow to Shaowu (300 miles).

This has been the coolest summer that I have ever experienced in China—never over 90 degrees, and frequent rains in the evening. Foochow had a terrible time with typhoons this summer, and that kept Shaowu cool, as it is just on the edge of the storm belt. But the natives say the "tiger" (fierce heat) will come in September. Here's hoping they are wrong!

Love to each one and many, many more happy birthdays!

Martha

"Dozens trained in the Woman's School
are now army nurses."

SHAOWU, FUKIEN   SEPTEMBER 1, 1943

Dear Anna and William,

A typhoon carried on for a good part of the time at Foochow and blew off the crop of peaches, but the rim of the storm reached us in cooling breezes and showers, and I have never known such a cool summer in China. And the terrible diseases, which raged at Foochow—bubonic and pneumonic plague, did not reach us this summer. Just this week the bubonic plague has started here and 47 of the people in a block or two have been taken. I have been going to a shop to buy maltose but will not go again for a while. Malaria has been bad here, but dysentery cases in the school have been mild compared with last year, and no meningitis since the spring. One teacher went to Foochow to the hospital for examination and was kept there, dying of tuberculosis in three weeks.

[Excerpt of partial story written by Martha: "At one time 77 students who were quartered in an old, deserted Buddhist temple seemed to be sure to eventually face death—when Catherine remembered seeing her grandmother gather a certain kind of herb and make a tea to give to the people. . . . (Catherine administered the tea, and not one person treated, died of malaria.)]

[Note: Chinese herbalists have used the leaves of the Artemisia annua, or sweet wormwood, (Quinghao) for more than a thousand years.]

A student is passing on this week it seems, also of TB. He took the highest rank in the whole school. The dean tried to make him go home in the spring but he refused. He lived to study. He had no interest in religion. I went to see him often when he took down, but he always answered me that he did not understand.

Right here I stopped, until the noise of passing enemy planes stopped. How I wish that those devilish things would be put an end to! They come and tear up our neighboring cities often enough to keep a person excited when they go overhead. I guess they are gone for this time.

Donald got back a week ago, and has been working day and night to get things here in shape to go back to Ingtai, where he will have Junior one and Senior one. He takes charge there and leaves the dean here at Shaowu with the rest. The reason being that the new students refused to go to Shaowu, and teachers newly hired also refused Shaowu. The students that have got established in Shaowu are willing to return. It is very expensive to divide forces, and we hope and pray that by the end of the year everybody may go back to Foochow permanently. This summer thousands have died of plague so it was good to be out of that mess—we had such a time last year. Donald just dropped in to say that $10,000 relief for poor students has failed us. Must plan.

It seems to me that I have crowded more into this five years than into any previous ten, but the Lord only knows whether this is the case or not. Dozens of women trained in the Woman's School are now army nurses.

Every old dress that I have not given away or made into refugee clothes, I have been wearing this summer. You would laugh to see so many of your antiques in good preservation. Now I can wear anything that was for a while too tight. One missionary asked me for white cloth for a patch on her sheet. I cut the end off one of mine and took it to her—and did she have a sheet. It was patch after patch. I would have given her my sheet if I had known before what she had. A sheet here is now worth from $600 to $1,000. I still have more than two.

How did you get the idea that the Board had cut our salaries? They have been doubled. I must not have written clearly. Of course the government rate of exchange has not advanced as the inflated prices have, but we get on all right. With the special gifts, I can help the poor. An old student who is an official showed up during the summer. He had finished traveling over most of free China and said that Fukien still had the lowest prices in China. I pity the others. I had rice and "morning glories" (a vine like morning glories) and cucumbers and onion fritters for dinner.

Yesterday I walked a mile or two to a mill and bought two pounds of wheat. We will roast that and grind it in a stone hand mill, and it makes good porridge. I always have a good breakfast—milk, toast, porridge, an egg, and fruit in season!!! So no one needs worry about my food. I have two hens that between them provide me with an egg a day and sometimes I can buy a few. The trouble with fresh eggs is that someone always needs them more than I do. When the cook gets back, I plan to have some cookies made with a kind of wheat syrup and the Hsuehs and I will have a feast. Bread in the shop is about $30 a lb., flour $14 upward.

The old timers are profiteers. It is the refugee and migrant population that suffer—the white collar people. One can use a thousand dollars of this money and never know what has been bought—a basket of peanuts (46 lbs. with shell) for about $400 and six loads of charcoal (600 lbs.) for $600 and my thousand was gone.

September 2 —— Pneumonic plague took a Catholic nun and a Chinese nurse yesterday. The Catholic compound is about half a mile from here. Strange thing, that disease—it dips down and takes a person here and there without warning. I will stay away from that region for a while, but the germs come by air.

Yesterday received letter from ROSE, Josephine, Emily, Mrs. Hinman and others including yours—grand mail. Emily S. Hartwell's letter full of holes—too much hot stuff, (censored).

September 3 —— Cook pulled in on his two feet last night, half dead! Bubonic and pneumonic plague in all towns on the way. One of our best students drowned on the way upriver.

Love to each and all,　Martha

"I make the servants keep quiet about the prices or
I would have no desire to eat."

SHAOWU, FUKIEN, CHINA　NOVEMBER 30, 1943

Dear sister,

The subject, which everyone gets enthusiastic about now, is PRICES. Flour is now $20 a lb.—lard, $70—fruit, none—one seedy, sour little orange, $10 a 3 lb. chicken, $200—pork, around $64 a lb. When I sit down to a meal I make the servants keep quiet about the prices, or I would have no desire to eat. This morning I paid the month's milk bill—scant pint a day costing $300. We are told: "Trust in the Lord and do good and verily thou shalt be fed." I always have enough and some to share with my needy neighbors—thanks to the friends in good old U.S.A.! My typewriter paper is almost gone—just a little carbon paper left—and when that is gone I will have to trust to a pen or even a lead pencil.

Mr. Faurot, Foochow College music teacher, has taken Mabelle to Foochow and Nanping to give concerts, and expected to go to the Provincial Capital—but two weeks ago the "Joneses" bombed out of existence two-thirds of the city, and those that are left do not feel very joyful—so that much of the tour is off.

Love to each and all,　Martha

*"I do not have enough money to have a home in the U.S., but
I can live very comfortably in Foochow on my income."*

FOOCHOW COLLEGE, SHAOWU, FUKIEN, CHINA FEBRUARY 15, 1944

Mr. H. B. Belcher
14 Beacon Street
Boston, Mass. U.S.A.

Dear Mr. Belcher,

Will you kindly read this letter and pass on to the Secretary who handles such requests as mine? Mr. McClure has written me that "the Board wishes more data" in regard to my request to retire on the field.

Perhaps I should simplify my letter of about October 1, 1943. First of all the question of a home is permanent in my thought. If I should return to the U.S., after a few weeks of visiting with friends, I would have no place to live permanently. My retiring allowance must be my dependence in old age. My savings account in the U.S. is a negligible amount, as you know for many years the American Board grant for Woman's Work in Foochow was only a nominal sum. The rest I had to make up, and that left very little on my personal account. I do not have enough money to have a home in the U.S., but I can live very comfortably in Foochow on my income.

In Foochow I can have a small home of my own near the Hsueh family and other Chinese friends, with my servant who has been with me for more than 20 years. There would always be something that I could do among the poor of a large city like Foochow.

The friends of my younger days in the U.S. are nearly all dead and their children and grandchildren scarcely know my name. But in Foochow I count three generations of Christian families as friends.

I dread those cold winters in the U.S. where one is shut in most of the time. In Foochow, where I can be out of doors every day, my health is good. These two and one half years in Shaowu, I have not missed any classes on account of ill health.

By the time this letter reaches you I will have begun the 45th year of service under the American Board. After so long a residence away from my native land, I am unused to the American gadgets, speed, noise, conveniences—in fact, life as a whole. The quieter (though less convenient) ways of the Chinese are more familiar to me.

In spite of refugee conditions, these years in Shaowu, in touch again with student life in Foochow College have been a very great satisfaction to me.

Sincerely yours,   Martha Wiley

"During this hard life as a refugee Martha has been stronger than any of us—either Chinese or Missionaries."

[letter from Catherine]   FOOCHOW COLLEGE   SHAOWU, FUKIEN, CHINA   APRIL 17, 1944

Dear Mrs. Achelpohl: [Anna]

The Fairy Bridge Compound, which had been Miss Wiley's home (and also Donald's and mine) for 25 years, was sold to Miss Wiley and Donald and me. It was sold very cheap to us because we are all mission workers, and also because so large a place is not needed by the Woman's School any longer. Miss Wiley paid half and we paid half. There are four Chinese acres (1½ U.S. acres) inside the city. The buildings are very poor and badly eaten by termites, so we will need to build or repair our homes.

Foochow College and the Synod and many personal friends have asked the American Board to let Miss Wiley retire on the field. The Board has not answered yet, but we feel sure it will all agree, though it has a strict policy to the contrary. Old missionaries are expected to go to the homeland. But so many have asked her to stay that I feel sure that she may have the privilege if she wants it. The Hsueh family certainly wants her to be near them.

During these three years of refugee life she has taught the children every day. Donald and I will do all that we can if she is sick, but here during this hard life as a refugee she has been stronger than any of us—either Chinese or Missionaries.

I want to tell you about a gift for her BIRTHDAY celebration. She was given a set of scrolls sent all the way from Chungking. They were made by Admiral Chen Shao-Kwan, also a member of the National Council, and expressed admiration of her character and thanks for her long service in China.

My children and I remember the good things you sent us when we were in the U.S., and the girls still think that the dresses that you made for them are their best. When they go to Foochow in the summer they will wear them again. We are very happy that Jean has two sons. If she were a Chinese she would be very proud. We recall the happy day in Chicago when Jean and her husband took charge of us. It has always been a regret that we have not met you and your daughter Doris. I have heard of your family so often that I seem to know them all. I hope that when the war is ended you and Mr. Achelpohl will make a visit to Foochow. We will all try to make you have a good time. I must now try to write Mrs. Woodhouse [Belle]. All of you seem as near as real relatives.

Sincerely yours,   Catherine Lin Hsueh

[letter from Admiral Chen]   CHUNKING, MAY 31, 1944

Dear Miss Wiley,

I thank you very much for your kind letter of April 30th which Mr. Ting has brought to me when he arrived in Chunking and from him I am very glad to learn that you have always been in good health.

I do hope the Board can let you to remain in Foochow after the war. If you have to go home we should miss you very much. Should I happen to be in Fukien during or after the war I would certainly not miss the opportunity to visit you.

God bless you.

Yours sincerely,   Chen Shao-kwan

*"When I land in the U.S. I am like a stranger—
not knowing where to turn."*

JULY 24, 1944

Dear Anna,

The American Board has not agreed to my retiring at Foochow, so when the war is over I must go to the U.S. for furlough at least, and probably permanently. If I stay in the U.S. I will have an income from the Board of $75 a month. That is now not enough for room rent in the U.S. If the Board would let me stay here, I could live on that and have a home of my own. When I land in the U.S. I am like a stranger—not knowing where to turn and for the rest of my life with no settled place that I can call my own. But why worry? The Lord knows all about it. When I think of Emily Smith and a host of other single women living like outcasts I do not like the prospect.

Now you can understand why I did not go to the U.S. when every other foreigner fled to the U.S. from Shaowu—I was not leaving here until I had to. Of course you will never give up your home. Always stick to that. I wish that I could talk with you half a day and clear up my mind. Of course, if one has money enough, the U.S. is far more comfortable than China—but if not, China is better and cheaper. Chinese friends may be personally biased when I talk with them. So I cannot talk freely with them or be too much influenced by their opinion.

I hope that you keep well and do not worry about the future. It will be a new experience for me to be shut down tight on money, as I have always had enough to use freely for myself and others. I think that I grow lazy, and I do not want to think of work in the U.S. In fact there is nothing that I could do. Here I could earn good money tutoring. I wear on

Belle's nerves with too much talking and company. Just think! She will be 75 this fall. Tell me what expenses are for you now—then I will know about what I should plan for.

Lots of love from,   Martha

AMERICAN BOARD OF COMMISSIONERS FOR FOREIGN MISSIONS
Foreign Department

CHINA BULLETIN (#71)   October 10, 1944

NEWS FROM FOOCHOW

Confirming the fall of at least Foochow City, the American Board today received a radio message from Rev. Elmer W. Galt, acting treasurer of the Foochow and Shaowu Missions, sent from Ingtai (Yungtai according to the spelling in the national language) and reading: "WILEY LANGTREE ARMSTRONG GILLETTE TOPPING FAUROT GALT UNHARMED. INGTAI DYER NUEMANNS JACOBS HOUSTON WILCOX INTERNED MISSION PREMISES FOOCHOW."

We understand this to mean that the Westerners on the staff of the Willis F. Pierce Memorial Hospital in Foochow, the Union Hospital, chose to remain with the hospital patients and Chinese staff when the Japanese approached the city and were interned on the mission premises immediately adjoining the hospital.. . .

It is probable that Miss Martha Wiley, Miss Lucy B. Langtree, Miss Susan E. Armstrong and Mr. Albert Faurot were already in Ingtai, where Foochow College and the Orlinda Childs Pierce Memorial Girls School (Wenshan) presumably opened their fall term in late August or early September.

. . .

Ingtai is about 25 miles southwest of Foochow, up the Ingtai River. It is not on a main strategic route, and may escape occupation by the Japanese, as their declared purpose is to occupy a potential friendly landing point for the American forces. In 1941 when the Japanese occupied Foochow, they did not go more than half way to Ingtai. A letter from Mr. Galt sent July 2nd, after the ten American Board Missionaries had decided to stay in Foochow and vicinity, said that those who remained were convinced that "if the need arises for us to join the ranks of the mobile, there are mountain fastnesses not at all far away where we can live very tranquilly and comfortably for any period of time that may become necessary."

It is very possible that the hospital staff in Foochow will be given a certain length of time for clearing the hospital of patients, and then later all Foochow internees will be transferred to the central internment camps in Shanghai, as it seems to be the Japanese policy to remove isolated groups of internees to the main internment centers.

. . .

A word of caution: In our newspaper release, we carefully avoided mentioning the name of Ingtai or reference to the "mountain fastnesses," presumably in the mountains beyond Ingtai. Please see that these facts do not get into print, as we have evidence via Argentina or otherwise even copies of Life are reaching Japan; and identification of the whereabouts of this little group of missionaries might stimulate a Japanese raid in that direction.

Wynn C. Fairfield

1944

BOSTON, OCTOBER 11-(AP)-THREE CONGREGATIONAL MISSIONARIES OF THE AMERICAN BOARD OF FOREIGN MISSIONS WERE INTERNED IN MISSION PREMISES AFTER OCCUPATION OF FOOCHOW, CHINA, AND SEVEN OTHERS WERE "UNHARMED" AT ANOTHER OF ITS STATIONS IN THE MOUNTAINS, THE BOARD ANNOUNCED TODAY.

THE INTERNED MISSIONARIES WERE MEMBERS OF THE STAFF OF THE WILLIS F. PIERCE MEMORIAL UNION HOSPITAL IN FOOCHOW.

THE MISSIONARIES AT THE MOUNTAIN STATION INCLUDE MISS MARTHA WILEY OF YAKIMA.

CHINA BULLETIN #71 A   October 25, 1944

On October 21st we received a cable from Mr. Elmer Galt bringing us the sad news that Rev. and Mrs. Ling Iu-cu (Lin Yu-Shu) of Foochow died on October 8th. Mr. Galt's message read as follows:

"SYNOD INFORMS YOU WIDESPREAD MOURNING TRAGIC DEATH OCTOBER EIGHTH LING IU-CU AND WIFE. TOPPING TEMPORARILY ONLY SECRETARY. MISSIONARIES FOOCHOW HAVE CONSIDERABLE FREEDOM."

Our interpretation of this message is that Rev. and Mrs. Y. S. Lin were killed in connection with the occupation of Foochow by the Japanese. Mr. Lin was the secretary of the Mid-Fukien Synod and an outstanding leader of the whole United Church of Christ in China. . . . As the cable notes, this throws sole responsibility for the Synod secretary-ship on Mr. Topping.

We are very grateful for the information Mr. Galt sends us that our missionaries in Foochow have considerable freedom. When the first message came advising us that the medical staff had stayed on in Foochow, we had hoped that they might be permitted to carry on their work in the hospital, and this second message would seem to give increased grounds for that hope. The Union Hospital immediately adjoins the missionary residence compound and can be reached without going on the street.

Wynn C. Fairfield

To relatives, Foochow active and retired missionaries and staff.

[letter from the Christians]   368 S. McClellan Ave.   Decatur, Illinois   December 12, 1944

Dear Friends,

Many of you already know that our beloved Foochow Mission is suffering the darkest hours of its hundred years of history. In the spring, when the Japanese began the drive southward along the railway, all Fukien missionaries were advised by their Boards and by the U.S. government to evacuate as far as possible; and that those who decided to remain must be prepared to be shut in for the duration, because if the drive succeeded there would be no road open to them to leave the province until the coastal blockade is lifted.

After there had been much debate and indecision, in June a sudden opportunity came for a group to ride out on some Chinese military trucks. With only four hours notice, ten Americans packed their most needed possessions into duffle bags and suitcases, and climbed into small box-like trucks for their first 40 miles. That night they slept on boards, which normally were the front wall of an inn, but had been stretched across stools to provide sleeping accommodations for ten 'foreigners'—without a speck of privacy!

The story of that trip is still coming to us in its many aspects of danger narrowly escaped, privations cheerfully met, hearts wrung with anguish for China's helpless sufferers, and yet, over all, a sense of God's loving guidance, as four of the group headed for work in West China, and the rest toward India and the road home. This latter contingent landed in California just about the same time the Japanese took over Foochow.

Meanwhile, those who remained in Foochow had still been counting on the possibility that invasion might not come their way, that the enemy might be so busy using the railway line, after they captured it, that they would not have time to invade the surrounding provinces. But they counted without the Japanese Navy, which decided on further conquest along the coast to make doubly sure there would be no place for American aviators to use China airfields.

. . .

Loyally yours,   Agnes M. Christian
Leonard J. Christian

AMERICAN BOARD

BULLETIN #71 F   **December 21, 1944**

PART OF THE FOOCHOW STORY

December 4, we received a letter from Rev. William H. Topping, secretary of Mid-Fukien Synod, dated October 23, in which he said: "I trust that you will have received our cable dated October 20 telling of the death of Rev. and Mrs. Y.S. Lin, at the hand of local Chinese ruffians, and also my letter dated October 16, telling in some detail the circumstances of the tragedy. I do hope these communications get through to you."

. . .

I am sending out these extracts that Mrs. Topping has sent, as well as two or three more sentences of news from the letter first referred to. I am sending the extracts just as they have come to me, except that I have added a few explanatory words or phrases in parenthesis. Please do not publish any of this without permission of Mrs. Topping or myself.

Wynn C. Fairfield

Extracts from Mr. Topping's other letters

6:45 A.M., October 2/44 —— The city has been in great excitement. This A.M. I hear cannons very clearly, and it seems to be getting nearer. Also machine gun fire very clear. Many people have evacuated and some are on boats on the river. I don't know how serious it is. Foochow College crowd are starting from Water Gate in a boat this A.M. for Ingtai. I'll have to get some things together in case we have to get out yet. I'm glad you're not here.

Oct. 2 —— 5 P.M. This has been a very hectic time but now I'm quietly sitting listening to a broadcast from San Francisco. I'd like to tell you about today's excitement, but it would not get through. The facts seem to be that pirates landed to capture a store of rice at Santuao. Half the force got what they landed for and the other half went further inland and last night were surrounded by our two friends' forces (Gen. Lee), and at daylight we heard the terrific noise and it was witnessed from the tennis courts where we spend the summer (Kuliang). Expect another day will complete the task. There was an Extra out today of the Central News giving many details. Many Chinese officials and foreign friends are sitting on boats at the Upper Bridge.

Those who were at the stone church last night are mostly on boats now. Susan Armstrong, Bert Faurot and Martha Wiley are on Foochow College boat headed for Upper Bridge. Lyda Houston would not go. If there's further trouble, the fewer here the better. Dr. Dyer and company plan to stay on no matter what happens. Elmer Galt and I sent some more things on the Foochow College boat. We're having Seng Seng hire three husky coolies to stay in our basement with Do Ming. They could carry our loads to Upper Bridge if we should suddenly have to go. I expect we'll stay right here. I can hear occasional big guns but the big noise of this A.M. lasted only two or three hours. I think the worst is over.

Lyda has just been in discussing what to do; then Dr. Dyer, Lyda and I had a talk on the lawn. The telephone rang up at the hospital just now from Miss Wray's Consul who is supposed to be on the river and he wanted to know if Miss Wray, who is in with a broken hip, could walk to the boat. He thinks the crisis is over and the situation well in hand. I hope we'll all sleep easy tonight.

9 P.M. —— Bert, Susan and Miss Wiley came back to sleep in their own beds, their sampan stuck on a sand bar. . . . Foochow College was evacuating to Ingtai, quite regardless of the present crisis. The staff is all on the boats.

Oct. 3, 6:45 A.M. —— Not much sleep, as I had one ear open most of the night listening to cannons and the rattling of machine guns, which kept up on and off during the night. As I write now the booming is terrific, sometimes making the table vibrate. I'm hoping the news in yesterday's Extra is correct and the situation is well in hand. I see Dr. Dyer out watering her flowers. Too bad so many boys have to be killed. I expect there must be a lot of casualties with all this shooting. It was bright moonlight most of the night. Many of the wounded have come into Cha-cang Hospital, none have come in here yet. It is nerve wracking.

12 noon —— Things about the same. I went over to Seng Seng's house last night to see why he had not sent the coolies. He had just left for the compound. We did a little further talking about the men and they are to come right after lunch. They will live at Lincoln Hall at Foochow College so that we can get them easily, and if we should have to leave they will return here after seeing our loads off at Upper Bridge. They in that case would act as a sort of guard for the compound, with two coolies already on guard at Foochow College. If they met armed resistance of course they'd have to get away, but they could offset local stealing especially if Seng Seng stayed here too, as he plans to do. He knows all the bad actors around here. I went to inform Lyda and told her to have all her girls leave, as we could not be responsible for them. She's going to do that. Lyda would be free to walk with us to Upper Bridge with her loads—she has two.

There is a lull in the fighting, which I assume is the calm before the storm—another Extra out today saying there was to be an all out attack on the pirates. Our General is at the front and am told is optimistic. Henry Lacy has all his office staff in a boat ready to leave if necessary. Dr. Dyer and Jakie (Jennie Jacobs) plan to stay longer than the rest of us to care for the remaining patients. Miss Wiley will either walk to Upper Bridge with us or with Dr. Dyer and Jakie. We all hope that none of us will have to go, but are planning for it if necessary. Last night I heard a lot of shooting in the streets.

Oct. 16 —— Rev. Leu Soi Ling went to Fairy Bridge where Catherine Siek [Hsueh] had been staying incognito. He was getting jittery, as they had been pressing him for information about the Foochow College rice. He had a hang-hang (a traitor or spy) with him and had told the hang-hang that Mrs. Siek [Hsueh], the principal's wife, knew everything and where she was. As soon as they left Fairy Bridge, Catherine hustled and got Seng Seng to take her to Southside, where she stayed hidden a week until Seng Seng could get her to Ingtai.

The 80th division seems to be waiting outside North Gate for the Japanese to retire and meanwhile they are looting the city clean. The guerrilla attack on the 8th was described to me by Catherine Siek [Hsueh], who saw part of it from Do Suek. About 5 A.M., firecrackers, bugles, etc. could be heard from the direction of Uang Bieng Gaek and eventually guerrillas came in sight, about 1,000 strong. A few Japanese waited on the hill until they got within range and then they fired, killing some, and the rest fled. Some of the wounded have arrived here and I have talked with some I know.

I wish I could tell you the situation in Foochow—it would be ridiculous if it were not so tragic. Gong Li Tung arrived here and told how the Japanese had entered his home and threatened him with bayonets six times, and made him open his safe and boxes. Seventeen guerrillas were carried though the streets here last night to the enthusiasm of all the people. They did the best they could with the equipment they had.

There is a long account in our Ingtai Daily Local sheet of the murder of Pastor Ling Iu Cu and his wife by the Japanese. They were torturing him until he died, to find out where funds were secreted, and then at 9 P.M. on the 8th they burned the house down. Ling Iu Cu had sealed up that back door into the college grounds and made a new outlet from his house into a narrow lane in the rear. It was this way that the ruffians could enter without having to pass the Foochow College gateman. He seemed to have had an obsession that he was going to be attacked in his home and had all the doors bricked up. Madeline Chen, principle of U.K.T.S. [Union Kindergarten Training School], is stranded at Mintsing with 18 girls, and Elmer and I wrote to Henry Lacy to give her $10,000 or anything she needs.

"The risk of going was far greater than the risk of staying."

JANUARY 16, 1945

Dearest Sister Belle,

This letter will soon be on its way to you, but if it or any previous letters have got across the seas is a question. Your last letter to reach me was dated the last week in July, so six months have gone by with no word from any one at home in the U.S.A. I have kept writing even oftener than in the past, hoping that at least a few letters would get though.

You may get more news by radio about Foochow than we at Ingtai get. It will soon be four months since we came up here, and we missionaries are not faring badly—but the Chinese refugees are crowded and miserable.

I had dreaded the winter on the mountainside, with the house poorly heated, but up to date there has been no weather as cold as at Shaowu.

A week or ten days ago a telegram came to our mission secretary from the Methodists at Mintsing, in a neighboring county, saying that all were starting to the U.S. via west China and India, and advising us to get out at once. Our secretary walked over the mountains to consult with them and see if there were any new developments in war news.

He came back all "het up" and saying that we four women were to pack up as soon as possible and get out and on our way. One woman had just been here a year after furlough; one was the English lady who would not spend the funds for travel; one was my hostess Miss Langtree, who has been here eight years with no furlough; and the last my humble self. The three flatly sat on the proposition, and I could not take that wild trip alone, especially as I do not speak the dialect used in the West.

I would need to walk to Mintsing—one and a half days—take a sampan to Nanping—up river two or three days—then by some unknown way get to Aing-Yang airfield, wait for a plane to somewhere, take another plane over the enemy lines—with insufficient warm clothing for the west China trip and no summer clothing for the heat of India, and no companion. So I also just kept quiet and made no preparation. The risk of going was far greater than the risk of staying. Sleeping in Chinese inns, with the "lice-sickness" (relapsing fever) and the "bed-bug" fever (typhus) taking a heavy toll of lives in the interior, it seemed to me the part of wisdom to just sit tight where I am. The men were pretty mad for a few days but are cooled off now. They had thought that as the Methodists were going it would look fine for some American Board to go—especially for me, "at my age"!

If the Japanese start up here we have a plan—that is, if there is time to carry it out—to walk on two days to a village up river where there is a church. There is a lot of air activity over our heads, and one day last week empty machine gun cartridges came down from the sky back of the compound. The school boys were out hunting them as souvenirs. Today several waves passed over—but we can learn no more of what was done. It is aggravating to be so ignorant of up to date news. In the meantime the Japanese have gutted Fairy Bridge and Foochow College and the Orphanage Industrial (across the street). They have moved into the Peace Street compound, occupying our homes and the hospital. It is reported that they have said that all British and U.S. property must be destroyed by fire, when they are through with it.

Often I have a great urge to see you all but the trip, by India now is too hard. It was not so dangerous a year ago. Reviews and exams will take all my time up to January 27, as I have classes in both Wenshan and Foochow College. Today was very cold in the classrooms. It makes me shiver to see men wading up the river towing boats. It is 50 steps from the river to the highway and 137 stone steps from the highway to the house. All water has to be carried up from the river. And we have to go down and up the stairs wherever we go.

Love to all,   Martha

"How will the hundreds of Chinese women ever get back their self respect."

Dearest friends,

When I returned to Foochow it was like a dead city. When I hear "co-prosperity," I feel like screaming so loud that all the world can hear that only death and desolation follow the Japanese invaders. How long will it be before the people can begin to live again? Everything is stripped from the houses. Shops are closed for want of anything to sell. Livestock is all gone. Poultry has been eaten by the Japanese soldiers. Worst of all, how will the hundreds of Chinese women ever get back their self respect and look at the world again unashamed.

Each house must furnish its quota of men and women for forced labor on the aviation field, the roads, the bomb shelters, and as cooks, and washer-women. If there are no able bodied persons in the house, a money payment is expected—$300 a day for each person exempted. Think how impossible for the poor people to pay this exorbitant fine.

Miss Wiley is very well and strong and herself very busy all day long. She lives with a missionary lady about two miles from here. She comes here to teach her classes in the morning and in the afternoons we are very thankful to have her with us. I teach ten hours a week besides my house work. I hope the war will be over soon so that we can go back to Foochow.

With heaps of love to you both, dear friends, we owe you both a great deal. May our dear Lord bless you and take good care of you.

Affectionately yours,   Catherine Hsueh

"The Japanese are tearing down Foochow College as they need fire wood."

Mrs. Norman Woodhouse
Wiley Rural Station Yakima, Wash. U.S.A.

Dear Sister,   (The first section of this letter was censored.)

. . .

The last home news was from Anna and dated July 1944, so it has been over six months since any mail has come through, and we are "isolationists" against our will.

The Japanese are tearing down Foochow College as they need fire wood. I can't tell yet if I have anything left in Foochow. It is a great temptation to the Chinese to carry off what the Japanese leave. Japanese officers are living in our mission houses at Foochow.

Our food is limited in variety but enough: eggs $20 each, meat $90 a pound. Flour in Foochow $4,500 a bag—when it can be bought. Ingtai is now one huge bouquet of plum and peach blossoms.

Our schoolwork goes on as usual. The boys have a hard time with very crude conditions and their food is scarce and very expensive. We are profoundly grateful that we did not have to flee from Ingtai in the winter months. The mission men tried to get us started in January! It took considerable strength of will to refuse, especially for me, a retired missionary, but for an old lady to set out on that journey would have been almost suicidal.

I am happy in the work here. I teach from 7 to 8 at home, then walk a mile and have two classes in Foochow College, walk home for lunch, and have three hours some days and two, on others, also at the end of a walk of a mile—so I have four miles a day of walking and five or six classes a day. The only means of going anywhere is on foot or by boat. I am glad to be able to walk, or else I would be shut in.

Donald gave me my annual birthday dinner. He never leaves that out. A rich man up country ordered a cake for me—$1,500! I could have used the money to better advantage.

He was my student 40 years ago—after all, that was only $10 U.S. The Hsueh girls helped to dispose of the cake at $10 bites!

Please share this with the relatives near and send on to Anna.

Love to all from,   Martha Wiley

"What the tigers left the grasshoppers took."

FOOCHOW, FUKIEN, CHINA   JULY 4, 1945

Dearest Sister,

Am again in the old City compound but not in my former home. When the school year ended in Ingtai we all came tumbling down here—but may have to go there again. When the enemy left some other people moved in, which makes this compound crowded with no place for me to move in and keep house. I need to control my diet—which cannot be done when I board. Fairy Bridge was a wreck when the enemy left. Nothing left but walls and some floors. We have been trying to repair enough to live in, but the weather is hot and labor is $800 a day for some old coolie to sit around and smoke half the time. Four years with no electric lights or kerosene lamps have made it very necessary for me to have my glasses changed, but that is impossible nearer than the U.S.A. Some times I have an overwhelming desire to see all of you again and nevermore hear a siren, but no one can predict just how long it will be before traffic is again established.

All my sheets, pillowcases, table linens etc. etc. etc. are gone. Sheets sell for $6,400 each just for cloth; these were taken by the natives, but the enemy took what was in the house.

They scrambled everything. It is funny to find a tea table across the City, and a chair at Pagoda Anchorage, ten miles away. All mattresses are gone or polluted. If a giant typhoon had struck our things they could not have been more scattered or more wrecked—what we can find! The natives did not show themselves in a good light—what the tigers left the grasshoppers took. As soon as the roof is mended and some shutters on the outside, street side, of Fairy Bridge house, I will move over there. Every fragment of glass was stolen from the windows. Not a foot of electric light wire in all of Fairy Bridge or Foochow College. One meter costs thousands of dollars if you can find one.

Donald is pretty much discouraged. If the Japanese had pulled down Foochow College it would have been better. One can stand on the basement floor and look up to the sky—just the walls standing. We do not know what we will do in the fall, go back to Ingtai or stay here.

Foochow College after Japanese bombing.

Today is the glorious 4th. Last year we were in Shaowu worrying how to get money from the banks there. When I think of the running here and there that I have done, and just missed the robbers and the bandits and wrecks on the rivers, I am filled with gratitude. Coming down from Ingtai we planned to leave on June 20th, but Donald made us hurry and start on the 18th. He followed on the 19th—the next day bandits stopped riverboats and looted them. If they had got my few suitcases of clothes I would have been in a plight, for nothing was left in Foochow—but we arrived safe, thanks to God.

Today all the men Americans are having a dinner. We women Americans are not invited—perhaps too much booze wanted. How I wish the war would end! Eight long years of it is too much with deterioration and dry rot set in from top to bottom.

Hurrah for Missouri! A president from your state! Eisenhower is from Kansas, is he not?

This letter will not be cut up, as it is so stupid. Interesting things cannot be written.

Love to all,   Martha

[newspaper clipping, September 7, 1945]

MISSIONARY TELLS OF WOE IN CHINA

Letter Describes War Conditions

WILEY CITY—Starvation, looting and horrors of war were described by Miss Martha Wiley, missionary in Foochow, China, in a letter to her sister, Mrs. Norman Woodhouse. The letter, written September 7, arrived Friday, the quickest delivery since the war started.

"The unexpected has happened," Miss Wiley wrote. "The Japanese have moved out after months of rape, looting, shooting, starving, gambling, opium and other humiliation to the Chinese people. No one has had enough food and the population looks like famine sufferers in India."

Gifts of Rice Seized

The Japanese would not let United States wheat enter Chinese ports, seized gifts of rice and sold it at outrageous prices, gorged on Chinese crops and burned what was left before they moved out, Miss Wiley reported. There is not a chicken and very few animals left in the district. All vegetables are used up. There is little milk and only dirty water. When villagers protested the Japanese greediness, their homes were burned or torn down for fuel.

"Please send me some seeds by first class mail in your next letter," Miss Wiley appealed. "We have been unable to get seed and heavy rains have spoiled what was grown here."

Martial Law Prevails

Foochow was under strict martial law during the four months it was occupied by the Japanese. When they left, they all boarded their ships and then directed a heavy bombing on the city, Miss Wiley wrote. She described the horrors and suffering caused by this departing blow. Even if the Japanese do not return, it will be hard for the Chinese people to recover, she said.

Miss Wiley wrote that she had been packed since August 20 to go to Shaowu, but that she was not permitted through the lines encircling the city. Later, bandits loomed up and made travel extremely dangerous. In Shaowu, the home of the Donald Sieks [Hsue-hs], who visited in the Yakima valley three years go, was destroyed and all their belongings taken.

There is no iron left in Foochow, the Japanese even taking the hinges off doors. Nails are now selling for $6 a pound. Fresh fruit and vegetables were consumed by the Japanese and very little other food is available. Salt is selling for $9 a pound in Shaowu and $2 a pound in Foochow for dirty salt, she said.

"I have a bit of pith in a saucer of oil for my evening light."

FOOCHOW, CHINA   OCTOBER 31, 1945

Dear Anna,

I get so little news that I often wonder what is really going on. No mail is coming in yet except a stray bit one or two years old. There is not much on the radio, and I seldom go to the Peace Street Compound to listen. There is no electricity until night, and then it is not certain. Our section of Foochow has already been without electricity for two weeks. I have a bit of pith in a saucer of oil for my evening light. Naturally I go to bed early. The streets are as dark as they were 40 years ago. The electric company is cleaning the engines, they said. Fairy Bridge house has had no repairs since the war began, and with Japanese and Chinese looters it is pretty well wrecked. Catherine and I are trying to get it in better condition.

This morning I went out to the drill ground to see about 40,000 students assemble in honor of the Generalissimo's birthday (59). I was the only foreigner tramping about among the throngs of Chinese. I quite enjoyed seeing the youngsters!

Love to each,   Nana

[partial letter]   FOOCHOW, CHINA   FEBRUARY 3, 1946

When Mrs. Hsueh and the children returned from the U.S. in 1940, it was necessary for them to go to a country place called Ingtai for a year to escape the Japanese, and to be with Mr. Hsueh who is principal of the American Board High School, which had moved to Ingtai. After a year the school had to move farther into the interior, to Shaowu, and remained there three years. After that there was another year of refugee life in Ingtai again. So Mabelle has taken three years of junior high and three of senior high in the boys' high school, of which her father is principal.

The Chinese idea of the inferiority of girls' minds received a shock when, in the term examinations of this January, Mabelle's grades were highest in her class of 100 boys, and highest of all in senior high, and averaged second in the whole school—her sister Marian ranking first in the whole school of 800 boys.

Yours sincerely,   Miss Martha Wiley

"I had some men come and tear down the dugout bomb shelter."

FOOCHOW, CHINA   MARCH 8, 1946

Dear Anna,

There has been no cold weather this winter, not even a frost, so now every abominable disease is raging—bubonic plague, meningitis, cholera, typhoid, relapsing fever—all the "insect diseases" and "rare diseases." People are inoculated with good U.S. serum, by the thousands. This week I plan to get a couple of shots for the "rat sicknesses." My cook has been gone for nearly a week to his village to "bury his mother" who has not yet died! He heard that she had bubonic plague, but I think not as she has lasted a week.

This week I had some men come and tear down the dugout bomb shelter, smooth down the yard and plant a lot of bulbs, but the spring garden is yet to be planted. Now it is too cold for the seeds to sprout. The cook's wife will plan for her "many month." She went off and bought four piggies to take the place of two big ones. The pig man brought six and swore that she ordered six. So I took one and Catherine took one. Now that I own a pig my troubles have begun. The pig cost $10,000 and bran this month $3,000! I guess that I had better get out of the pig business before I go broke. Lard is now over $1,000 a pound.

Love to all,   Nana

"We had a time getting his concubine diverted while we took turns talking."

FOOCHOW, CHINA   MARCH 29, 1946

Dear Anna,

Donald got started on a new gymnasium for Foochow College. We planned on one million dollars, then prices went up two times higher. The frame of the gymnasium stood there grinning like a skeleton, and work had to stop. Then Catherine and I got busy. We went to the "Tea King." He is my old student and most courteous to me. Catherine has taught his son every day and lets him board in the house, so we had a pull. We had a time getting his concubine diverted while we took turns talking. She opposes all contributions.

To make a long story short, we got a promise of lumber and money to one million of this inflated money. The rest can be managed and the work is going on today. Yesterday, Catherine and one of the men teachers went to the sawmill and arranged for the shipping by boat of the lumber, and this morning she is off to get the half-million cash promised. Donald was tied up all that day in long sessions of the "Board of Managers of Foochow College." It was just as well, for women are the most successful beggars. I could not leave my school work yesterday but contributed the ricksha fare.

I got my cook cleared of debt, and then he sold his pig and paid me back. Then his mother had a month of illness and died—expenses $55,000 which he borrowed, at 10% interest a month. I advanced him this to save the interest and now he has a big pig almost ready to sell that he is offered $120,000 for ($60 U.S.). My pig, which he insisted on buying for me, is a healthy child.

Yesterday our neighbor parked her pigs in our front door with natural results. I told her that the next time I would report her to the health department. Just that minute a young dandy came along, and said that he was in the health department. He just grinned—pigs in the front door did not phase him. When rats died in Foochow College not long since, the health department said they "had no time to fumigate." The governor's son, who is a student here, telephoned his father and those lazy louts came on the run and fumigated for two whole days.

Love to each and all,   Nana

"My book of English Phonetics has sold well."

FOOCHOW, CHINA   APRIL 21, 1946

Dear Sister Belle,

I have been very busy in school work this term and there will be no let-up until June. My book of English Phonetics has sold well. I had it printed for Foochow College, but other schools are using it also. Everything that I do now is done with my departure in view. After nearly half a century here, my roots are down deep. All my old cronies that hear of my going to the U.S. soon come in to get a donation. The widow of my first servant, now in the poorhouse, came this P.M. to get a gift. How glad I am to have something to give them from the gifts sent by friends!

With love to each and all from,   Martha

"Eight years as refugees have taken their toll on our resiliency."

[letter from Donald and Catherine]   FOOCHOW COLLEGE   FOOCHOW, CHINA   APRIL 27, 1946

Dear American Friends:—

The last stroke to befall Foochow College is the loss by fire of the largest and best of the campus buildings. Yesterday, April 26, at 11:30 P.M., a great outburst of flame swept over the basement floors, spurted through the arches and upward into the second storey, soon wrapping the stairways in flames.

In this building, 48 boys of the Senior Middle graduating class and several teachers had rooms. The library occupied the third floor of one wing; class rooms were in an adjoining wing; rice stores occupied two rooms. All the students and teachers had gone to bed at 10 o'clock. Suddenly the roar of the fire awakened them, which was so violent from the start that students and teachers barely had time to save themselves.

A few snatched their quilts and a book or two as they ran, but many lost their clothing, bedding and all their books. Teachers ran to the students' rooms to warn them and so lost the time to save their own things. Some of the boys turned about and tried bravely to put out the fire.

Junior High boys swarmed out with pitchers, wash basins, pails and tried to get water to the boys near the fire. Conspicuous among the young fire fighters were three lads from the Governor's family.

In the meantime fire companies came in and did their best, but it had not rained for weeks and wells were nearly dry. Neighbors threw open their doors and school boys and firemen drew from the small well holes every last drop of water. But before the fire could be checked in one wing, all the water in school wells and in the neighboring areas had been exhausted. Nothing could be accomplished by trying to tear down parts of the building (as Chinese stop fire in their own homes) for these were solid walls, built in foreign style. We could only stand aside and watch the floors fall, and finally the roof. As yet we have no knowledge of the origin of the fire.

There was not a breath of air stirring or else all our buildings would have been a total loss. If the long tongues of flame that shot straight upward had been blown to the west, the whole of the Junior High dormitory, classrooms, and gymnasium would have caught fire. And if they had veered even slightly to the east, the church would have taken fire, and flames would have jumped a narrow alley to the offices and from there to the primary school building. Since there was not water enough to save one building, it would have been impossible to save a group of buildings.

It was all over by daylight except the smoldering rubble and bare gaunt walls that stood mocking us just as they did after the Japanese left the campus. Ruins left like that seem to be sentient, and stand grimacing at puny human beings that are not strong enough to cope with disaster.

As this morning moved on, we could realize some of the facts confronting us. The library had just been put in shape. Yesterday was the first day that a new librarian had taken over the evening work. In the afternoon, he had received a consignment of books to the value of $480,000 N.C. [National Currency] from the Commercial Press and had placed them in stacks for the students. Students had been invited to begin to use the reference books and to make use of the library from 7 to 9 as a study room just that evening. All those books were burned, also a previous consignment of $300,000, besides all the cases of books that we carried with the school when at Ingtai and Shaowu. Many Chinese books can never be replaced. War and fire! How destructive are both!

Then how badly the school needs the space! The boys from the burnt dormitory carried their few pitiful belongings to an old Chinese building that has been used as assembly hall. It will take some days to plan even beds for them.

Now, these walls will have to be torn down and an entirely new building put up that will be fire-proof, or nearly so. The head of the Construction Bureau estimates that not less than $50,000 U.S. will be required to build at present prices. That will be a staggering sum in our present cheap, inflated currency. God only knows how it can be done. Today the weight of this disaster, added to all the other rehabilitation problems, seems to daze us. Eight years as refugees have taken their toll on our resiliency.

The rice stored in the two rooms was the subsidy that each student had to bring for the teachers. That was the half-year quantity from which rice was weighed out each month. Today the price of rice is $35,000 N.C. for a "load" of 150 lbs. The pre-war price was seven dollars a load, and during the war the highest price was $3,000 a load. How can the school refund these millions of local currency? But it must be done, or see these families suffer before our eyes. He who feeds the sparrow will not forget His children in Foochow College.

We are deeply grateful to God that not one person lost his life last night. The military trainer roomed in the third storey. He was unselfishly looking to see that no student was left in the rooms until it was too late to get down a stairway. For months, the scout master had been trying to get a large canvas sheet to use in teaching the boy scouts to jump into it. Last week it was finished. When the military trainer was cut off from escape by the stairs, the scouts and their master dragged to the building the heavy canvas and the trainer jumped to safety. This same man was one of the Foochow College group of 71 persons who joined the church Easter Sunday.

Many of the students who lost all that they have are poor boys. One Chinese quilt cannot be bought for less than $30,000. A mosquito net is priceless. UNRRA [United Nations Relief Rehabilitation Administration] does not help in individual relief cases.

There are several bright spots in this calamity. The school spirit of the boys, and their bravery in trying to help check the fire, showed the good training of the teachers and the scout master and the loyalty of the boys to the school. The military trainer will be considered in a new light by his boys after showing his willingness to risk death for them. The uncomplaining sympathy of the teachers, even when they knew that the rice stores had been swept away, was a new phase of their character.

Yours in His service,   Donald Hsueh

Catherine Hsueh

College Recitation Hall repairs

*"These seven years have gone by like a dream,
thanks to bombs, boats, buses, bandits
and bubonic plague."*

MAY 31, 1946

Dear Miss Williams,

Everyone connected with Foochow College has had inoculation against bubonic plague. Having done all that we can, we go on as usual. The lighting problem here is worse than when we were refugees. The electric machinery breaks down of old age, and for a week at a time—when the City is blacked out—we have to depend on the native candles, now made of anything but oil, so it is impossible to work at night. I tried to write this letter by the flickering light, so "please excuse."

I am now looking forward to seeing all the dear ones in the U.S.! These seven years have gone by like a dream, thanks to bombs, boats, buses, bandits and bubonic plague. Perhaps all of us have lost some "pep" during that time, but how wonderful that our lives have been spared so long!

In the hope of seeing you sometime this year,

Affectionately yours,   Martha Wiley

"The Buddhist monks hold all life as too sacred to be used."

FOOCHOW, CHINA   JUNE 30, 1946

Dear Anna,

Your last letter of May 29th, reached Foochow May 29th (1 year). Air mail is not so very much faster since there is no air route to Foochow any more.

Yesterday I got a letter from the Passenger Agent in Shanghai, and he said to write him again in two months and he would do his best to "fix me up." That is all right with me as it would be terrible to start off now. There are cholera cases on the coast steamers, generally, and a long uncertain wait in the heat and sickness of Shanghai would be unbearable. Only transports are on the Trans-Pacific Line now. Soldiers are being moved here and there on the coast and carry diseases with them.

Bishop Lacy was at Sharp Peak recently, and he said that all that was above ground of my house that the Kinnears gave me were five or six empty window arches. That is more than I had supposed!

The care taker of the Kuliang bungalow says that the house is stripped of everything, even the locks on the doors. Catherine had the roof repaired to protect the walls. If we can rent the house, and use the advance rent money to repair the place, it might be advisable to put the place in order again.

In the meantime a Mr. Chen (millionaire tea merchant) has invited the Hsuehs and me to go to Kushan Monastery, on the same range of hills as Kuliang, and spend part of the summer. He keeps a part of the monastery rented all the year for his family and friends. We will have to eat with the Buddhist monks—rice and vegetables. They allow no meat, eggs, or anything pertaining to animals to be on the premises. They hold all life as too sacred to be used.

Marian and I exclaimed that we were afraid of bedbugs—but the son of Mr. Chen says that his father will have the place gone over with DDT frequently. So we may go during the last two weeks of July and the first two of August. If it is comfortable we may stay until September. Catherine says that we will take oil paper to paste on the bed boards—sounds comfortable, doesn't it? This morning it is not as hot as yesterday, when the sweat dripped off my hand so that I could not write.

Lots of love to each and all from,   Nana

"Farewell to Miss Wiley — The graduating class of Junior High, Foochow College, June 28th, 1946" — Marian is second in from right.

"Every evil that comes as an aftermath of war is rampant."

FOOCHOW, CHINA   JULY 17, 1946

Dear Miss Williams,

. . .

It is very difficult for anyone but officials to get a passport, as the government wants to keep at home its cheap money. (Now from $2,000 or $2,500 to one U.S. dollar!)

Yesterday I helped Donald and Catherine draft a letter to the American Board asking permission to go to the U.S. this autumn to raise funds for Foochow College. Next month salaries will increase 100% bringing the current expenses up to $8,000,000 N.C. a month ($4,000 U.S.). Donald has gathered all that he could from every possible Chinese source and Catherine has worked night and day keeping a stream of letters going to America. Foochow College needs $25,000 from the U.S. It has not been the policy of the American Board to permit institutions to raise funds, so we wait the outcome with some uncertainty. They sent an airmail letter and asked for a cable reply. Unless they go to the U.S. for funds or the Board wakes up and makes a large appropriation, Foochow College is on the rocks after 95 years of splendid service.

In case Donald and Catherine are permitted to go to the U.S., we will plan to go together. If not I will be going on by myself, sometime in the autumn. We are preparing our minds for either eventuality—Donald and Catherine on the way to the U.S., or for closing up Foochow College.

This post-victory year has not brought the blessings of peace and prosperity. I have never seen the better class of Chinese so utterly discouraged with their government. Every evil that comes as an aftermath of war is rampant. Naturally eight years of confusion cannot be put right quickly. A university student recently dropped in and remarked: "America is disgusted with China—and rightly so."

Always affectionately yours,   Martha Wiley

"The cook says he saw the ball of fire divide."

350 KULIANG   AUGUST 17, 1946

Dear Sister,

On August 1st, the three Hsueh girls and I and my cook came here. All July was full of typhoons and fairly cool. August came on with a hot blast. We all pitched in to clean off the eight year collection of dust and cobwebs. In the midst of this, I stepped off the lowest step of the porch and sprained one ankle and the arch of the opposite foot. For a few days I had to keep the sprained foot off the floor, and move about on a chair for a week. The girls went in swimming twice a day in a rather dangerous pool, and I worried all the time they were gone unless I sent the cook—and he had all that he could do to feed the group as there is almost nothing to buy! What we brought up here melted like snow. A small chicken costs $5,000 and everything else in proportion. Vegetables are hard to get at any price.

Today I walked over a hill to look at Miss Ward's house repairs for her. Kuliang is now a ghost town. Dozens and dozens of houses are just rubble. Ours is among the best preserved, and yet we have not a pane of glass left and every lock and bolt is gone—cut out. The roof is pretty good. The beds had the rattan bottoms cut out. My spring cot broke down beyond repair. We had to borrow beds from the Chinese tailor. He is very obliging and tells often that when he was a child I used to give him cakes to eat.

I did not care much to come here, but I had no other way to shake loose from the students who wanted to study English all summer. I was thoroughly bored by so much tutoring. Mabelle and Marian are both fine students and got the highest average in three years among nearly a thousand boys. Catherine wants them to have some girl friends, as all their school life they have been in a boys' school. Our house will be quiet when they are gone.

If Donald and Catherine can go to the U.S.—and get enough funds for Foochow College to get through a couple of years—I will feel free of that obligation, and can settle down to knit. Donald had to raise teacher's salaries from pre-war $50 to $100,000 plus a rice subsidy at $400 a pound, to each teacher. The fire damaged the school terribly.

Last Sunday evening, Catherine and Elizabeth and I were sitting just inside the dining room door when a bolt of lightning instantaneously dropped. There had been no previous thunder to warn us. We each thought the other had been struck. It seemed to me that the lightning fell right between us. The cook says he saw the ball of fire divide, and part strike at the end of our porch about six feet from us, and part strike a tree about 20 feet away. Our watchman says that it came down on our house. We three first fell back and then began to call the others to see if they were alive. Then with one breath we called out, "Thank God, Thank God!" The cook came in and cried out, "We are all risen-from-the-dead people."

The tangible results of the scare are that a big tree about 20 or 30 feet from us was snapped off at the base and blasted to splinters, and a tree near it had the bark on one side peeled off. When Elizabeth had picked herself up, she said that if we had been killed by lightning then all Chinese people would believe that we were very wicked and God had killed us. The natives will not touch the splinters of the tree. And for a day Catherine could hardly hear. No bombing raid ever equaled this episode, though we have been close to falling bombs.

Much love to each one of the three families from,   Nana

"Almost all my pre-war friends (villagers) have starved to death."

350 Kuliang- Foochow   August 20, 1946

Dear Miss Williams,

It seems strange to be here in this ghost village. The old foreign summer colony had over 4,000 houses, but now a large percent of them are just rubble, from two Japanese occupations and years of local banditry.

My cook is with me and one of us has to watch the house if the other leaves as "thieves are thick as trees." Almost all my pre-war friends (villagers) have starved to death, so no wonder they take whatever they can lay their hands upon. Most of the large trees are missing.

Even the weather has become erratic. Most every night a fierce wind would roar over the house, and with the morning light a fog would settle down—not at all like the lovely cool, bright August days I remembered.

August 23 —— I came down the hill yesterday, leaving the cottage before day to escape the heat of the plain, and it was well that I did for I had a walk of about three miles at the end of the sedan chair route. Real sedan chairs are no more. The coolies found a foreign armchair, tied a pole on each side, and I rode down the mountain elevated above the common crowd like the pope. When I came down the mountain and came trudging into the Fairy

Bridge house, even before I'd had a cup of water I was asking for mail—and your precious letter was the first to hand and the first read.

I believe that the Lord knows how much you and Miss Katherine are needed, and will keep you much longer and continue to make you the joy and blessings that you have always been. I hope to see you face to face and tell you how much of the good (if any) that I have done in China has been because of you. Donald could never have had his education without your help and neither could Miss Wang, principal of Wenshan. And the Woman's School could have not been as successful, and dozens of others have shared your beauty.

Up to this time, I have felt myself essential to Donald and Catherine's success in this post-war period of discouragement. But now they seem to be emerging into a more hopeful frame of mind. The better class of Chinese are in depths of hopelessness about their government and more or less about the church, and the middle-aged—in charge of Synod schools—are breaking under the strain. Idolatry is rampant again. Since I came back from the country I have heard "foreign devil" and "foreign hag" shouted at me by Chinese children more than in the past 30 years.

With love to you and Miss Katherine,

Affectionately,   Martha Wiley

"Whatever I take now is all that I will ever have."

FOOCHOW, FUKIEN   SEPTEMBER 12, 1946

Dear Anna,

Your letter of August 5th reached me September 11th. Not so bad for regular mail. You said that the last letter from me was dated April 29. You should have had three more up to that date. I have been using regular mail as air costs $750 a letter. You see I am using your paper; this sheet costs over $50 here. You certainly would have gone broke to have had such a lot of company in Foochow. One ordinary dinner for a few friends costs at least $10,000 N.C. I seldom invite guests, but for years I have never had so many invitations as now to eat in Chinese homes. School has begun again with 900 boys. I am teaching part time, so that if I need to stop it would not be hard to plan my work.

I hate to start out now on the steamers as they are so terrible, but other people can stand it. Steamer runs to San Francisco only, from here (Shanghai). I will have: a large trunk of clothes and bedding; a steamer trunk; a large trunk of photos, etc.; a box of books; a box of dishes—besides my hand luggage. Now what to do when I get to San Francisco is a puzzle. To ship that stuff to Belle's place will cost a fortune, but she has lots of room. To ship it to your place would fill your cellar or your attic. Besides, what would I do with it? You and Belle have your house well furnished and extra stuff would only clutter up your house.

On the other hand there are some things that I would like to keep. If I leave here, I will not be able to return, as my retirement is long overdue, so whatever I take now is all that I will ever have. Also, if I arrive in San Francisco in March, it would be nice to have the spring and summer in Yakima, and if you could come out there for the summer I could go home with you in the fall. Of course this is just tentative.

September 5 —— Catherine started to Shanghai, deck passage with the two older girls, on the steamer, which is an old U.S. freighter. She "bought two beds" for the three at $40,000 each, and so planning reduced the travel one half. But if she could not have "bought beds" they would have had to stay on deck and take the weather and the waves as they came. Mabelle wrote me from Shanghai, as I had given them money for an ice cream treat, that a slice of ice cream cost $750. It is eight years since I left the U.S.—there must be many changes by this time.

Love,   Nana

⟍

"I remember Admiral Chen as a little chap
playing around my home—and now
a disillusioned patriot."

NOVEMBER 11, 1946

Dear Sister,

Yesterday was Sunday and I planned to write you then, but instead I went off to play. Mr. Ling, a former member of the National Plenary Council, my old student, invited the Hsue-hs and me to go to Admiral Chen's place for a visit—call. At 8 A.M. he and his 2nd lady drove up in his automobile, and we piled in and went to the dock and took somebody's private launch—big and clean and so comfortable. After two hours down river by launch, we came to a village landing and piled out.

It was only an hour's walk across the fields by a single-stone path to Sieu-kwan's home. He came to the door himself, and how different he seemed without his uniform and gold braid. Also looked thinner. But his home was literally "ship-shape." His gardens and flowers and vegetables looked nice, but what a lonely life! He hustled his man around and we had a bowl of refreshments and talked a while in his summer garden pavilion and then left. He walked with us to the landing, and the last we saw he was still standing on the river-side watching our boat.

Admiral Chen and Martha

The government got down and crawled to get him back after ousting him. There was a complication about the ships from western countries being turned over to a competent party and he was needed. He was like Earl, he "paid no tintion" to the invitation. I remember him as a little chap playing around my home—and now a disillusioned patriot. Too bad he has no family. I've told you his story a dozen times, I am sure.

We got back to the Foochow dock at three plus and the men rushed us up to the Y.M.C.A. in rickshas. We had a "splendiferous" dinner to Chinese thinking.

Martha

TIMELINE 1947–1960

1947 — Martha leaves China for U.S.

1949 — Establishment of People's Republic of China (PRC), KMT retreats to Taiwan

— Students of Foochow College refuse to pay tuition, salaries cut in half

— Admiral Chen joins communist government

1950 — Admiral Chen now vice-governor of Foochow

— Martha is teaching in Piney Woods, Mississippi

1951 — Martha receives news Admiral Chen is killed, finds this to be incorrect, years later

1952 — Foochow College becomes a public school

— Donald is re-appointed as an English teacher and head of library

1953 — Martha retires and moves to Pilgrim Place cottages for retired mission workers in Claremont, California

1957 — Donald retires

6

UNDER COMMUNISM

Dear Doris,

. . .

The cook has come in to set the table. I keep a low fire in the dining room and live there except to sleep. In the living room we still only have half the glass, so the wind blows through even when the shutters are closed. So far this winter the temperature has not got down to freezing. My sweet peas are beginning to bloom. For several days the wet winds made it seem awfully cold and bleak.

3 P.M. —— A special [?] is just taking off carrying a woman doctor. She had to take an injection for dog bite and is now having paralysis creeping toward her lungs. She will be in Shanghai in two hours and under an iron lung. What strange things can happen! Three days ago I saw her dashing around the hospital beautifully dolled up, I praise the Lord for every day that passes without tragedy.

M. W.

Dear Anna,

Today I was in the Bank of China. The manager told me that now exchange was to be $12,000 N.C. for one U.S. dollar, and no black market or free market allowed. Now prices will shoot to the stratosphere. We certainly live in a chaotic government. Yet we muddle along. Foochow College began with over 900 students this term, in spite of $200,000 entrance fees. Today, at the faculty prayer meeting, over half the teachers attended, so we are getting a large per cent of Christian teachers again.

Donald had good news that Foochow College had just received $10,000 U.S. from Boston by this mail—also $3,000 U.S. insurance—but Donald has had to buy school rice at $1,000 a pound and upward. Every Chinese wants at least one pound a day.

Belle said that sometimes she was without sugar. We can get sugar here, but the present price is $3,750 a pound. Miss Houston and I have to entertain the Anti-Cobweb Society on the 22nd of February; it happens to be our turn. Think of the sugar it will take to provide cake and coffee for 50 people. We have to do it. This will be my last time to help entertain them. All the foreigners gather into these literary afternoons once a month.

I am glad that I had this warm dress made or I would shiver to death, even though it cost around $100 U.S.

Mabelle has come in to spend the evening, but has found a story and is buried in it. She has matured a lot this year and is a very attractive girl now. We hate to have her start off. The China coast is lousy with pirates, but on a large steamer there is less danger.

Affectionately,   Martha

Office staff of Foochow College—Elizabeth is behind Martha.
"Taken on the occasion of Miss Martha Wiley's return to her native country (U.S.)."

[Speech and poem written to honor Martha, before her departure to the U.S.]

Miss Martha Wiley came to Foochow from America toward the end of Kuang-su's reign in the Ch'ing Dynasty. She has taught in Foochow College and given great contributions in the promotion of public welfare for more than 40 years. Her friendliness, together with her deep interest in educational work has, won the respect and admiration of her students. With appreciation of her teachings and regret at her departure for home on account of her age, I beg to write these four stanzas to remember myself to her on her return and to show my highest regards:

> Across the seas you found your way
> To teach the youths here day by day.
> For fifty years you worked with zest
> And turned out men we call the best.
>
> Upon the hill my school looks grand,
> For modern thoughts the first to stand.
> With other lads I stayed here long;
> I think of days already gone.
>
> Your manly traits deserve high praise;
> I like to hear your word and phrase.
> As age can't fade your healthy glow,
> You look as fine as years ago.
>
> Can men just meet whene'er they please?
> Your presence is welcomed like a breeze.
> Beside the Min we'll walk around
> To see you're off and homeward bound.

Written and presented by her student Ting Ch'ao Wu on the 28th of June 1947, corresponding to the 28th day in the sixth month of the 36th year of the Chinese Republic.

"This is my last letter to you from Foochow forever."

FOOCHOW, CHINA   JULY 5, 1947

Dear Sister Belle,

This hot July morning I will rest myself by sending a letter to you. My ticket is bought on the General Meigs leaving Shanghai, August 10, so this is my last letter to you from Foochow—forever. Seems impossible to realize.

So many callers and sitters come all day long, and I have to get my work done at night. As soon as the inoculations required by the health department are finished, I think I will go to Kuliang for a week of rest and sleep. Catherine and Mabelle and I will have to leave Foochow around the 10th of August, and reach San Francisco the 25th. My plan is to proceed from there to Yakima. If Catherine has time before college opens, she and Mabelle will come with me to Yakima for a week and on to Chicago from there.

It is a wild time to get out of port. There are dozens of regulations, but I have most finished up. When I get to Shanghai I will have to get busy to get a passport. Everything is hard to do—not like the old, easy-going way.

When we reach San Francisco, I will send you word from there. Catherine has some speaking dates along the way if she can manage to go to Yakima.

I am looking forward to seeing all the relatives, new and old, and the friends that are left. Nine years is quite a while. Well, I'll be seeing you!

Love to all from,   Martha

"More and more babies are laid out in the street to be
picked up by the police—the people
are so terribly poor."

MONDAY, JULY 14, 1947

Dear Anna,

Just now a man from the City came up with a letter confirming my passage on the General Meigs. The Lutheran Center will give all three of us a cot each in Shanghai, at $2.50 U.S. each a day ($50,000 N.C.)

Oh, my goodness sakes! Catherine and my cook have been out here on the porch talking over the cook's problems. A new baby on the way and he says that they are so poor that they have to give it away. My old neighbor here is begging me to find a place for one of hers who was given to a heathen family, and they beat him and even tore off a part of the lobes of his ears to punish him. He made his home by hiding in the brush in the daytime—he only ten years old! It is a frightful thing to give a child away.

But now more and more babies are laid out in the street to be picked up by the police—the people are so terribly poor. This typhoon will damage their crop of rice and up the price. What a country! What a world! Kuliang is just a ghost town. A Chinese independent evangelist made a fortune in drugs during the war. He has bought up the larger part of the hills of Kuliang and is letting them go back to forest. The people who sold under duress have no potato fields and are in abject poverty. I would hate to get the curses that fall on his head.

I will get some photos of the cook's four fine children and see if I can get money for the family when I get to Yakima. Wages are low compared to prices. A man gets his board and $100,000 N.C. = $10 U.S. a month. Then what about his family? I am just getting one peach at $1,000. I can't bear to eat it when I see the sitters on my porch — $1,000 N.C. would buy 2 ½ pounds of rice. My old caretaker eats that much at a meal — if he can get it! It will be both a relief and a sorrow to get out from underneath the conditions here. When I leave, the special gifts for the poor will be very much decreased. But I think that I am too old to keep up the pace longer. The Woman's School is needed and wanted, but no one will undertake it.

If I ever lay my travel-weary head on one of your good beds, I will stay there a while.

Love from,   Martha

***"Everyone tells me that America is so changed
that I will feel like a stranger."***

SUNDAY, AUGUST 17, 1947

Dear Anna and the Girls,

My good pen has been stolen, so I must use a pencil. The last days in Foochow were very full of details. We left there Sunday, July 28th, took a steamer to Shanghai August 10th, also Sunday, and now it is Sunday, August 17th, three days distant from Honolulu.

Catherine and Mabelle are in a cabin of 18 persons, most of them Foochow friends. All the berths are three tiers high, as they were for soldiers. I was fussing around to get a lower when the steward said, "You've got the best in the room. Climb up there and keep still." The stewards are used to handling soldiers.

I have written ahead for a room in San Francisco. If none is available I will go to Chinatown, with Catherine, to some Foochow friends. How long we stay in San Francisco depends on the customs and the meetings there. Catherine is determined to go to Yakima if there is time.

Everyone tells me that America is so changed that I will feel like a stranger. After this wild trip nothing will seem very queer, I believe. The sea has been as calm as a mill pond. A typhoon was reported, but it did not come near us. Yokohama seemed like a ghost town. The great dock was deserted. A few launches flying U.S. flags flitted about the harbor. A half dozen large ships were at anchor well out. It was a far cry from pre-war days.

Lots of love to each and all,   Nana

"I have just completed a year of 'trial and error' in this country."

1103 MADISON ST.,   ST. CHARLES, MO.   SEPTEMBER 10, 1948

Mr. H.B. Belcher
14 Beacon St.,
Boston, Mass.

Dear Mr. Belcher:

Today I have written Dr. Ward about securing permission from the Board to return to Foochow with Donald Hsueh when his furlough comes to an end. You know the conditions in Foochow and you know me personally, hence your approval will have much influence for a favorable consideration by the Board.

Since I have a home in Foochow, I need not embarrass any of the missionary families by using their much-needed house room. Both Donald and Catherine Hsueh are anxious for me to be back, as they say—their "guest."

Also my financial problems would be greatly simplified if I were permitted to return to Foochow to live. I have just completed a year of "trial and error" in this country and believe that I would be far more comfortable in Foochow on the missionary allowance than I am in the United States. And supposing my income should ever be a little short I could easily add to it by private tutoring. I would enjoy doing this.

I would appreciate the privilege of USING the few good years that are left to me and not have to RUST them away—use them in a way that would not conflict with any young missionary's "sphere of influence."

Catherine Hsueh writes that she has been overwhelmed by the number and variety of the demands upon her time this summer. We have worked together so closely for many years, that I would be able to relieve her of a considerable part of the time taken by visitors in our home. The English correspondence of both Donald and Catherine is growing year by year. This is another place where they might use my help.

I wrote Dr. Ward that I can take care of my travel expense, and my personal preparations are already pretty well in hand. I do not consider my return to Foochow in the light of an experiment. During my last term of service I did not have a day of hospitalization and my medical examinations have been satisfactory during the past year. But even so, there would be no extra expense to the Board for my going, or for my recall in case that was necessary.

Will you kindly see what can be done about this matter? Before Donald would be ready to return to Foochow, I would like to spend some time with friends and relatives in Washington State; perhaps after the holidays, and go on to China from there.

With much appreciation of your helpfulness in the past,

Sincerely yours,   Martha Wiley

"Miss Wiley has a sympathetic understanding of my people
and would be a definite blessing to those who
love her and want her back."

[letter from Donald] GRAND RAPIDS, MICHIGAN OCTOBER 11, 1948

Dr. Earl Ballou
14 Beacon Street
Boston, Massachusetts

Dear Dr. Ballou:

I am writing this letter chiefly for the purpose of asking the Prudential Committee of the American Board to consider my request that my beloved teacher as well as a beloved member of the Hsueh family be permitted to return to Foochow for as long as she wishes to remain with my family.

After staying a week with Miss Wiley in St. Charles, Missouri, I realized that Miss Wiley has practically no satisfying work to do in this country. She is still very strong and full of energy, and still can render many more years of valuable service to the Chinese people.

Since Catherine and I have made so many contacts with American people in this country, I feel more strongly than ever the need of someone to help us with our English correspondence and other work where English is used.

So far, considering the difficulty of meeting the financial needs of the school, I have not thought it feasible to ask anyone for help in this capacity, though I have constantly felt the need of such help.

Now, with a retired missionary available, who has an intimate relationship with the Hsueh family and a very cordial relationship with the alumni of Foochow College and who will cost the American Board no additional expense, I feel strongly that to return Miss Wiley to Foochow would be very helpful to my work and a great relief to me personally and would be a great satisfaction to her. I believe she would be much more comfortable in Foochow than in this country, where she has no home of her own and would be more happy because of having something to do.

Dr. and Mrs. Hinman, already retired, came out to assist me from 1934-1938. Those were the best years Foochow College ever had as far as the relationship of the College and the alumni was concerned; and the interest of the alumni in Foochow College has continued to the present time. Just now the sympathetic interest of the alumni needs to be strengthened where it was weakened during the war years.

Miss Wiley is specially fitted to help this interest to grow, because she has a long and unusual background of our College, and a sympathetic understanding of my people. You all know of the reverence of the Chinese for an elderly teacher. For instance, Admiral S. K. Chen, and Honorable C. W. Ting, two of her oldest students, were willing to be chairman and a vice-chairman of the College Board of managers for several years, largely through the bond of friendship established by their former teacher, Miss Wiley.

Miss Wiley was a good teacher and is still an excellent teacher with her long experience in teaching Chinese students. We need her work in phonetics. The phonetic book, which she prepared and printed, went up as far north as Shanghai and Nanking, to be used in some schools. This made Foochow College outstanding in pronunciation and gave Foochow College prestige in English among all schools in south China during the last five years. That printing is used up and we need a revised reprint, which only Miss Wiley can do, because of so many years of experience in teaching elementary English.

There is an unlimited field for personal work among students and personal contact with parents of our students. I have more than 1,100 students in Foochow College, and among them are many children of Miss Wiley's former students. So I prefer to have her do this work along with Catherine; but Miss Wiley would not be considered a regular worker.

Mr. Belcher knows that Catherine and I have the big Fairy Bridge house. It was our desire, and still is, that Miss Wiley should live with us after her retirement from the American Board, where she already has her own apartment. She would not occupy any of the needed homes in the American Board compound.

To my mind, a capable, consecrated, experienced, elderly woman missionary like Miss Wiley, would be a definite blessing to the Chinese people who love her and want her back.

I do not know whether it is a rule of the American Board that a missionary should not return to the field after retirement, but just in case it is, I beg of you to present Miss Wiley's case before the Prudential Committee and make an exception to the rule and consider favorably my request that Miss Wiley be permitted to return to Foochow with me next spring.

I hope to get your reply around October 18, when I get to Oberlin, Ohio. Meanwhile, in behalf of Foochow College and the Hsueh family, I would like to express in advance my deep-felt gratitude for all you can help.

With best wishes for the success of your work,

Gratefully yours,　　Donald Hsueh

Loo-Toi, Foochow,
Dec. 28, 1948.

Dear Miss Wiley,

Many many thanks for your very kind message and Xmas card of this year and that of the last. I have also recived many copies of the Reader's Digest which I believe are ordered from you. You are really too Kind to do so. For all I appreciate profoundly your kindness.

I am extremely glad to Know that you will come back to Foochow soon. I do pray God will guide the achievement. Hoping to see you again in Foochow before long.

Wishing you a Happy New Year and best of health.

Yours cordially,

Chen Shackwan

Letter from Admiral Chen

"The State Department is issuing passports only in cases of an urgent and important nature."

[letter from Walter H. Judd]

WASHINGTON, D.C.   MARCH 1, 1949

Miss Martha Wiley
1103 Madison St.
St. Charles, Mo.

Dear Miss Wiley;

In reply to your recent letter will advise that in view of the disturbed conditions in China at this time, the State Department is issuing passports only in cases where it has been established to the satisfaction of the Department that the travel is of an urgent and important nature.

As you know, Americans are being evacuated from China unless they have a compelling reason for remaining there, and the Department is not encouraging travel to China at the present time.

However, if you want to forward your passport to the Passport Division, State Department, together with a letter setting forth the purpose of your trip, how long you expect to remain in China, and giving information as to your background, they will advise you definitely in the matter. In view of the fact that your passport is valid until July 31, 1949, that you have spent many years in China, and plan to return there with the President of Foochow College, the Department may give you permission to make the trip. I will support the request as strongly as possible.

With kind wishes, I am

Sincerely yours,   Walter H. Judd

"I make an earnest request that I may return to my work and my home in Foochow."

1103 MADISON ST.   ST. CHARLES, MO.   MARCH 21, 1949

Passport Division,
Department of State,
Washington, D.C.

Today I am mailing you my passport, No. 918, issued by the Consulate General in Shanghai, July 31, 1947, and valid until July 31, 1949. You will please find enclosed a statement of Principal Donald Hsueh, of Foochow College High School, a statement of the American Board of 14 Beacon St., Boston, Mass., and a recent photo of myself.

I send these enclosures in order to make an earnest request for an extension of the passport for two years, that I may return to my work and my home in Foochow City, Fukien, China.

My work, for the greater part has been in a Boys High School, but I have also had much experience in Relief and Industrial Projects during the many crises of the past few decades. The principal of Foochow College, an American sponsored institution, wishes me to return at an early date. I leave no dependents in the United States. My return would involve no one. My long residence in the province of Fukien has given me familiarity with the language and the people.

I will be deeply grateful for an extension of my passport for two years so that I may return to Foochow, Fukien, China.

Kindly address all replies to:

Miss Martha Wiley

1103 Madison St.,

St. Charles, Mo.

"American and British Consuls have again sent out strong warnings to their nationals to get out of South China."

[letter from Margaret Ballard]   PAGODA ANCHORAGE   AUGUST 1, 1949

Dear Miss Wiley,

As you have undoubtedly heard, the American and British Consuls have again sent out strong warnings to their nationals to get out of S. China, while it is possible to do so. The Americans included Fukien, while the British only mentioned Kwangtung and Kwangsi. I have not yet heard what the reaction of Foochow missionaries is, but certainly recent happenings in Shanghai plainly show that the new rulers are fundamentally anti-foreign, and plan the ruin of all foreign trade, as you have probably read or heard. The American Vice Consul was beaten and imprisoned for 3 days for an infringement of some traffic regulation—they acknowledge no international obligations, nor the ordinary usages of countries.

It is said that 700 foreigners in Shanghai, after attempting life under the new rulers, are anxious to get out as soon as possible, but it is a question whether they will be granted Exit permits, though the slogan is out: "Drive out the foreign vermin." As a Hong Kong paper said, we have heard the epithets, "imperialists"—"running dogs"—"capitalists" before, but this last is a new one! Please do not refer to any of these matters in writing to me, in case we should have changed hands! There is much more that might be said, but you probably get plenty of details in various papers.

Local bandits calling themselves Communists are active all over Fukien, except in the villages actually occupied by Nationalist soldiers. They make heavy demands upon the landowners for large amounts of rice, also for guns, and woe betide those who do not obey, unless they are able to vanish. These bandits have all the slogans and methods of their masters, so probably have trained leaders, though it is almost impossible for the soldiers to deal with them, for they appear just ordinary peasants and keep well hidden, usually coming out at night.

Yours with love and gratitude,   Margaret Ballard

"I can hire a man to take a bicycle
and I will sit on the back."

[letter from Catherine]   DUNG-ANG   SEPTEMBER 20, 1949

Dearest Gu-gu [Martha]:

I am at Dung-ang now, 20 miles from Amoy. I can go back by high way now. Some places have busses. Tomorrow I will leave here—there is no bus from here but I can hire a man to take a bicycle and I will sit on the back where it is used for things or books. Of course it is uncomfortable but so many people can do it, and I can do it too. This afternoon I have tried it. I think it is all right. I am sure that I can go back safely. It is a very interesting story I am going to tell you. When I got to my brother's home on September 3rd, that evening I prayed to God earnestly to open a way for me to go back to Foochow. That night I had a dream that a man was coming to see me telling me, "On 14th day you can go back." The next morning I told the family I would go back to Foochow on September 14th. Every day I was looking for the day to come. When 14th of September came, there was no sign at all that I could go back.

On September 15th, Daik-ho telephoned asking me whether I would like to go back with a group of Foochow people. I immediately decided that I would go—September 17th I left Amoy. It was just exactly the 14th day since I had the dream. When I got to Dung-ang, people told me it was a very hard and dangerous trip for me to take. They said it would be much better for me to return to Amoy. Two people turned back, but I believe it was the time God had prepared or arranged for me to go back, so I said to Daik-ho that I would stay in Dung-ang for a day or two and see what I could do—here I can go through easily. From Dung-ang to Foochow all are occupied by the Communists now.

Love,   Catherine Lin Hsueh

P.S. From now on I will be cut off from you—you would not hear from me for how long I do not know. When you write to some of my friends, please tell them that I could go back safely. We believe that we will have a very hard time. I do not know whether this letter can reach you or not, but the Post Master will try his best to get it through. I must go back to Foochow, because I believe Donald and Elizabeth need me to be with them. Much love to you and Aunt Belle.

Catherine

"Foochow was liberated on August 17th but yesterday after noon 12 planes came from Formosa to bomb."

[letter from Donald]   FOOCHOW   OCTOBER 30, 1949

Dearest Gu-gu, Mabelle and Marian:

You can sense my difficult days and I need your constant prayers.

Foochow was liberated on August 17th—but since September 7th, the opening of the school, I have had no day of peace. We still have 860 students—but alas! two thirds of them refused to pay full tuition fees. You have got to receive them whether you like them or not. Everyone's salary has been cut down to only half pay for each month compared with last term. Everyone is suffering. Of course those teachers who have got many children suffer the most. Other schools are more or less the same. The Lord knows how long it will last.

Mother came back from Amoy on September 23rd when my trouble was developing. You can imagine how happy and thankful I was that she could help think of different ways to deal with different problems and absurd situations. Thank the Lord we are all well. I sometimes sleep only two or three hours a night, yet my high blood pressure does not get worse.

If this letter reaches you by Christmas time, our love and best wishes to you all.

Yesterday after noon 12 planes came from Formosa to bomb. We still do not know how many people were killed.

Please give our best wishes and love to all friends, (Auntie Belle and Auntie Achelpohl).

With much love,   Daddy

"We have been suffering from sporadic bombing by Kuomintang planes."

[letter from Margaret Ballard]   FOOCHOW   NOVEMBER 9, 1949

Dear Miss Wiley,

I am sure that you are thinking much about all your friends in Foochow these days, and longing to hear some details of what life is like.

For the last ten days or so, we have been suffering from sporadic bombing by Kuomintang planes, which is far from pleasant. Some Go-downs [store or warehouse] have been struck and burnt out, and various boats sunk, and houses demolished. How many people have been killed or injured is not made known, though I expect the number is small compared with "European blitz" casualties. However, it is grim enough for those poor creatures who have lost an arm or a leg or a home, and the chatter of machine guns and the ack-ack of the anti-aircraft guns are sufficiently disturbing, even when there is not much probability of one's own neighborhood being attacked.

We have had three days of quiet, but yesterday two planes came over, and dropped leaflets announcing a raid for today and warning the people to scatter—so far nothing has happened, and it is nearly noon. It was pitiful for several days to see the poorer people trooping out to the small outlying hills, with babies, bundles and often their bedding also, in case their houses should be gone when they returned. How long it will be before an end is arrived at is a question, also just what the end will be.

Affectionately,   Margaret Ballard

"Donald's salary is 309 lbs. of rice each month."

[letter from Catherine]   DECEMBER 14, 1949

Dearest Gu-gu:

In October Donald and I had a very hard time. Some naughty students and some teachers who were expelled used the opportunity to make great enemies of Donald, and told many lies about him in the newspaper. We thought that we would leave Foochow for Peking to work in the Congregational Church there. Mr. Harold Matthews has arranged it for us—for a month we did not have a bit of peace—our hearts were sore.

Since then I have not been in the school. Now the school is governed by committee. Two thirds of the members are teachers and one third are students and coolies—nine people in the committee. In September, when Foochow College was just opened, the students decided how much each one should pay and how much each teacher should get each month. Now Donald's salary is 309 lbs. of rice each month—about $7 U.S. for a load of 160 lbs. of rice now. The teachers get less than 300 lbs. of rice each, a month—compared with what they got last term, just half of it. Each teacher is very poor now, especially those who have a big family.

Daik-ho has eight children. They eat two meals of soft rice each day—still not enough. Many people are suffering from hunger, especially during the winter time.

Please give our love to Auntie Anna and Auntie Belle and the rest of your family. I should have written to them and Doris and Jean, but my mind is perplexed and I don't think it is wise to write many friends in America.

Affectionately,   Catherine

"Admiral Chen is now the vice governor of Foochow."

[letter from Catherine] NOVEMBER 6, 1950

Dearest Gu-gu:

Donald's salary this term is 400 lbs. of rice a month (about $17 U.S.) Well, we get along quite all right. I raise some vegetables enough for our family and also some chickens and eggs. You do not need to worry about us; 80 lbs. of rice for Hwa [Elizabeth] will be enough in Peking. I still hope that you will come back and live at Fairy Bridge.

Admiral Chen, your favorite student, is in Foochow now. He is the vice governor of Foochow. He asked about you. Ding chiu-ngu, your student, is also in a very high position. They both are still good people.

Will write you again.

Much love, Catherine

[Note: Martha accepts a teaching position at Piney Woods School, Mississippi]

DOVER HOTEL   DENVER, COLO.   NOVEMBER 19, 1950

Dear Belle,

After I left you I changed buses at Walla Walla, Pendleton, Twin Falls, Burley, two small towns, Ogden, Cheyenne—and here I am at Denver. Denver is my first stop-over. Spent Sunday here. Will leave Monday morning at 6 o'clock and go direct to Jackson with no stop-overs.

A lot of navy boys were on the buses and there were two in every seat and sleep was out of the question, except a few snatches.

Dover Hotel is a poor excuse, but it is only one door from the bus station and is cheap—room with bath—$2.50 for 24 hours.

Will write again when I arrive at Piney Woods.

Love, Martha

PINEY WOODS, MISS.   NOVEMBER 25, 1950

Dear Sister Belle,

I sent you a card from Denver. Then came on to Jackson without stop or incident. Young Mr. Jones met me at Jackson and it was a beautiful sun shiny day. Had lunch with the president and dinner. Then moved to my apartment.

. . .

Love to all from, Martha

"Fruit is scarce here at Piney Woods but the meals are good."

PINEY WOODS, MISS.   DECEMBER 1, 1950

Dear Sister Belle,

Last Saturday I went out looking for a store and wandered down the road until I came to a sawmill—a very big lumber company runs it—and there I found some fruit and bought a dozen each of apples (small ones) and oranges and lemons. The women teachers in this building were greatly surprised for they did not know there was such a store. I put my loot in a box in the kitchenette and told them to help themselves—which they did not do, so I passed out a portion—and found that the teacher across the hall had saved hers for a sick girl. Fruit is scarce here in Piney Woods but the meals are good and well-cooked and would suit you, Belle.

There are grits (cooked corn cereal) and bacon and eggs and toast for breakfast (no Postum). Lunch: sweet potatoes, meat of some kind, vegetable salad, corn bread—no dessert. Supper: cold meat, potatoes, one cooked vegetable. So you see why I had to get out and forage for fruit.

Love from,   Martha

"It has just about made me collapse."

PINEY WOODS, MISSISSIPPI   MAY 2, 1951

Dear Sister Belle,

Yesterday very bad news came from China. My Admiral—Chen Shao-kwan, was shot by the Communists at the time of the great purge about two weeks, or three, ago. I am glad that he was a Christian man and that he could go to his death fearlessly. He was quite a man, retired to a little field on an island near Foochow. Why should they want to kill him? Another Admiral, a friend who lived very near to my house at Fairy Bridge, was also shot. And four pastors, all of them friends, and one principal of a school in our mission, were shot at the same time. Besides these countless numbers, 50,000 in all, in our one province.

It has just about made me collapse. I have felt limp as a rag ever since as I really *knew* a few of the atrocities.

I teach the Junior College Bible class this evening, so I had better get this letter in the office before supper and be off to the class. No notice has been given as to the date of closing the term. Dr. Jones is off on one of his collecting tours and every one waits for him.

Love to Gail and Neva and all the others from,   Martha

[Note: In a 1957 newspaper article Martha states that a former student had written, some time later, to tell her the news she had received of Admiral Chen's death was incorrect. He eventually died of stomach cancer in 1969—three weeks before Martha's death.]

"The name of Foochow Middle School has been changed."

[letter from Frank Lin]   BETHEL SEMINARY   KOWLOON, HK.   AUGUST 2, 1952

My Dear Miss Wiley:

I am sure that you want to know something about Mr. and Mrs. Hsueh. Recently I got a letter from my brother-in-law. He said that the name of Foochow Middle School has been changed, because it has been combined with another middle school. They will have 1600 students next semester. Mr. Hsueh still holds the position of principal. I think that the missionary homes are used as student dormitories—otherwise how can they house such a large number of students?

Yours very sincerely,   Frank Lin

[Note: Martha retires to Pilgrim Place, a residence for retired mission workers, in Claremont, CA in December of 1953.]

"Most of what tourists see is just 'window-dressing'—masses of people are near starvation."

DECEMBER 1960

Dear Mrs. Carlson,

Again it is almost Christmas—so quickly have the days and months passed since we met in your hospitable home. I wonder if those grapes and other good things that you were so generous with, flourished during 1960.

My fig tree was unusually full of fruit for two crops so I had something to share. The one orange tree has not done well and there are only a few oranges—and what there is, the passers-by feel privileged to take! One grapefruit tree ripens in June, and the loquat tree is a total failure.

But I am like my sister Belle in one respect—we both loved to work among the flowers. I was saving the roses to give to my Chinese friends at Thanksgiving time—but the evening before I was to cut them—someone else evidently wanted them more than I, and they disappeared. I have about a dozen bushes. It gives me a very lonely feeling to think that she is never again to be in the garden she enjoyed so much, for so long. I hope that the strangers who have the place will love it as much as she did.

But how much more glorious is the HOME above, from which neither illness nor people can dislodge us! Pilgrim Place is becoming a very crowded settlement. When I came here there were 150 residents, but now there are 278 and more begging to come in. The place has lost its former homelike feeling, as there are many that one cannot know. I take

Sunday dinner at the hall and each time sit at the table with entire strangers. But during the week I do my own housework and cooking. And I am so glad that I am able to do this—it keeps me occupied.

At Thanksgiving holiday my Chinese friends from Pasadena came and we had the day together—the mother, two sons, two daughters, a son-in-law, and a grandchild! We had lunch at the INN and the boys certainly enjoyed the food. The mother, who came to the U.S. in August, is simply a shadow. The head of the family is a minister in Hong Kong. He writes me that most of what tourists see is just "window-dressing"—that masses of the people are near starvation. His own people in Foochow beg him for food. When he sends it, the P.O. confiscates it. Poor people!

Now Christmas is next and what a pleasure it is to take this occasion to write to all those whose memory is dear to me! My remaining sister is in St. Charles—so far from here, but she is very good to write. Every Tuesday I receive a letter from her. She is alone, too, as she has one daughter in Detroit, and one in Chicago. She does not like to travel by herself so her daughters have to come to her.

A reading club that I joined when I came here has gone to pieces—most of the members have passed on, so I have joined and Adult Forum in Pomona that meets every Monday evening. The lectures are excellent and I get more than when the Club was in existence. A doctor and his wife, very kindly take me with them.

I am sure that you will have a good time with your family at Christmas time. It is grand to be with younger people and children. They really provide the Christmas cheer.

My love and best wishes to you at this season when we miss those who have gone before—but who are praising God in a more glorious realm.

Millions would love to have our privilege of worship, but are denied it.

May this Christmas bring you an even deeper sense of the Saviour's nearness!

Affectionately,   Martha Wiley

DECEMBER 28, 1965

Dear Connie,

Thank you, my dear, for remembering me so very generously. The years are running by and it will not be very long until an entirely new generation will have taken over. Anna and I are the only ones left of the large family of nine!

She is far from well; and would it not be strange if I were left the longest though I have had the most rugged life of all the brothers and sisters? But only the Lord knows, and we can trust his wisdom.

A Mrs. Curtis, who used to work in a bank in Yakima, has sort of adopted me and drives where it is necessary for me to go. Yesterday she brought me home from my shopping trip.

Ivy Craig is my nearest neighbor and feels that she has to look after me, though I can out-walk her on our evening walks. She is around 75 years—had a long siege in South Africa work. A new couple from Japan are in the apartment above me and are very fine folks—but they do not have a car!

After all is said, no one can take the place of your VERY OWN KIN! I hope to get to Yakima again, but can hardly expect to make it. The travel to St. Charles is easier for an old person than to Yakima. I got on very well this past fall going both ways by myself. Anna worried a lot about me—but she need not.

Can you realize that this coming February I will reach "the exalted age" (as the Chinese say) of 92? If your Aunt Belle were living she would be 97. Our generation has almost passed out.

Former Chinese students and other Chinese have become quite friendly now. One, a paper manufacturer in Massachusetts, another a business man in San Francisco, a teacher in the public schools of L.A. and one in the Fuller Seminary, in Pasadena, and a few others. Needless to say, they were cared for by me when small—most of them.

How fortunate you are to have all your family near enough to visit on occasions! If any of them remember me give them my love.

Do let me thank you again for your kind thoughts and good "eats." You surely deserve all the good that comes your way.

Much love from your   Aunt Martha

[This last letter was written to my grandmother, who was the initial inspiration for compiling this book. With this letter our exploration into Martha's life comes full circle.] Kathy

AFTERWORD

And so we come to the last saved letters—although Martha did continue to write in her diary every day, until just a few weeks before her death. These entries were very brief, mentioning social engagements with friends, along with a general summary of the day.

After returning from China, Martha eventually took a position teaching Bible studies in the Piney Woods School—an all black school in Piney Woods, Mississippi. The school was established in 1909 by Dr. Laurence C. Jones and employed both black and white teachers. Martha taught there for three years before retiring in December of 1953 to Pilgrim Place, the Claremont, California retirement home for mission workers.

Martha lived in Pilgrim Place for fifteen years and was active until the end, attending lectures and book groups and socializing with friends. It was during this time that she donated various artifacts along with her suitcase of nearly 700 collected letters, to the Yakima Valley Museum in Yakima, Washington.

Considering Martha's life of turmoil and her extensive exposure to various diseases it is surprising that she was the last surviving sibling of her eight brothers and sisters. Martha's six brothers had all passed on in the two decades previous: her sister Belle died in 1960, and Anna, in 1967. Until Martha's death in 1969, at the age of ninety-five, she was also the oldest living graduate of Whitman College.

As for the Hsueh family, Donald and Catherine's two eldest daughters, Mabelle and Marian, came to live in the United States to continue their education. Mabelle became a university staff member, and Marian, an internist. The third and youngest daughter, Elizabeth, was unable to leave China. She eventually married and both she and her husband died during the Cultural Revolution. In 1979, Donald also died in China, from an infection acquired after an injury. After his death, his wife Catherine was brought to America to be near her daughters, but lived only one month.

During the Cultural Revolution, Foochow College became a public school, and was later shifted to middle school status and is still in existence as of this writing.

As an odd coincidence, just three weeks before Martha's death in 1969, her old student and friend, Admiral Chen Shao-kuan, died of stomach cancer.

Martha witnessed great change during her years in China. As with all changes in life, we find our place in this web of humanity in perpetual flux—demanding that we adapt to new situations and rise to meet new challenges. Martha's legacy is clear: to stand amid turmoil with honor and hope, diligence and respect, humor and integrity. We are delighted to have known a part of her life through these letters—to have known one of many who do good.

[Excerpt of 1962 newspaper clipping]

Almost anyone would concede that Miss Wiley lives up to the definition of a "tough old Yakiman."

Last Feb. 24, just a day after her 87th birthday, she was hospitalized by an automobile smashup in which she received numerous injuries, including a shattered kneecap. Today she walks about, freely and vigorously, with no sign of a limp, reads and busies herself with countless affairs.

Around her home in Pilgrim Place in Claremont Miss Wiley has made an enchanting little garden, a medley of brilliant tropical exotics and such sturdy flowers as the pinks and daisies that may well have bloomed around her pioneer home near Yakima.

. . .

Her home, in a colony of cottages occupied by retired ministers and missionaries, is a pleasant place, but it is not what Miss Wiley wishes for herself. She wants to be in China, from which she is barred by the Bamboo Curtain.

"I would never had left China had I dreamed I could not get back," she grieves. "I wanted to see my own people again, and then was planning to return to China to end my years there."

"Of course, if I were in China I'd be dead," she admits, matter of factly.

She worries constantly about "my girls" and "my boys" about whose fate she is unsure. She is sure of one thing—that they are hungry.

"It's hard to eat," she sighed. "When such good food is placed before me, and I start thinking of their hunger, I just cannot do it."

She gets out a box of pictures and pours over the bright and serious faces, explaining them. Many of them are boys and girls she saved from starvation or slavery, and brought up and educated.

. . .

Every penny she can spare goes to an organization that can ship food to those in China, but that can give no assurance it reaches its destination. Miss Wiley goes on hopefully contributing, believing that if even an occasional parcel reaches her friends it is worthwhile.

But she doesn't know what to think of communism and its impact on the Chinese.

China was regarded an inferior nation for so long that its rise as a world power may stir the pride of its people, she believes. She does not go along with the theory that the Chinese absorb any foreign influence and make it Chinese; and, if they did, it would be a slow process, covering many generations.

"Conditions change and customs change," she explained. "The world is different today than when I was young. And who can tell about communism?"

. . .

Miss Wiley returned to the states in 1913 to raise money to build the home for the Chinese where she was living until her return to this country after the war. And it is in that home that her heart is today.

"Now, don't glamorize me," was her final admonition. "Don't do that."

ABCFM NEWSLETTER

Miss Martha Wiley of Claremont, California, and Yakima, Washington, in educational and evangelistic work in Foochow, China (and Shaowu briefly) for [44] years (1900-1916, 1919-1944, died at the McCabe Rest Home in Claremont on August 21, 1969. She was 95.

Born on February 22, 1874 in a log cabin in Yakima, to parents who pioneered in the Northwest Territory, Martha Wiley attended Washington State University, obtaining a bachelor of Pedagogy in 1895, and Whitman College in Walla Walla, receiving her B.A. in 1898, and M.A. [honorary] in 1909 during her first furlough. Her research studies were on the early pioneers of Central Washington State.

Miss Wiley began her educational service in Foochow in 1900 as a teacher of mathematics at the Boys' High School, which later became Foochow College. In time she added English and Bible classes to her teaching schedule. At the time of the Chinese revolution and the overthrow of the Manchu government in 1911, she did a great deal of relief work among Manchu women and children in the East gate area of Foochow. Later on, with her colleague, Emily Hartwell, she started a Women's Bible Training Center in Foochow, and was its able and forward looking principal for many years. In later years she emphasized Christian education and evangelism more and more among her students and women of the area.

World War II caught Miss Wiley in China. Instead of returning to America, she made her home in Foochow with the family of Donald Hsueh—one of her former "boys," who was then principal of Foochow College. During the Japanese occupation, when the Christian schools had to evacuate to Shaowu in the northwest part of Fukien province, she went with Mr. and Mrs. Hsueh. In 1944, when the U.S. Embassy ordered all Americans to leave Shaowu, Martha Wiley retired on the field instead, and stayed on until 1947.

She became a resident of Pilgrim Place in 1953 and remained active and alert to the end. With her keen sense of humor and her buoyant outlook she endeared herself to all.

MARTHA WILEY OBITUARY

Valley pioneer dies at age of 95.

Miss Martha Wiley, 95, died today in the Pilgrim Place Rest Home at Claremont, California.

Miss Wiley, a retired missionary-teacher to China, was the last surviving child of Mr. and Mrs. Hugh Wiley, founders of Wiley City.

She was born in the homestead at Wiley City, attended Whitman Academy, Whitman College, and later was graduated from the University of Washington in 1895 with a degree in pedagogy. In 1898 she also received a B.A. degree from Whitman, and in 1910 a masters degree from Whitman with membership in the Whitman Phi-Betta-Kappa honorary. She taught school in Ahtanum, Wenes, and Yakima City schools until leaving for Foochow, China in 1900.

Miss Wiley did evangelistic work at Formosa while a refugee there in 1927, and also did educational and relief work while a refugee in Central Fukien, in 1941 to the close of WWII. She was appointed by the American Board of Commissioners of Foreign Missions in 1900, when she left Yakima for Foochow College, Foochow, China. She was a teacher and did relief work and adult education.

After 47 years in missionary work for the American Congregational Missionary Society, she returned to the United States in 1947. In past years Miss Wiley gave a collection of material gathered while she was stationed in China to the Yakima Valley Museum.

She was a member of the Yakima Valley Pioneer Association and the Ahtanum Pioneer Congregational Church.

PHOTOGRAPHS & ILLUSTRATIONS

CHINESE NAMES

Martha — Oi-Su-gu, Gu-gu, (Su–gu means teacher, aunt)

Siek — Foochow dialect/Hsueh (pronounced shweh) — Mandarin dialect

David — Ding bing (Donald's older brother)

Donald — Ding Goi

Catherine — Uong Suk-ing (trans. — Snow Gold)

Mabelle — Ting mi (mei)

Marian — Ling-ing

Elizabeth — Ling hwa (hua)

Chen Shao-kwan (kuan)

Boys riding water buffalo

GLOSSARY

A. B. C. F. M. — American Board of Commissioners for Foreign Missions

B. M. I. — Board of Missions of the Interior

Boxer Rebellion — 1898-1901 — Uprising opposing foreign imperialism and Christianity

Boxers — A nationalistic Chinese secret society that flourished in the 19th century

CCP — Chinese Communist Party

Jones — Martha's term for the Japanese

KMT — Kuomintang, Chinese Nationalist Party

Li — Chinese unit of distance equal to about 0.6 km or 0.4 ml

Manchu — A member of an indigenous people of Manchuria who formed the last imperial dynasty of China (1644-1912).

M. E. — Methodist Episcopal

Mex. — abbreviation for Mexican silver

W. B. M. I. — Woman's Board of Missions of the Interior

Yamen — office or residence of a Chinese public official

Barnabus and Timothy

Hills of Foochow beyond North Gate

INDEX

Send inquiries to:

Kathy Langhorn
P.O. Box 328
Silverdale, WA 98383
or
lettersfromthedragonbook@gmail.com